FabJob G

Become a
Life Coach

BRENNA PEARCE AND ALLAN M. HELLER

FABJOB® GUIDE TO BECOME A LIFE COACH
by Brenna Pearce and Allan M. Heller

ISBN: 978-1-897286-16-6

Library and Archives Canada Cataloguing in Publication

Pearce, Brenna, 1959-
FabJob guide to become a life coach / Brenna Pearce and Allan M. Heller.

Accompanied by a CD-ROM.
Includes bibliographical references.
ISBN: 978-1-897286-16-6

1. Personal coaching--Vocational guidance. 2. Counseling--Vocational guidance.
I. Heller, Allan M. II. FabJob III. Title. IV. Title: Become a life coach.

BF637.P36P42 2008   158.6   C2008-900503-1

Important Disclaimer: Although every effort has been made to ensure this guide is free from errors, this publication is sold with the understanding that the authors, editors, and publisher are not responsible for the results of any action taken on the basis of information in this work, nor for any errors or omissions. The publishers, and the authors and editors, expressly disclaim all and any liability to any person, whether a purchaser of this publication or not, in respect of anything and of the consequences of anything done or omitted to be done by any such person in reliance, whether whole or partial, upon the whole or any part of the contents of this publication. If expert advice is required, services of a competent professional person should be sought.

About the Websites Mentioned in this Guide: Although we aim to provide the information you need within the guide, we have also included a number of websites because readers have told us they appreciate knowing about sources of additional information. (**TIP:** Don't include a period at the end of a web address when you type it into your browser.) Due to the constant development of the Internet, websites can change. Any websites mentioned in this guide are included for the convenience of readers only. We are not responsible for the content of any sites except FabJob.com.

FabJob Inc.
19 Horizon View Court
Calgary, Alberta, Canada T3Z 3M5

FabJob Inc.
4616 25th Avenue NE, #224
Seattle, Washington, USA 98105

To order books in bulk, phone 403-949-2039
To arrange a media interview, phone 403-949-4980

www.FabJob.com
THE DREAM CAREER EXPERTS

Contents

About the Authors

Lead author and editor **Brenna Pearce** has been a contributing writer, editor, and researcher on a number of other FabJob guides, including the *FabJob Guide to Become a Business Consultant*. As a former elementary and high school teacher with degrees in Education, History, and English Literature, Brenna understands and appreciates the deep satisfaction in facilitating the self-discovery process in others. For this FabJob guide, she interviewed a variety of experts in different coaching specialties from across North America. Brenna is currently lead editor of FabJob Inc., an award-winning publishing company named "the #1 place to get published online" by *Writer's Digest*.

Allan M. Heller is a freelance writer, based in Pennsylvania, who has written more than 300 articles for newspapers and magazines, and has published poetry and short fiction as well. His interest in coaching began when a family member became a life coach. To write the *FabJob Guide to Become a Life Coach* he conducted extensive research, personally experienced 12 weeks of life coaching, and interviewed numerous experts including psychology professors at various universities, instructors at coach training schools, and administrators at the International Coach Federation.

Acknowledgements

Many life coaching experts have contributed their valuable time and wisdom to make this FabJob guide a success. Thank you to the following individuals (listed alphabetically), whose time, assistance, and willingness to share information has been invaluable in the preparation of this book:

Ken Abrams	Laura Meyer
Jenna Avery	Meg Montford
K. Denise Bane	Janine Moon
Jennifer Bergeron	David Noer
David Brenner	Kevin Nourse
John Capsule	Marilyn O'Hearne
Jill Chongva	Sophie Pachella
KC Christensen-Lang	Rinatta Paries
John Fox	Steve Rhode
Timi Gleason	Ann Ronan
Scott Haney	Roberta Rosen
Tracy Heller	Amber Rosenberg
Debra Jackson	Christy Seawall
Larry James	Barbara Sher
Tom "T.J." Jones	David Steele
Anna Kanary	Barbra Sundquist
Marlee LeDai	Katy Taylor
Stanley J. Lieberman	Nancy Theodore
Terri Levine	Chris Ullman
Marguerite Manning	Joe Vitale
Sybil McLendon	Christy Whitman
Christopher McCluskey	Schaunon Winter-Gilman
Lynn Meinke	

1. Introduction

1.1 What is Coaching?

Welcome to the *FabJob Guide to Become a Life Coach* and congratulations on choosing an exciting career that helps so many people to succeed in their lives. You've taken the first steps to your own personal success by purchasing this guide.

We all know people who help others achieve their goals, who inspire friends and family to persevere in the face of adversity, and refuse to allow them to wallow in the seeming security of a mediocre job or life. They inspire others to greatness by gentle persuasion, constant encouragement, or a kind of in-your-face inducement. Perhaps you know someone like that. Or perhaps you are someone like that, which is why you are reading this guide.

It's a myth that the reason so many people never accomplish their goals is because they don't really want them, or don't want them badly enough. Life coaches understand that. People use life coaches for the same reason that they use sports coaches or personal trainers: they want someone to work with them, to encourage them, to push them. It's easy to find excuses for not exercising when you don't have someone to push you; not as easy when your personal trainer shows up at your door three times a week wearing a jogging suit.

 As a coach, your job is to provide objective, unbiased feedback to clients. Yours is not to judge or determine what clients should do or what they need, but to act as a facilitator so that they can figure it out for themselves. Well-meaning though they may be, friends and family members may think that they know what is best for someone, and their ideas often conflict with what the individual thinks is best for him or her. Life coaches free their clients from expectations imposed on them by others.

Life coaches can help people who are trying to do too much, and guide them towards what they would really like to be doing, and what gives them the most satisfaction. Often clients find that it is not what they are currently doing at all.

 People sometimes spend their entire lives doing what they are told that they should do, what their parents expect of them, or what they think that society expects of them. What about doing what they really want? Some of them have been caught up in this cycle for so long that they are not even sure what they want. But they can still find out. Life coaches do not have an agenda. They leave that up to the client.

Another big issue in life coaching is helping people prioritize, helping them to find balance in their busy lives. Coaches report that a lot of their clients are already successful people, many whose upper level positions in the corporate world have left them feeling isolated. They want someone who is both willing to listen and provide honest, sometimes blunt feedback. They need to hear what employees and subordinates won't tell them, which is why a lot of executives are turning to personal coaches.

Life coaching does not carry the stigma that therapy does. Men in particular are often reluctant to see a therapist, and even more reluctant to admit to seeing one. But life coaches report that their clients are about evenly divided between the genders.

Over the past decade, the number of self-employed individuals has skyrocketed. Surveys indicate that more than half of the population is not satisfied with their jobs, their lives, or both. Some are disillusioned, feeling that their employers do not value them, and subsequently come to the conclusion that they owe them no loyalty. Others want the independence and flexibility that self-employment offers, and enjoy facing new challenges and responsibilities. Whatever the reason, the trend is evident. Perhaps this is one reason why so many are turning to life coaching, as both clients and coaches.

Another issue that has become increasingly important to people in North America recently is global warming. The debate surrounding ratification of the Kyoto Protocol and Al Gore's Academy Award-winning film, *An Inconvenient Truth*, especially have had a major impact on people's awareness and perception of their own, individual impact on global warming, and closely associated with this is the "carbon footprint." As a result, people are turning to carbon coaches to help them understand and reduce their contribution of CO_2 into the atmosphere. This field is wide open since carbon coaches are still relatively rare in the U.S. and Canada.

We've all heard of the "Baby Boom Generation," people who were born between the end of World War II and the early 1960s when birth control pills were introduced. Approximately 76 million babies were born during this period, a time of growing affluence in North America. This is also a generation that can expect a longer life than previous generations. Now that many in this affluent group of people are retiring or are close to retirement they are seeking advice about what to do with their retirement savings and what to do through their retirement years to maintain a healthy and productive lifestyle.

As a result, a need for retirement coaches has arisen. Like carbon coaching, this is an area of opportunity with many potential clients for life coaches. Issues surrounding the sudden loss of friends and coworkers as a result of retirement, loss of status, uncertainty about the future, or even if retirement is the right course of action, all create a need for retirement coaches. Retirement coaches help people sort out important questions about retirement and assist them in setting fresh goals.

1.2   The Growth of Coaching

The world is quickly becoming faster, more intense and more chaotic. People are turning to life coaches to help sort everything out, to prioritize, and to make sense of things. Various estimates put the number of life coaches practicing in the United States and Canada between 10,000 and 15,000. Some have turned to practicing full time, while the rest have incorporated coaching with their regular occupations.

The vast number of coaching organizations and practicing coaches has created a market for dozens of online coach referral services, as well. Many of these services charge the coach to be listed, but allow potential clients to freely search the database.

According to a recent article in the *National Post* by Ray Williams of Premier Career Management Group in Vancouver, Canada, coaching is one of the fastest growing professions in the world, second only to information technology. Hundreds of newspaper and magazine articles have explored the topic, among them *The New York Times*, *USA Today*, *Harvard Business Review*, *Kiplinger's Personal Finance* and *Family Circle*.

In addition, coaches have been interviewed on television programs such as *The Today Show*, *Later Today*, *American Journal*, *NBC Nightly News* and *Oprah*. But the market is far from saturated, and there are still plenty of people who have never heard of life coaching.

Thomas J. Leonard: The Father of Coaching

The late Thomas J. Leonard has been called "the father of coaching." A former financial planner, he began in the early 1980's by assisting his clients to lead more fulfilling lives, before this was officially called life coaching. By nature a workaholic, he authored six books on coaching, and traveled extensively — lecturing, teaching, speaking and appearing on talk shows. Leonard founded Coach U in 1992, International Coach Federation in 1994 and Teleclass.com in 1998. His premature death of a heart attack in February, 2003, at age 47 was a serious blow to the coaching establishment. Memorial services were held for Leonard throughout North America and Europe.

Admittedly, not all of the press about life coaching has been positive or inspirational. Like any new field, it is not without its detractors, but life coaching thus far has proven to be a juggernaut that won't be slowed by a few naysayers. And for every naysayer, there are people sharing their personal success stories like these:

"My experience with life coaching was integral in helping me make a life-changing decision," recalls John, a real estate developer. "I had been employed for 12 or 13 years with a real estate company, and coaching helped me realize that I needed to start my own business, and that I had the aptitude for it. I wound up quitting my job and starting my own company, and now I have two companies. Recently, I successfully completed a major real estate development, and in the process, secured my personal freedom."

"My coach's assistance was invaluable," says Katherine, an investment planner. "She skillfully assisted me through a mid-life job search and career change in a new city. She helped me perfect my interviewing technique, made excellent suggestions about job search strategies, offered enthusiastic support and helped me through a successful negotiation process. Her efforts made a real difference in my securing the ideal job."

1.3 Who Becomes a Life Coach?

Although life coaching is relatively new as a profession, a lot of people who enter this field have already been utilizing the skills required for a long time. Many come from careers that involve significant interaction with people—human resources managers, public relations officers, and educators, as well as personal trainers, hair stylists and massage therapists.

Others have no formal experience working with people, but are very social individuals who enjoy becoming involved and derive great satisfaction from assisting others. They are accustomed to listening, asking questions and giving feedback. They just never thought of it as life coaching before. One common denominator for coaches is that they are used to and enjoy working with people. Obviously, this encompasses a wide range of professions and individuals.

Nearly a third of coaches are former therapists, and although coaching is distinct from therapy, there are some overlapping aspects. Both are skilled at listening closely, observing behavioral patterns and asking powerful questions. Neither attempts to pass judgments or decide what clients are supposed to do. Both assist people to look inside themselves to find solutions. Many therapists become life coaches because they are tired of dealing with pathology; they are sick of sickness. They want to work with people who are well but want to be better; who are happy but want to be happier. Many are also exasperated with insurance companies, mountains of paperwork, referrals and other bureaucratic burdens.

Members of the clergy often go into coaching, some tailoring their practice with a religious or spiritual slant. Retired people can be very effective coaches, as they have lots of life and business experience. Many coaches who specialize in corporate training or career development are former job counselors, business consultants, CEO's or teachers. To some extent, their previous professions entailed what they now know was coaching, and they bring with them a wealth of practical experience. They are accustomed to guiding people, to helping shape young minds or to putting motivated individuals on the track to success. They have seen countless examples of what works and what does not.

Carbon coaches also come from a wide variety of backgrounds, and you don't need a science degree to become one. While some are architects or engineers, most come from all walks of life and have one thing in common: a concern for global warming and a desire to help others do something about it. All a carbon coach needs is a good understanding of the effects of carbon in the atmosphere on global warming and a knowledge of what solutions can be implemented by individuals to offset this.

Coaches are an eclectic lot, and not all of them hail from careers typically associated with coaching. Those from "non-traditional" backgrounds often find themselves drawn to coaching because it offers them the opportunity to extract what they liked best about their old jobs—working with people—and make that the focus of their new endeavor. Bartenders, merchants, sales people, reporters, nurses and restaurant workers can all be great coaches. There are even those who have never worked closely with other people as part of their job, but become coaches because they realize that they have always wanted to do so.

Coaches have something in common with their clients: both want to succeed, to become the best that they can be, to move their lives and careers in a bold new direction. When clients succeed in attaining their goals and realizing their dreams, life coaches succeed as well. Coaches have already taken the first step towards changing their own lives for the better by committing to doing the same for others, and it is on this common ground that the coaching relationship begins.

1.4   Are Coaches Consultants?

Webster's *New World Dictionary* defines a consultant as "an expert who is called on for professional or technical advice or opinions." Generally speaking, people who hire consultants are looking for specific recommendations. They want someone who will tell them the best course of action or develop solutions designed to fit their unique situations. They don't want someone who is going to ask them a lot of questions and insist that they figure it out on their own.

Like consultants, coaches occasionally work with clients on short-term projects or very specific situations. Coaches can help someone design a marketing plan for a business, come up with a diet and exercise regimen or prepare for an upcoming event. They can help management and executives reduce their stress levels or create new management policies. However, the key distinction is that the coach is helping others to do these things, not doing them him or herself.

According to the *National Post* article mentioned above, a coach is not "a therapist, counselor or management consultant" although sometimes consulting and coaching overlap. Typically, individuals who provide both coaching and consulting services will refer to themselves as a coach and consultant. This guide focuses on coaching as a career. If you are also interested in doing consulting work, you can find useful advice in a guide such as the *FabJob Guide to Become a Business Consultant*.

1.5   Coaching is Not Therapy

Coaching is sometimes confused with counseling or therapy. According to the *Occupational Outlook Handbook* published by the U.S. Bureau of Labor Statistics, "Counselors assist people with personal, family, educational, mental health, and career decisions and problems." While counseling may sound similar in some ways to coaching, there are fundamental differences.

As mentioned, coaching clients are generally well-adjusted, successful individuals who would like to be more successful. As a coach, you are there to help them achieve a more fulfilling life, a more rewarding career, or more effective interaction with others. Establish up front that you are not, nor do you intend to be, a therapist. While a lot of mental health professionals do transition into coaching, they are not acting in the capacity of therapists when they do so.

There are several major distinctions between coaching and therapy. The primary difference is that therapy deals with what is wrong with the individual. This is why coaches have clients as opposed to patients. Secondly, therapy digs into the past, in order to establish the roots of current problems. Life coaching occasionally explores a client's past, but does so in order to recall successes and sources of inspiration, not hang-ups. Life coaches start in the client's present and work with them toward a better future.

Finally, life coaches are their clients' equals, their collaborators in success. They are not authority figures. Therapists typically address their patients by first name, while the patients call them "doctor." Coaches are often characterized as having a skilled friendship or being in partnership with their clients. Some coaches will consent to see clients who are in therapy, with the clear understanding that the coaching relationship is entirely separate. However, you would do best to avoid coaching clients with psychological issues. *Not totally sure I agree w/ that*

You may begin a coaching relationship with the belief that a client is well-adjusted, and then start to notice warning signs that suggest psychological problems. According to Lynn Meinke, a life coach and former psychotherapist, a coach should be aware of certain behavioral patterns that suggest psychological duress. These include lack of interest in accomplishing stated goals, sudden mood changes, or excessive fatigue or excitability. Also, the client may begin to persistently have negative thoughts or feelings of self-doubt or worthlessness.

Everyone has a bad day or a bad week occasionally, but if a client fails to follow through on a plan of action for two or three weeks in a row, or keeps missing or canceling appointments, the coach needs to ask the client to consider re-evaluating his or her goals. Perhaps focusing on more appropriate goals is the solution to the flagging motivation.

If this approach is ineffective, the coach needs to ask the client if he or she has experienced this type of decrease in motivation before, and if so, whether he or she has sought help from a mental health professional. The situation is a delicate one, but the coach needs to tell the client what the coach is observing in order for the two to explore options for dealing with the situation.

Meinke says that dropping a client who needs therapy is tantamount to abandonment and could be psychologically devastating. Continue with the coaching, but make the immediate goal to have the client consult an appropriate mental health professional. This allows the client to decide whether or not to continue coaching while in therapy.

In the event that the client refuses to consider therapy, then the coach may have to stipulate that the continuation of the coaching depends upon it. If the coach is forced to end the coaching relationship, he or she should continue to remain compassionate and supportive of the client and give referrals. If the coach does not know any therapists or mental health counselors to recommend, he or she can call a hospital or mental health clinic in the client's geographic area, or call the American Psychological Association's Public Education Information line at 1-800-964-2000.

1.6   Inside This Guide

The *FabJob Guide to Become a Life Coach* will take you step-by-step through getting started and succeeding as a life coach. These steps, and the chapters they appear in, are as follows:

In Chapter 2, we will introduce you to the many specialty areas in which life coaches operate. From carbon coaching to weight loss/body image coaching, we'll introduce you to a variety of coaching niches from which you can choose.

In Chapter 3 you will learn more about what is involved in life coaching and find sample questions, exercises and coaching sessions. You will also learn about various delivery systems for getting your services to clients, such as e-coaching, workshops, and retreats and offer some of the advantages of each. This chapter has a wealth of information for you to learn more about the basics of what's involved in life coaching.

In Chapter 4 you will discover how to learn life coaching through educational programs, mentoring, volunteering, and self-study. This chapter lists a variety of organizations that offer programs you can take to become certified as a professional life coach. We'll also offer tips on how you can learn coaching and get coaching experience in other ways.

Chapter 5 focuses on starting your own business. As a life coach you will be a small business entrepreneur, and as such you will need to be prepared for the many exciting challenges to opening your own business. Whether you choose to do business in a home-office or rent office space, you will need to learn about creating a business plan, choosing a name for your company, legal issues and more. We'll also offer you some suggestions for setting up your office space and point you to further resources you will find useful as you start out on your new business venture. This chapter also addresses that all-important topic: Setting Your Fees. We'll show you how to set your rates for individual and corporate clients, for a variety of different services.

Your business will need clients, of course, so that is the focus of Chapter 6. You'll learn about choosing a target market and about the promotional tools many of our experts have told us they have tried and found effective. The information you will find in this chapter includes tips about what print and electronic tools to use as well as information about a variety of marketing techniques, all of which will help you find new clients and let people know you're in business. We'll also offer some additional advice about marketing your services to a corporate clientele in this chapter.

In Chapter 7 we have included a number of tips from our experts. We're sure you will find their advice both helpful and encouraging.

So let's get started. Your new career as a Life Coach is just pages away!

2. Coaching Specializations

As a life coach you may decide to assist anyone who wants coaching, in any area of life. However, most coaches choose to specialize in particular areas. In addition to calling themselves life coaches, coaches who specialize may also describe themselves using terms such as business coach, career coach, executive coach, relationship coach, etc. to more accurately reflect what they do.

While you may initially want to assist people with any life issue, chances are you will have greater expertise in some areas or find particular areas more rewarding. For example, if you decide to become a career coach, you will assist clients with job searches, and may help them to prepare their resume, determine the best job-seeking strategies, and support them in their transition to a new line of work. Obviously, the work you would do as a career coach is substantially different than the work involved in couples coaching.

When choosing a specialization, there are other considerations beyond the types of issues that you will be coaching clients in. Specializing in a particular area may contribute to the success of your business by helping you market your business more effectively than if you were trying to sell your services to everyone. Being a specialist coach can help to draw clients to you who are looking for someone to coach them in a particular issue (i.e. the one you specialize in).

> *"Despite the fears that many new coaches have around limiting their income and potential client base by selecting a niche to specialize in, it is an incredibly valuable way to focus your efforts in terms of marketing. When potential clients are looking for a coach, they most often have a particular issue they are concerned about. Having a niche makes it much easier for them to find you."*
>
> — Jenna Avery, spiritual coach and mentor
> **www.highlysensitivesouls.com**

As you will read later in this section, you might choose to specialize in anything from alternative lifestyles to work/life balance. Popular specializations in coaching include the following, listed alphabetically:

- business coaching
- carbon coaching
- career coaching
- corporate coaching
- executive coaching
- relationship coaching
- retirement coaching
- spiritual coaching   *spiritual + wellness coaching whole-person coaching*
- time management coaching
- weight/body image coaching
- work/life balance coaching

It's important to note that specializations may overlap. For example, if you're doing executive coaching for a client, the issues of time management and work/life balance may arise. Likewise, a spiritual coach may also deal with areas ranging from relationship coaching to weight/body image coaching.

The following is an introduction to specializations that many new coaches are interested in breaking into. This part of the guide includes some samples and resources for these particular coaching specializations. You can find some additional tips to help you choose a specialization in Section 5.2 ("Creating a Business Plan").

2.1 Business Coaching

Business coaching typically involves coaching small business owners, however, the term "business coaching" is sometimes also used to refer to coaching executives and employees in any size business.

In this guide, you will find information about the key areas of business coaching in two sections: 2.4 (Corporate Coaching) and 2.5 (Executive Coaching). If you are interested in business coaching, start your research by reading these two sections. But you may also find useful information in other sections covered in this chapter.

As part of a business coaching practice, you might assist clients with areas many businesspeople are concerned with such as Time Management Coaching (covered in section 2.9) and Work/Life Balance Coaching (section 2.11). In addition, if you decide to become a Carbon Coach (covered in section 2.2) you might work not only with individuals, but also with businesses that are concerned about environmental issues.

Likewise, as a Relationship Coach (section 2.6) you might help businesspeople to develop better relationships in the workplace, as a Spiritual Coach (section 2.8) you could help businesses integrate spirituality into the workplace, as a Career Coach (section 2.3) you could be hired by companies to coach employees who have been downsized.

As you can see, business coaching can encompass many areas of coaching. Before deciding on a specialization, take a look through the rest of this chapter to learn about the many different options that you have.

2.2   Carbon Coaching

An excellent opportunity for life coaches is in the field of carbon coaching. This is a relatively new sphere of coaching, but one that has great potential for someone like you starting out in a career in life coaching. As mentioned earlier, the Kyoto Protocol and Al Gore's 2006 film, *An Inconvenient Truth*, have had major impacts on awareness of global warming and people's individual impact on it.

Although coaches have been active in the U.K. and elsewhere in Europe for some time, most carbon coaches in the U.S. and Canada come from organizations like the David Suzuki Foundation or architectural firms specializing in environmentally-friendly building techniques. Since they are so rare, carbon coaching is a wide-open field.

You don't have to be a scientist, architect or engineer to be a carbon coach, though. You will need a good understanding of the issues surrounding how CO_2 emissions contribute to global warming and understand the ways in which individuals can reduce, neutralize or even reverse their impact (known as their "carbon footprint").

You can offer your services to a variety of clients, including individuals and corporations, as well as municipal and other governments. In addition, you can offer carbon coaching services in conjunction with any other life coaching services you offer. Not only will you be working with a variety of interesting people, but you will be contributing to their knowledge and awareness of global warming as well as making a positive impact on the environment to the benefit of future generations.

2.2.1   A Client's Carbon Footprint

One of the central goals in carbon coaching is to help people reduce their carbon footprint. A person's carbon footprint is the amount of carbon each person contributes to atmospheric carbon increase each year. For example, one round-trip airplane flight from Los Angeles to New York and back contributes an additional 2,500 pounds of CO_2 to the atmosphere (about 1 lb. of carbon for every mile of air travel).

Since the carbon footprint is such an important concept as part of carbon coaching, let's take a closer look at it. We have been hearing the term carbon footprint more and more frequently recently as it is becoming widely used in the media. Carbon dioxide emissions are closely bound to the major issue of climate change, contributing to the greenhouse effect in warming the Earth's atmosphere. One particularly sobering fact is that North America produces more than 19% of the total of all CO2 produced on the planet by human activity.

In February, 2007, the U.N.'s Intergovernmental Panel on Climate Change released its first working report on climate change, followed in April and May by the second and third reports in the series. These reports point out that greenhouse gas (GHG) levels in the atmosphere have increased by at least 70% between 1970 and 2004. Carbon dioxide produced by human activities in particular has actually increased by 80% over that time, mainly from burning fossil fuels like coal, natural gas, and oil.

The focus of carbon coaching is on how (and how much) the individual contributes CO2 to this increase in emissions and how they can reduce that amount. There are, in fact, many ways that we as individuals contribute to CO2 emissions. Some of the more obvious are burning gasoline in car engines; heating/cooling our homes and heating water for household use (showers, laundry, dishwashers, etc.) using natural gas, propane, or electricity from coal-fired electrical plants; and on and on.

As a carbon coach you will consult with clients on ways they can reduce their use of carbon from sources like these. Some coaches travel to their clients' homes in order to identify overuse or misuse of energy sources and point out solutions. For many clients, this can mean making significant changes to their lifestyles.

If you would like to read about one family's lifestyle-changing experience with their carbon coach, you can check out a two-part article published in the *Globe & Mail*, entitled "Carbon coaches get family to conserve: Lifestyle change helped save energy." To find the article go to **www.sustainablebuildingcentre.com** and search for *carbon coaches*.

As the two-part article by Deborah Jones illustrates, even people who think of themselves as environmentally conscious can contribute to global warming in unconscious ways. The choice of cars we drive, the amount of electricity we use, and even whether or not we go to a restaurant or a movie theater, all produce carbon in one way or another. The first step in identifying a person's (or family's) carbon footprint is to look at their lifestyle.

One way to do this is to have clients use one of the many carbon calculators available online. You can also use the Sample Carbon Calculator shown on the next two pages.

Clients input a variety of annual data such as the amount of miles they drive and fly, how much natural gas, propane or fuel oil they use to heat their homes, how many kWh (kilowatt hours) of electricity they consume, and even how much garbage they throw away. The national average carbon produced per person in the U.S. is about 8 tons (16,000 pounds) per year and averages about 4 tons per year per person worldwide.

The more detailed input an online carbon calculator allows, the more accurate it will be. If you do plan to use one of the online calculators, be sure that it is as detailed as possible. To find online calculators type "carbon calculator" into a search engine like Google. The U.S. Environment Protection Agency has an excellent, detailed carbon calculator at **www.epa.gov/climatechange/emissions/ind_calculator.html**.

Some coaches will visit clients to check how much electricity each of their clients' appliances use, using a device like the Kill a Watt. This inexpensive (about $40) device is plugged into a wall outlet then the device you want to monitor is plugged into the Kill a Watt, which then measures that appliance's kWh usage. The output reading can then be used to determine if the device is using more than it's supposed to or can be compared to energy ratings for similar but newer appliances to see if the existing ones should be replaced.

You can find a list of common household appliances and the amount of electricity each uses at **http://michaelbluejay.com/electricity/howmuch.html**. For example, according to the list at this website, a typical CRT computer monitor uses 120 watts, while a newer LCD monitor of the same size uses only 40 watts of power. Changing to an LCD monitor will help clients realize electricity (and money) savings while at the same time reducing their impact on global warming if their electricity comes from fossil fuel-powered generators.

Sample Carbon Calculator

According to the Kyoto Protocol (1997), each person should produce no more than 5.4 tons (11,000 pounds) of carbon per year as their individual "carbon allowance." The average American currently produces about 8 tons per year.

For most people, the bulk of their carbon output comes from automobiles, household utilities use such as electricity and heating fuels, and the garbage they produce.

Answer all the questions below so that I can help you determine your contribution to global warming.

Automobiles

Car #1

Make/Model/Year: _____

Miles per gallon:
(visit **www.fueleconomy.gov** if you're not sure)   _____

Number of miles traveled in one year: _____

Car #2

Make/Model/Year: _____

Miles per gallon: _____

Number of miles traveled in one year: _____

Other Vehicles

Provide additional information for any additional cars/motorcycles/boats/ATVs, etc., in your household as follows:

Vehicle: _____

Miles per gallon: _____

Number of miles traveled in one year: _____

Air Travel

Include information for business/personal/vacation travel.

Person #1 _____

Number of miles traveled per year: _____

Person #2 _____

Number of miles traveled per year: _____

Person #3 _____

Number of miles traveled per year: _____

Provide additional information about air travel for other persons in the household if more than three.

Public Transportation

Number of miles traveled by bus or train for all
persons in the household: _____

Number of miles traveled by taxi or limousine _____

Household

For each of the following, look at household utility bills for the last 12 months.

Electricity (kWh per year) _____

Heating Oil (gallons/liters per year; note: 1 gal.=3.79 liters) _____

Natural Gas (therms per year; note: 1 therm=0.106 GJs) _____

Propane (gallons/liters per year, for barbecues, torches, etc.) _____

Garbage (pounds produced per year; note: 1 lb.=0.454 kg) _____

Calculating the Amount of Carbon Used

In order to use the carbon calculator, you will need to know the amounts in pounds of carbon associated with each activity. The calculations are very basic and you could put these into a spreadsheet like Excel to calculate the totals automatically for you. Following are the calculations you will need for each activity:

- **Automobile:** Miles traveled divided by MPG X 22 lbs of CO_2 per gallon. Repeat this calculation for each automobile in the household.

- **Air Travel:** Miles traveled divided by 0.9 lbs of CO_2 per mile

- **Public Transportation:** Miles traveled X 0.5 lbs of CO_2 per mile for bus/train and X 1.5 lbs per mile for taxi/limousine

- **Electricity:** kWh per year X 1.5 lbs of CO_2 per kWh

- **Heating Oil:** Gallons per year X 22 lbs of CO_2 per gallon

- **Natural Gas:** Therms per year X 11 lbs per therm

- **Propane:** Gallons per year X 13 lbs of CO_2 per gallon

- **Garbage:** Pounds per year X 3 lbs of CO_2 per gallon

After you have totals for each single activity, add them up and divide by 2,000 to get the number of tons of carbon. This is the client's carbon footprint. Be sure to compare the client's total to both the national average and the Kyoto Protocol's suggested carbon allowance. Another resource is the UN's Intergovernmental Panel on Climate Change (**www.ipcc.ch**) which also has recommendations for maximum individual emissions in its "Working Group" reports.

2.2.2   Ways to Reduce Carbon Impact

Once you and your client have calculated their estimated annual carbon contribution, you will have a fairly good idea of what areas in their home and lifestyle are causes for concern. You can then help them put together a list of ways that they can reduce their carbon output and create a goal worksheet and checklist for making and tracking changes.

For example, your client might decide that using public transportation during the work week is an easy solution to reducing the carbon impact from driving their car to work. According to the government website, **www.fueleconomy.gov**, the average newer, mid-size family sedan contributes 4-10 tons of CO_2 per year depending on the make, model and year. By choosing public transportation, your client can reduce CO_2 emissions considerably.

Following is a list of some options you may advise your clients of a variety of ways to reduce their carbon impact. Most involve some sort of alteration to habits and lifestyle. Others may require making changes to building structures, appliances, and so on. Strategies for reducing a carbon footprint include:

- Reducing the amount of garbage thrown away (e.g. by recycling and composting)

- Using public transit

- Purchasing a more fuel-efficient car (fuel economy is directly related to GHG emission, i.e. the higher the MPG, the lower the GHG)

- Reducing the number of airplane flights

- Lowering hot water heater temperature

- Replacing incandescent light bulbs with compact fluorescent bulbs

- Turning off electrical appliances when not in use (and unplugging them since many, e.g. TVs, continue to use electricity even when turned off)

- Washing laundry in cold water

- Turning up the temperature setting of air conditioners in summer

- Monitoring groceries purchased (produce that comes from further away and highly processed, packaged foods create more CO_2 due to transportation and manufacturing processes)

- Turning down the thermostat in winter

- Using a low-flow shower head to reduce hot water needs

- Drinking tap water if it's safe to drink rather than bottled water (bottling and shipping creates carbon dioxide)

TIP: Using a power bar or surge protector with a switch to plug several appliances into (such as a coffee maker, toaster, electric kettle in the kitchen or TV/DVD player/video game console in the family room) will make it easy to cut the power to multiple devices at once.

2.2.3   Low Carbon Diet

Like the phrase "carbon footprint," the term "low carbon diet" has appeared frequently in the media lately. In a 2006 article in *Time* magazine, entitled "The Low Carbon Diet" (available at **www.time.com/ time/health/article/0,8599,1552237,00.html**), author Stacie Stukin characterizes a low carbon diet as "tightening your own personal pollution belt." Just like people on weight loss programs, clients need a coach to help them achieve their low carbon reduction goals and get through the highs and lows.

Like the more conventional weight loss diet, the low carbon diet can be a short-term undertaking. Carbon coaches use the notion of a low carbon diet as a "hook" to get clients interested in their services by offering people a relatively low-cost, quick fix to their concerns about contributing to global warming.

Offering clients tips like those listed in the previous section, coaches help clients understand the value, both in financial and environmental terms, to hiring a carbon coach to help them lower their impact on global warming. In addition, coaches can offer a two week low carbon diet program to get clients interested.

This entails having clients monitor their daily life for things like auto and air travel, garbage produced, electricity used, etc., for one week and totaling the results. The next week, they try to cut back on their habits in order to lower their carbon output. Use an online carbon calculator or the one provided above to determine the results.

2.2.4 Buying Carbon Offsets

This is another relatively new concept that allows the individual to reduce their global warming impact, making the individual "carbon neutral." Carbon offsets have been used for years by companies in various industries in order to offset pollution they cause to the environment. However, carbon offsets have only recently been offered to individual consumers.

If you know how a balance sheet works in accounting then you can easily understand the basics of a carbon offset program. On the assets side is the carbon offset; on the liabilities side, the individual's (or company's) share of carbon emissions. The carbon offset credit exactly matches and balances the debit of produced carbon pollution. These offsets can be purchased to counter individual or family impacts at home, and they are also available to offset carbon produced by vacation and travel activities.

Carbon offsets are big business today. As the David Suzuki Foundation website explains, "they are bought and sold through international brokers, online retailers and trading platforms." One of the major trading platforms for carbon offsets is the Chicago Climate Exchange (CCX). The CCX is the second largest offset exchange in the world and the first established in the U.S. Visit their website at **www.chicagoclimatex.com** to learn more.

The David Suzuki Foundation advises that individuals should choose the type of offsets they purchase carefully, since some projects, like tree-planting, are impermanent and do not address fossil fuel dependency issues. Instead, the Foundation advises consumers to purchase those that meet the international "Gold Standard" that includes only projects that incorporate renewable energy, energy efficiency and low environmental impact among their features.

In order to purchase a carbon offset, an individual will first need to know how much carbon they actually contribute to the atmosphere, using an online carbon calculator, for example. Once they know how much carbon they contribute they can take steps to reduce their impact using methods suggested by their carbon coach to positively adjust the initial carbon footprint amount. Then they can purchase the offset to any remainder to become carbon neutral.

There is one real drawback to this concept, though. People can create even more pollution and in their minds keep a clear conscience because they have purchased an equivalent offset. Be sure your carbon clients know that carbon offsets are bought in order to both offset their own CO2 and to contribute to finding real solutions to global warming problems.

You can find a report called *The Consumers Guide to Retail Carbon Offset Providers* at the Clean Air-Cool Planet website. The report explains how the carbon offset market works, offers a glossary of terms you'll encounter in the retail offset market, and offers a number of criteria for choosing an offset retailer. In addition, it provides a list of carbon offset retailers (see p. 24 of the report). The report is available at **www. cleanair-coolplanet.org/ConsumersGuidetoCarbonOffsets.pdf**.

If you would like to read an overview of carbon offsets and how they work, and more about the Gold Standard, visit **www.davidsuzuki.org/ Climate_Change/What_You_Can_Do/carbon_offsets.asp**.

2.2.5   For More Information

There are many ways carbon coaches encourage clients in addition to making simple changes like those in the list above. These include everything from using renewable energy sources to planning a low-carbon wedding. You can read more about climate change and environmental issues at the following websites:

- *U.S. Environmental Protection Agency*
  www.epa.gov/climatechange/wycd

- *Union of Concerned Scientists*
  www.ucsusa.org/greatlakes/glsolutionsperson.html

- *Carbon Footprint*
  www.carbonfootprint.com/Minimisecfp.html

- *David Suzuki Foundation*
  www.davidsuzuki.org/climate_change

- *Friends of the Earth International*
  www.foei.org

- *World Watch Institute*
  www.worldwatch.org/node/5393

2.3 Career Coaching

Career coaches help people search for a new job. As a result, they are often hired by individuals who are dissatisfied with their current job and want to find something better, or by parents who want to help a child identify a career path and get help with job search techniques.

With layoffs and downsizing commonplace, career coaches are also often hired by companies to assist workers in finding new jobs. This type of career coaching is often referred to as *outplacement consulting*. The coaches may help displaced employees prepare a resume, re-assess goals and values, or practice interviewing techniques. The company usually provides the coaching as part of a severance package.

Career coaches work with their job-seeking clients every step of the way, from exploring job options, to helping them write (or writing for them) their cover letter and resume, to practicing for job interviews. Career coaches generally are experienced in matters of human resources, personnel, hiring and employment policy. Many are former school guidance counselors, have worked at employment or temporary agencies or were business owners.

2.3.1 Exploring Career Options

As with other branches of coaching, not all career coaching clients will know exactly what they want at the start. They will generally have a basic idea that they are unhappy at their current job, and anxious to explore alternatives. They might have always wanted to work in a specific industry, but aren't sure how to get started.

Discovering the client's strengths and weaknesses is the first step. This can be accomplished by various assessments, or by simply having clients list what they like and don't like to do, or the best and worst jobs that they have ever held. After discovering what they like to do, clients can then come up with lists of what types of jobs would allow them to do that.

Next, they need to find out what kinds of companies to approach. Some questions to ask the client can include:

- Do you prefer large, small, or medium companies?

- In what geographic area would you most like to work?

- Do you primarily want money, job satisfaction, or security?

- Do you prefer working with people, information, or things?

- Do you prefer a highly structured environment, or do you like to have more flexibility?

- Do you like working on team projects, or do you like to work in-dependently?

- How do you typically get along with co-workers?

- What types of co-workers do you find most/least compatible?

- How well do you delegate responsibility?

- What hours would you prefer to work?

- How far are you willing to commute on a daily basis?

There are many excellent career assessment tools you can use with clients to help them identify career options. For example, the Perfect Career Interest Inventory helps narrow job choices using interests, and is available free of charge at **www.iccweb.com/perfect_career.htm**.

A comprehensive source of information about career tools, ranging from free online tests to sophisticated instruments such as the Myers-Briggs Type Inventory, can be found at **www.quintcareers.com/career_ assessment.html**. The same site compares features of various free and inexpensive online career assessments to help you choose assessments that will be best for your coaching clients at **www.quintcareers.com/ online_assessment_review.html**.

2.3.2   Informational Interviews

If a client wants to find out more about jobs in specific areas before searching and applying for open positions, you can help them plan for informational interviews.

To start, the client makes a list of contacts in an industry he or she is interested in, and simply requests an appointment to learn more about a company. The informational interview is not to ask the contact for a job or be pushy, but to gather information. Many professionals are more than happy to impart their knowledge and expertise to others.

Career coaches can help clients practice for informational interviews. As with an employment interview, certain protocols must be followed: the client should be prompt, should do as much research as possible about the company or industry in question, pay careful attention to the person being interviewed and take notes, and always send a thank-you note. Possible questions that a client might ask during an informational interview are:

- How long have you worked here?

- How did you get started in this career? How do most people get into it?

- What do you like best about this job? What do you like least?

- How many hours do you typically work per week?

- What are some of the challenges facing this company?

- What do you wish you had known when you were first getting into this business?

- What are typical duties in this type of job? What are typical duties in entry-level positions?

- What advice do you have for someone just getting started in this career?

- What are the three things you look for when you are hiring for this company?

- Based on a quick review of my experience to date, what training or experience do you think I should pursue next?

- What do you anticipate happening with this business/industry in 5/10/20 years?

- Which professional associations, websites, or publications should I look into?

- Do you know anyone else who would be good to interview?

2.3.3   Resumes and Cover Letters

Not all clients who come to career coaches want coaching per se; they just want an effective resume. Some clients are not interested in the details of resume writing, and are perfectly willing to pay a career coach to do it for them. Or there may be clients skilled in their particular fields, but not great writers.

> **TIP:**   If someone hires you just to write a resume and a cover letter, offer to give him or her a free career coaching session. At worst, the client will not be interested; at best, you'll add to your coaching practice.

A 2005 HotJobs.com survey found that 84 percent of recruiters prefer chronological resumes so it's a good choice for your clients with a solid work history. However, for career changers who don't have previous paid employment in the career they want to break into, a functional or combination resume is a better choice.

If you are like most people who become career coaches, you likely already have experience preparing effective resumes and cover letters. You can further develop your skills with resume-writing resources. There are many books that provide advice on writing resumes and cover letters, and include samples. At the time of publication of this guide, the bestselling book in the resumes category at **Amazon.com** was *Resume Magic: Trade Secrets of a Professional Resume Writer,* by Susan Britton Whitcomb. You can also find valuable free advice on writing resumes online at:.

- *FabJob Resume Resources*
  www.FabJob.com/advice.html#resume

- *Resume and Cover Letter Tips from Monster*
  http://career-advice.monster.com/resumes-cover-letters/ careers.aspx

- *Resume and Cover Letter Writing*
  http://jobsearch.about.com/od/resumes/a/resumecenter.htm

A number of career coaches hold the designation of Certified Professional Resume Writer (CPRW), which is bestowed by the Professional Association of Resume Writers and Career Coaches (PARW/CC). More information about this certification can be found at the PARW/CC website at **www.parw.com**.

2.3.4   Interviews

Practicing for job interviews is an important part of what career coaches help their clients do. Career coaches understand that making a good first impression in an interview is essential. Unfortunately, too many job seekers take the attitude of "Just relax. Be yourself. You can't really practice or rehearse what you're going to say." Wrong!

As a career coach you can help job-seekers prepare for the interview by having them role play, with you in the role of employer. You can ask them questions such as the following:

- What can you tell me about yourself?

- Why are you looking for a new job?

- What are your strengths?

- What is your greatest weakness?

- Why have you had so many jobs?

- What are your short-term and long-term goals?

- What are your salary expectations?

- Why do you want to work for us?

- Why should I hire you?

- What questions do you have for me?

In addition to giving the job-seeker an opportunity to practice answering, you can use this exercise to give feedback and coach the client about appropriate answers to give. You can also help clients determine the right questions to ask prospective employers during an interview.

How clients answer questions can be as important as what they say, so you should give them feedback on their vocal qualities, body language, and appearance. Did they project confidence? Were they dressed professionally? Were there any problems you noticed such as using too many "uh"s and "um"s or avoiding eye contact? By identifying any areas for improvement during practice interviews, you can help them make a positive impression when they go on real interviews.

There are also many books available that provide advice on preparing for an interview and answering interview questions. At the time of publication of this guide, the bestselling book at **Amazon.com** on the topic of interviewing for a general audience (as opposed to interviewing books aimed at specific groups of job seekers such as computer programmers) was *301 Smart Answers to Tough Interview Questions*, by Vicky Oliver. You can also develop your interview knowledge and skills with online resources such as the following:

- *FabJob Interview Resources*
  www.FabJob.com/advice.html#interviews

- *Interview and Networking Resources*
  **http://jobsearch.about.com/od/interviewsnetworking/
  Interviews_Networking.htm**

- *Job Interview Resources at Monster*
  http://career-advice.monster.com/job-interview/careers.aspx

2.3.5   Thank-You Notes

A survey of 650 hiring managers by CareerBuilder.com found that nearly 15 percent of hiring managers say they would not hire someone who failed to send a thank-you letter after the interview, while 32 percent say they would still consider the candidate, but would think less of him or her. Yet only about 50% of people who interview for jobs send thank-you notes.

As a career coach, you can help give them a competitive edge by having them send thank-you notes after an interview. Some clients are just not writers, and don't really know where to begin. Writing thank-you notes is another service that you could offer.

A thank you email should be sent within one day of the interview. To really stand out, an applicant can follow-up the email with a hard copy, either hand-written or typed. Rosemary Haefner, Vice President of Human Resources at CareerBuilder, recommends that a thank-you letter have three paragraphs. "In the first paragraph, thank the interviewer for the opportunity. Use the second to sell yourself by reminding the hiring manager of your qualifications. In the third paragraph, reiterate your interest in the position."

Job-Hunting Support Groups

Members of job hunting groups fall into three categories –unemployed, underemployed or unhappily-employed. If you are working primarily with the former two, consider reducing your fees significantly or even coaching some members for free. This will help you establish yourself as a career coach, and you will be doing a valuable service for clients who really need it. People change jobs, and former clients may return at some point in the future. Also, they may know someone who is looking for a job or career change, and will gladly refer that person to you.

In many respects, you work with a group of job-hunters much the same way that you work with individual clients. Group members could offer feedback to each other, and could pair off to conduct mock interviews while the other members watched and critiqued. For larger groups, divide them into smaller groups of three or four. Also give the members weekly assignments. For example:

- Read the first two chapters of *What Color is Your Parachute?*
- Rewrite your resume, and bring a copy to show to the group
- Make a list of 10 companies where you'd like to work
- Make a list of the five most important factors for job satisfaction
- Write a sample cover letter for a job at your ideal company

Section 3.2 has more information on how to run a coaching group.

2.4 Corporate Coaching

Coaches have made significant inroads into the corporate world. Major corporations such as Kodak, IBM, and Marriott are just a few examples of the companies that have hired coaches on a temporary or ongoing basis to meet business objectives and improve overall performance. Large companies don't have a monopoly on corporate coaches, though; coaches are also hired by non-profit organizations, government agencies, and small businesses. Though most corporate coaches work on contract for a variety of clients, a few are permanent employees.

2.4.1 Goals of Corporate Coaching

Many return on investment studies have been done regarding the effectiveness of corporate coaching, factoring employee retention, greater productivity and increased sales. Intangibles such as employee incentive and better motivation have also been included in these studies. The consensus is that coaching has been effective in overall improvement of the workplace.

In a 2002 white paper titled "How Is Coaching Used in Your Organization?", career services consulting firm Lee Hecht Harrison (**www.lhh. com**) identified the top five reasons why organizations provide coaching for their employees:

- For leadership development—70%

- For skill development or style differences—64%

- To retain top talent—40%

- As part of management succession planning—34%

- To ensure success after promotion or with a new hire—30%

Corporate coaching may involve coaching individual employees, or working with groups. When companies hire coaches to work with individual employees, the coach will normally be working with employees who are considered key to the organization's success, primarily those in leadership positions. While sometimes referred to as _leadership coaching_, this type of corporate coaching is more commonly known as executive coaching. Executive coaching is covered in depth in section 2.5, so this section will focus on working with groups.

While coaches may work with groups for any of the reasons indicated in the study mentioned above (such as leadership development, succession planning, etc.), much of the work that coaches do with groups involves one or more of the following:

- developing employee skills to ensure success on the job

- teaching employees to interact effectively with people with different communication or behavioral styles

- helping companies retain employees

To achieve these results, companies often hire coaches (also known as *trainers*) to present training programs to groups of employees to address such issues as: reducing burnout, improving customer service, increasing sales, understanding communication styles, conflict resolution, stress management, and other areas ranging from business ethics to time management. Training programs may be presented to a group of employees from all levels of the company, or a program may be offered to a group of employees at the same level, such as teaching supervisory skills to a group of new supervisors. Many coaches are retained by corporations to come back and follow up on previous programs.

In addition to training programs, corporate coaches may also be called upon to address issues unique to particular companies, such as significant changes in company policies or procedures, departmental reorganization, phasing in or phasing out certain work areas. The coach gauges employee response and helps them make a smoother transition. Employees are given the opportunity to voice concerns or complaints, or just sound off in an unbiased, non-judgmental setting. They may feel free to tell a coach what they might be reluctant to tell a supervisor.

2.4.2 Steps in Presenting a Training Program

There are three primary steps involved in presenting a training program for a corporation:

1. Conduct a needs analysis

2. Design the training program

3. Deliver the training program

Needs Analysis

The first step in training is to assess the needs of the organization. For example, if a company is experiencing high employee turnover, they may be looking for training that will help to reduce the turnover.

In some cases company representatives have a clear picture of what type of training will solve the problem, and may put it in writing in a "Request for Proposal" (RFP). An RFP is a document that provides information about the organization, their training needs, and what they require in a proposal to do the training work. RFPs and proposals are covered in section 6.4 of this guide.

However, most corporate coaches are hired without an RFP. In these cases, having a face-to-face meeting with a company representative, such as an executive, department manager or human resources person, will be your first step to defining the client's needs. Typically, this process begins when you first meet with a prospective client and may continue after you are hired to carry out the training. This is covered in more detail in section 6.4, "Marketing to Corporate Clients."

When conducting a needs analysis, it is important to remember that the company is officially the client, not the employees. Therefore, the outcome of the training program is whatever the company's goals are, not those of employees.

Program Design

Once the need for training has been established, you will likely be responsible for designing the training program (in a few cases trainers are hired to present programs that have already been developed by the company). This process is also known by such terms as "instructional design" and "curriculum development."

Some corporate coaches develop their own training programs that they market to different companies, tailoring those programs to meet the needs of specific organizations. For example, a corporate coach who spent years working in and then supervising a call center may have dealt with a lot of irate customers and have practical solutions for getting to the source of the problem and calming a caller down without seeming patronizing.

Alternately, the coach may have worked in a collections department and knows how to be both firm and diplomatic when calling on delinquent accounts. So he or she comes up with a seminar called "Connecting While Collecting," and targets collection agencies, banks and credit companies as clients.

Program design involves more than simply scripting what you will say to the trainees. Since most adult learning is interactive, you will also need to design group exercises and prepare instructional materials. Examples of group exercises and resources for program design are included in section 3.4 of this guide.

Training Delivery

Training delivery involves conducting training sessions through such methods as presenting information, facilitating group discussions, and directing participants through exercises or the use of interactive multimedia. Training may take place with participants in a classroom, or it might be conducted on the job. Another option is train-the-trainer sessions which teach employees how to train their co-workers.

If you want to improve your skills delivering training programs, the resources in section 3.4 may be helpful. Section 6.3.2 on "Speaking and Events" also offers some useful resources for coaches who want to develop their confidence and skills speaking to groups.

2.4.3 Considerations in Corporate Coaching

Worker attitudes play a significant role in determining how successful the coaching or training will be for a business organization. Employees of companies that hire coaches may have negative, mixed or neutral feelings about how training may benefit them. This is less of a factor in personal coaching, where clients contact coaches because they want to be coached, or are at least receptive to the concept.

If you are facing employee resistance, your training program should begin by acknowledging the resistance and explaining to the employees how they can personally benefit by participating in the training program. For example, in a customer service training program, you might explain how the training program can help participants reduce their stress by learning ways to deal effectively with difficult customers.

In some cases group training may not be appropriate for a particular employee. For example, high-level executives may not want to attend training programs on sensitive subjects that will involve employees at all levels of the company. Often it is better for the employees not to have high-level executives present at such training programs because the employees may hesitate to participate fully, fearing they may be judged negatively and possibly cause damage to their career. During the initial meeting with someone who might hire you to train their group, you can ask if there are any people who might prefer one-on-one training or coaching. This is covered in the next section.

Also during the initial interview with the company, the coach should clarify issues regarding confidentiality—what can and cannot be disclosed about coaching and training sessions. This is another departure from traditional life coaching, where what the person being coached says is never discussed outside of the session, except in rare cases. Because the coach may be privy to confidential company information, corporations often require them to sign non-disclosure agreements and carry some sort of liability or errors and omissions insurance (see section 5.3.3 for more information about insurance).

2.5 Executive Coaching

An executive coach works with important individuals within a company or other organization. Coaching may be provided for C-level executives such as Chief Executive Officers (CEOs), Chief Financial Officers (CFOs), Chief Operating Officers (COOs), etc. and managers, supervisors, department heads or other key employees. Like corporate coaches, executive coaches do much of their work for major corporations. However, they are also hired to coach executives in non-profit organizations, government agencies, and small businesses.

To work effectively with executives, most executive coaches have ample experience in the business world. They are former CEO's, presidents or managers. Others have worked as headhunters, recruiters or human resources personnel. This is not a hard and fast rule, however. The ability to connect, inspire and motivate is what really matters, and good coaches already possess this ability.

If you have been searching for information about executive coaching, you have likely encountered the statement that "between 25 percent and 40 percent of Fortune 500 companies hire executive coaches for their employees." This statistic comes from a study by Hay Group, an international consulting firm, published in the October, 2002 issue of *HR Magazine*. Although more recent figures are difficult to come by (various sites claim anywhere from 50% to 80% of the Fortune 500 now hire executive coaches) it is apparent executive coaching is a growing field.

The reason for this growth is the positive impact executive coaching has on a company's bottom line. A recent study by consulting and leadership coaching company MetrixGlobal LLC, conducted for a Fortune 500 firm looked at the business benefits and return on investment of executive coaching. The study found that "Coaching produced a 529% return on investment and significant intangible benefits to the business." You can learn more about executive coaching's ROI from the following:

- *Executive Briefing: Case Study on the Return of Investment*
  www.metrixglobal.net/images/pdfs/metrixglobal_coaching_ roi_briefing.pdf

- *Coaching ROI: "Wow" Your Clients with Real Results*
  www.managementconsultingnews.com/articles/battley_ coaching_roi.php

2.5.1   Why Executive Coaches Are Hired

As mentioned in the study cited in the Corporate Coaching section of this guide, the number one reason companies hire coaches is for leadership development (70% of respondents gave this reason). Other reasons companies hire coaches are: for skill development or style differences (64%), to retain top talent (40%), as part of management succession planning (34%), and to ensure success after promotion or with a new hire (30%).

A variety of issues arise within corporations in which the performance of a single person may have a great effect on the outcomes of certain situations or on the goals of the corporation as an entity. In these cases, the coach is usually hired to groom a recently-promoted executive for his or her new role or to assist one who may be having difficulty adjusting.

A recently appointed executive, manager or supervisor might need a coach if they are having trouble fitting into their new position. While they might be efficient managers of production or sales, for example, they may not have a lot of experience in managing the team of people they are now in charge of leading. They may not clearly understand what their new bosses require of them in their new role. Coaches can help such new leaders in developing goals and strategies to enable them to get the most out of their team's efforts, or assist with coming up with creative problem-solving solutions.

Coaching is also useful for executives who have been in their position for some time, but need to develop new skills. For example, this might include helping an executive or manager develop a better management style or hone leadership skills. The ability to work well with others as part of a team may need to be developed and nurtured. Clarification of an individual executive's role within the company with respect to corporate goals at large and how to transmit that information to others in the company might be needed.

2.5.2   Coaching Executives

Sessions between executives and their coaches are often intense, and can last up to two hours once or twice a week.

A coach might start by asking the executive to prepare a personal mission statement. Have the client answer the questions, "Who am I?", "What are my personal goals?", "What are my professional goals?", "What is my world view?", questions designed to help the individual clarify how they relate to others and how they will get the most out of their position.

The next step will be to create a list of issues that need to be addressed. These might include evaluating personal competencies, determining ways to inspire team members or thinking of ways to get employees to internalize company values.

The coach can help provide objective, non-biased feedback to the client with respect to his or her leadership skills, using methods such as 360° Feedback. This involves getting feedback from those who work the executive including peers, direct reports, and possibly key clients. One example of an instrument that can be used for 360° Feedback is the Profiles Checkpoint 360° Competency Feedback System from Profiles International (**www.profilesinternational.com**). The system measures a manager's performance with respect to:

- Communications ability

- Leadership qualities

- Adaptability to change (risk-taking, work environment, etc.)

- Interpersonal relationships

- Ability to manage tasks effectively

- How productive they are (assertiveness, decision-making, etc.)

- Ability to train and motivate others effectively

- Self improvement on the job (learning from mistakes, constructive criticism, etc.)

Consisting of 70 questions, the Checkpoint 360° Feedback System provides a comparison of the boss or manager's rating of his or her abilities compared to the ratings of the subject's boss or multiple bosses, direct reports, and peers. For each question, the assessor (whether self or others) marks a 1 through 5, with 1 implying that the subject never shows the particular skill, and 5 meaning that the subject consistently shows the skill. Often subjects are surprised by the discrepancy between their own assessments of themselves, and those of their boss, co-workers and employees. You can see a sample analysis of a completed Profiles Checkpoint 360° Competency Feedback at **www.assessmentspecialists. com/samples/cp.pdf**.

In addition to considering an executive's role within the company, the executive might also need help in balancing his or her personal life with the needs of the company. This might involve identifying ways to orga-nize one's workday in a more efficient fashion in order to get the most work accomplished and still have time to spend with family. A coach might help such an individual learn more about his or her own person-ality, leadership style, personal goals and so on. All of these things will help the busy executive better manage others in the company. They will also help increase productivity or other corporate needs while allowing the manager to feel more fulfilled in his or her role. (Work/life balance coaching is covered in more detail in section 2.11.)

After the major issues that need to be addressed have been identified, you will help the client develop an action plan. The action plan will prioritize each problem and establish how it will be handled. Perhaps your client might need to attend a few leadership seminars, or needs to interview individual team members to find out how each one fits into your client's vision of what he or she is trying to achieve. The plan will help your client identify possible options to solve the problems and then choose the best possible solutions.

In addition to prioritizing these actions, the plan will include a time-line for achieving each goal. This means that as each problem, issue or shortcoming is identified, a time frame will be established for ad-dressing it and creating a solution. In other words, "I will do X within Y weeks/months/years." This is important because some problems may be easily solved while others may take longer and might have multiple solutions that need to be implemented over time.

2.5.3   Considerations in Executive Coaching

Many of the same considerations involved in corporate coaching are also involved in executive coaching. This includes the fact that the com-pany is the client, not the individuals being coached.

With executive coaching, there must be some consensus at the onset about how potential conflicts will be resolved. For example, when the focus of coaching will be on a problem executive, organizational development and leadership coach Timi Gleason of Executive Goals (**www.executivegoals.com/coach.html**) advises her clients to "be prepared for the employee to make another decision rather than 'shaping up.'"

The executive may decide to resign after exploring his or her situation with the coach. Discussing potential issues with the client in advance of the coaching can help ensure that the coaching meets the needs of both the client company and the individual being coached.

2.6 Relationship Coaching

Relationships form the cornerstone of our existence, and are therefore a natural venue for life coaches. There are hundreds of relationship coaches throughout the United States and Canada (roughly two-thirds of relationship coaches are women, as well as several husband-and-wife teams) and about half of them hold credentials as therapists or counselors. While this branch of life coaching is still relatively new, schools and training programs specifically for this type of coaching now exist, and its potential for continued growth looks promising.

In establishing the need for relationship coaching, David Steele, founder and CEO of The Relationship Coaching Institute, cites the increasingly high divorce rate, number of single-parent homes and number of singles. Steele, a marriage and family therapist turned relationship coach, contends that most people want to have successful relationships, but they just are not sure how.

Most clients involved in personal relationship coaching tend to be married couples seeking a more harmonious existence together, or unmarried couples involved in long-term relationships who are not sure where they are headed. In both cases, the couples are usually inclined toward fixing whatever problems they have, since they are investing significant time and money in coaching. Other clients are "chronic" singles who are desperately looking to meet someone, and wondering why they are having no luck. This group tends to be an equal mix of men and women.

Relationship coaches work with clients face-to-face much more often than traditional life coaches, either through one-on-one sessions, workshops, group sessions or couples' retreats. Fees for relationship coaching tend to be similar to those for general life coaching. In cases where relationship coaches work with large corporations, though, they tend to charge what their corporate counterparts charge.

Relationship coaches deal with personal and sensitive issues, and these should be explored delicately. When meeting or talking with clients for the first time, stress that you will maintain absolute confidentiality. Still, there are certain questions that you need to ask clients, and certain information that you need to know in order to get a good general background on the client. For example, the coach may ask questions about past relationships, marriages, experiences, dating history, the types of people to whom the client is or was attracted, and so on.

2.6.1 Working with Singles

Having clients determine what they want is generally the first step in coaching singles. Are they looking for interesting people to date, a long-term relationship or to get married? Make sure that clients are as specific as possible. You will have a hard time helping people achieve their goals if they aren't even certain what those goals are.

Once the client has determined realistic goals, the next step is to help them put forth a plan of action. For example, if Bill wants to meet a woman interested in a long-term relationship, his coach might ask him to list what he has done so far in an attempt to find Ms. Right. Next to each item on the list, Bill would mark how effective each one had been, with 1 being the least effective, and 5 being the most effective. The two can then analyze why each step has been effective or ineffective. Maybe Bill's list looks like this:

- Went to weekly singles' dance at local nightclub–2

- Approached female co-workers I found attractive–1

- Visited Internet chat rooms–1

- Asked friends to fix me up with someone–1

- Volunteered at community center–2

Bill is understandably discouraged by the low scores, but he and his coach decide, based on these scores, that he will continue to go to the weekly singles' dances and to increase his volunteer hours at the community center.

Alternately, relationship coaches and their clients may determine that the client is not ready for a relationship at the moment and better off remaining single. This doesn't mean that he will never have an intimate relationship again, just that the timing is not right.

2.6.2   Working with Couples

In addition to married couples, relationship coaches also coach couples who are not sure where they are going, and don't know whether they should marry, live together, or explore other options.

As a sample exercise, relationship coaches working with couples might have each partner come up with lists—what they like about their relationship; what needs improvement in their relationship; suggestions for a better relationship; activities for them to pursue together. Afterwards, the couples compare their lists, and see where the similarities and differences lie.

A favorite activity that coach David Steele uses with couples is the "appreciation exercise." Couples take turns telling each other what they appreciate about their partner. This could take five minutes, ten minutes, or an hour, depending on how much they elaborate. One partner will start, and when he or she mentions each point, the other person will repeat if for emphasis. For example:

JEREMY: I appreciate how patient you were with me when I had a stressful day at the office Monday.

JENNIFER: You appreciate how patient I was with you when you had a stressful day at the office Monday.

JEREMY: That's right. Also, I appreciate how you picked up Jerry and Rachel from the mall Saturday after I told you that I was too exhausted.

JENNIFER: You appreciate how I picked up Jerry and Rachel…

This particular exercise focuses on the positive aspects of the relationship, and Steele recommends that every relationship coach employ this exercise when working with couples.

While relationship coaches work with couples who are experiencing difficulties, they do not want to coach couples in abusive relationships. Unfortunately, spotting this kind of trouble is not as cut-and-dried as obvious physical signs, such as marks or bruises. If you suspect abuse in a couple who come to you for coaching, inform them tactfully that you do not think that you can be of service to them. For further information, you may wish to visit the National Domestic Violence Hotline site at **www.ndvh.org** or the Canadian National Clearinghouse on Family Violence at **www.phac-aspc.gc.ca/ncfv-cnivf/index-eng.php**.

2.6.3 Divorce

Not all relationship coaching deals with finding and maintaining successful relationships; some of it deals with cleanly and effectively ending unhealthy ones. With 50% of all marriages failing, some coaches have found a niche in coaching people going through divorces. The crux is usually on parting amicably with an estranged spouse, starting anew following a marital breakup, discovering the reasons for the failed marriage or, in cases where couples have children, dealing with issues such as visitation and custody.

Coaches do not provide legal advice or counsel, but instead help clients work out an action plan, such as:

- Will they hire an attorney, or do an uncontested divorce?

- Have they worked out a custody arrangement?

- How are they going to tell their relatives, and when?

- What timeframe for the whole process do they have in mind?

- Are there any other potential difficulties that they had not foreseen?

All of these issues can and do come up, and thinking in a clear, logical, step-by-step fashion is not always easy for the client. Often, clients are faced with many issues at once and frequently have trouble knowing where to start or what to deal with first. Divorce coach Laura Meyer says, "My clients come to me with any issue relating to divorce and separation. The biggest challenge is narrowing issues down into bite size pieces, since in most cases my clients' entire lives are upside down. They may want to work on too many things at once and get overwhelmed."

Relationship coaches might also moderate divorce support groups, or even give speeches or presentations before them. If you are going to coach clients going through divorce, cultivate contacts and relationships with divorce support groups and similar organizations. But don't come on like you're giving a sales pitch for your coaching services. Besides seeming pushy, you might be seen as trying to take advantage of people who are particularly vulnerable, and that totally goes against life coaching. You can find information about working with support groups in section 3.2.

Parents Without Partners is the largest international non-profit organization for single parents, with over 50,000 members in North America alone. Although the majority of their members are divorced or separated, PWP also welcomes widowed and never-married parents. The organization holds regular meetings and events, and frequently hosts guest speakers and presenters. You can find information about Parents Without Partners at **www.parentswithoutpartners.org**.

2.6.4   Other Relationship Areas

Family Issues

Some relationship coaches focus on family issues, specifically between parents and (usually teen-aged) children. These coaches may work with the parents and children together, or on an individual basis. Single parents face many unique challenges in raising kids, and they also form a segment of relationship coaches' clientele.

Social Skills

There is also a branch of relationship coaching that deals with helping to improve social skills and self-confidence of clients who may be timid or shy. Some people just want to make more friends, or to have a better social life in general. They may be happily married or involved with someone, but still feel that their relationships are lacking in another regard. Maybe they want more male friends, or more female friends. Maybe they feel uncomfortable at parties or large gatherings, want to work on projecting their image or develop their public speaking skills. Some clients want to become more assertive.

Business

Relationship coaching has its applications in the business world, too. A client might have experienced a slump in work performance due to telephone anxiety, not connecting with customers, or not getting along with bosses and co-workers. Some relationship coaches work with business partners or bosses who can't seem to "connect" with each other or their employees. Relationship coaches can help individuals and companies to moderate disagreements before they blow up into lawsuits, by providing objective, non-biased feedback.

2.7 Retirement Coaching

Retirement coaching is one of the fastest growing areas of life coaching. There's a good reason for this. You've almost certainly heard of the "Baby Boom," the rapid increase in the numbers of babies born between roughly the end of World War II and the early 1960s. During this period approximately 76 million babies were born, and today many in this increasingly affluent and savings-conscious demographic are getting set to retire.

Even now, more than 11,000 people are retiring every day in North America. But the number of Boomers reaching retirement age will more than double in the next 10 years. It's no wonder that Fortune magazine reported in the June 2007 issue "with so many baby boomers getting ready to bow out of the workforce, coaching aspiring retirees is a fast-growing mini industry."

In addition to the large number of upcoming retirees, another factor is that people are living longer and healthier lives. The average life expectancy in the United States today is about 75 years for men and 80 years for women (these figures are slightly higher for Canada) compared to an average for both genders of about 68 years in 1950. This means that if people retire at 60-65 years of age they can expect to live an additional 15 to 20 years or even longer after retirement.

2.7.1 Services Provided by Retirement Coaches

There are a number of different aspects to retirement coaching. One of the most obvious concerns is, of course, having sufficient finances to live a reasonably comfortable lifestyle throughout retirement. But there are a number of other services retirement coaches provide. These might include helping clients in:

- Planning for retirement in advance of retiring

- Where to live during the retirement years

- What to do with one's time during retirement (for example, education, travel, etc.)

- Possibly working or opening a business after retirement

- Finding a sense of purpose in retirement

- Finding personal fulfillment in retirement

- Finding leisure activities (hobbies, etc.) to pursue in retirement

- Finding volunteer work

- Relationship coaching

- Deciding whether retirement is the best option

2.7.2 Retirement Planning

Retirement planning can include a number of different facets of retirement. The aspect of retirement that probably first comes to mind for most people is financial planning for the years after a person no longer works at the job they have had for a number of years. There are countless financial planning institutions and organizations available to people saving money for their retirement. Unless you are a certified financial planner or something similar, this likely will not be the focus of retirement planning for you as a coach. Instead, you will help people to think about all the different aspects of retirement they will face, although that may also include advising them to seek help for their financial planning needs.

Retirement coaching is more about lifestyle coaching. In other words, helping clients to identify what they would consider the ideal lifestyle in their retirement years. You will help clients start thinking about what they are planning to do after retiring. For example, they might decide to take that European tour they've been dreaming about for the past 25 years. Or maybe they want to spend a few months catching up with old friends and family they haven't seen in some time.

Other clients might be thinking about starting their own businesses after they retire, particularly if they are retiring at a younger age. They may already have a good idea of the kind of business they want to run. In cases like these, you can help point them to resources like the Small Business Administration website (**www.sba.gov**) or other resources for small business start-ups (see Chapter 5 for more information about these resources). Still other clients might have half-formed ideas about selling their houses and moving to someplace more to their liking. This could include concerns about a more pleasant climate or being closer to loved ones. You will help your clients take the necessary steps toward achieving those goals.

Retirement planning should, ideally, begin a number of years before an individual is ready to retire. The average retirement age in the U.S. today is well below the mandated 65 years of age, so many retirement coaches market their services to clients much younger than sixty-five. Some coaches even characterize retirement as just another step in the career development process in light of the fact that many more people than ever before are using their "retirement" years to recreate themselves and try new things. In fact, helping draw out of clients their inner passions and goals can also be a major part of your focus as a retirement coach.

2.7.3   Pre-Retirement Assessment

One way to help clients start thinking about retirement and what they might like to accomplish in retirement is to use a questionnaire such as the one below. Some clients may be ready to retire long before the mandatory age and are financially secure enough to pull it off. Many people get into trouble, though, once they actually have the leisure time to do the things they've always dreamed about doing because once they've done a few of them they don't know what to do afterward.

Sample Pre-Retirement Questionnaire

Are you ready to retire?

Read each statement and decide whether you agree or disagree with it.

Question	Agree	Disagree
1. It is important that I accomplish something meaningful with my life.	☐	☐
2. I feel financially secure and ready for retirement.	☐	☐
3. I usually set and achieve my goals.	☐	☐
4. My boss/spouse/government says its time to retire. (I can't wait!)	☐	☐
5. I find it easy to stay busy when I'm not at work.	☐	☐
6. I have at least one hobby that I really enjoy and can spend hours at it.	☐	☐
7. I don't need to be the person in control of every situation.	☐	☐
8. Someday I would love to travel and see the world.	☐	☐
9. I believe I am in excellent physical, mental and emotional health.	☐	☐
10. I've always wanted to start my own business.	☐	☐
11. I am self-motivated.	☐	☐
12. I wish I had a job I really enjoyed doing.	☐	☐
13. No one would ever consider me a workaholic.	☐	☐
14. I live too far away from my adult kids and would like to see them more but my job is here.	☐	☐
15. I currently do volunteer activities or would like to volunteer.	☐	☐
16. I have a secret dream to someday do something I've never accomplished.	☐	☐
17. I would prefer a more leisurely lifestyle than I now live.	☐	☐
18. I have a good relationship with my spouse/partner.	☐	☐
19. I have a lot of friends outside of people I work with.	☐	☐
20. On the weekends I never think about work.	☐	☐

How to Score This Questionnaire

Generally, if a person checks off "Agree" more than "Disagree" then they are probably ready for retirement. The questions are designed to discover whether or not the client is emotionally and mentally ready for retirement. If they agree with most of the statements, chances are they have a number of personal internal and external resources that will allow them to be happy and productive in retirement.

For example, if they like to stay busy, have friends outside of work, have a hobby, and so on, then they won't likely miss their job even though you might need to help them discover some coachable goals as far as finding something meaningful to do once they've retired.

Some of the statements will help you determine if the client is happy about the notion of leaving their job. From this assessment, you can learn whether they will miss being in charge of things (statement 7), if they'd really prefer to stay at their job rather than retire (statement 4), whether they have aspirations of owning their own business (statement 10), or whether they've centered their whole lives around work (statements 12,13, 19).

Other statements will help to give you insights into what their dreams or aspirations are on a personal level. If they agreed that they'd love to travel or to move closer to their kids, then they probably won't miss the job too much and are ready to move on.

No questionnaire can ever be a precise model of a client's state of mind or intentions, of course. But you can use an instrument like this as a starting point to probe further into a client's mindset when thinking about retiring. You can also discover whether or not they are truly at ease with it or would prefer to keep working until they are ready for a more leisurely lifestyle.

Some clients may be facing mandatory retirement or are physically unable to work any longer at the same job. These clients may be on financial thin ice and really aren't ready to retire. Or they may be fine financially but they've never known any social life outside of their workplaces. A pre-retirement assessment will give you some insights into their general thinking about the retirement years.

2.7.4   Post-Retirement Coaching

Today's conception of an ideal retirement is not your grandparents' notion of a leisurely (even sedentary) lifestyle. In the old model of retirement most people left the workforce and gradually withdrew from any sort of active lifestyle. This also often had health consequences for many people due to inactivity and lack of exercise. Today, most retirees are not satisfied to waste their remaining years sitting in front of a television or knitting in a corner.

Post-Retirement Issues

People want to know what their alternatives are and how they can develop a more productive life after retiring. As you'll learn in the section on work/life balance coaching (section 2.11), many people can spend their working lives in a job they truly dislike because it pays well and they have never had the opportunity to work in a way that brings them pleasure and fulfillment. After retiring from their old jobs they may be looking for a way to move into a more fulfilling career.

You will help people identify their goals and their obstacles to achieving those goals. Consider the fact that many people lead three different lives: their professional or working life, their personal life (who they are as an individual) and their family life. At different times in their lives one or more of these may take higher precedence than another.

Some of the principle aspects of post-retirement coaching are:

- Reassessing career objectives (letting go of the old job and developing new career strategies)

- Recreating quality of life (being comfortable with the present, looking forward to the future)

- Personal fulfillment (taking charge of personal development, finding goals to better oneself as a person)

- Spiritual fulfillment (finding personal spirituality and connecting it with the present and future)

- Reorienting family connections (rediscovering a sense of family, revitalizing family relationships)

- Relearning leisure (becoming comfortable with not working, finding leisure activities to enjoy)

A person who has spent more of their time living their working life may find themselves floundering a bit now that their personal life or family life has suddenly become more important. For example, someone who has always led a busy life as an executive or some other kind of manager, may find real difficulty when they find themselves alone with no big projects to finish and no one to manage.

Relationship coaching can be another big part of the retirement coach's job. Spouses who have lived hectic working lives for years may have grown apart in many ways. Once they're both retired they might need to get to know each other again. This is something a retirement coach can help them with.

Above all, the retirement coach's job is to help people find fulfillment. This can be particularly vexing for people once they no longer have a job to go to every day. Some people might prefer a transition stage between full-time work and full-time retirement. That is, the solution to the problem of what to do with themselves may be to work at some sort of part-time job while drawing a portion of pension. Retirement coaches help people decide what works best for them.

A useful resource for retirement coaches is the book *Retire Smart, Retire Happy: Finding Your True Path in Life*, by Nancy K. Schlossberg, a professor emeritus at the University of Maryland. She identifies six main types of retirees – from the "Retreater" who is confused and upset about retirement, to the "Adventurer" who is ready for a daring life change. You can read more about the six types of retirees in an article at **http:// lifestyle.msn.com/boomers/article.aspx?cp-documentid=10799309**.

2.8 Spiritual Coaching

Spiritual coaching integrates core religious or spiritual values into various aspects of a person's life. Christian coaching is the leading form of religious coaching in North America, but this information applies to coaching in other faiths and forms of spirituality as well.

Spiritual coaching is, in a sense, religious coaching, but spiritual coaching can also have a non-religious slant, focusing on balance, physical and emotional well being, and greater consciousness and self-awareness. People seek out spiritual coaches when their basic needs have already been met. Instead of a concrete goal, such as finding a better job or buying a home, a client of a spiritual coach wants to delve deeper, to find some inner truth, to truly know themselves.

Spiritual coach and author, Marlee Ledai, whose coaching business, GoGirl Coaching, has been featured in publications like the *Chicago Tribune* and the *Los Angeles Times*, shares her impressions of clients who seek out spiritual coaching:

> "My clients want to synthesize their spirituality and worldview with their work…They are relieved and happy they've found a coach who understands their spirit-led orientation to life instead of by-passing it in favor of external goals and achievements. This is welcome to me

when clients want to talk about incorporating spirituality into life itself; the challenges are organic, the way forward makes itself apparent. The client is led by her own spirit and soulfulness."

Spiritual coaches often describe their services as an attempt to help clients reach an inner awareness and empower themselves to have control over who they are as an individual, rather than simply being acted upon by and reacting to external circumstances. Even so, helping clients open up to their own spirituality can be challenging. Spiritual coach Marguerite Manning describes the process this way:

"I always talk to the 'soul' or 'wise self' that exists in every client and I always talk the truth as I see it…I think I experience such a great amount of success because I tell each client ahead of time that I'm talking to their soul. As a result, they feel as if they must assume that higher level of consciousness…and they're not as defensive or closed to what I have to say as they would be otherwise."

2.8.1   Forms of Spirituality

Spiritual coaches are generally well-versed in philosophy and religion as well as more metaphysical fields, and tend to incorporate what they find most useful in their various studies and experiences. Although they may not necessarily concentrate on a specific religion or philosophy, many are familiar with the basic tenets of Christianity, Judaism, Islam, Buddhism, Native American beliefs and customs, and so on.

The main religions of the world and some of their subgroups are:

- *Christianity:* Catholicism, Protestantism, Eastern Orthodox, Mormonism, Jehovah's Witness, Christian Science, and many other subgroups

- *Judaism:* Orthodox, Traditional, Conservative, Reform, etc.

- *Islam:* Sunni, Shi'a, Sufi, etc.

- *Buddhism:* Mahayana, Theravada, Tibetan, etc.

- *Hinduism:* Vaishnavism, Shaivism, etc.

- *Shinto:* Jinja, Shuha, Minzoku, Kokka, etc.

- *Sikhism:* A few minor sects exist, but, mainly, a uniform system of beliefs is embraced by most Sikhs

- *Baha'i:* Grew out of Islam, with elements of Judaeo-Christian and Buddhist beliefs; a few minor sects exist

Some of the other forms of spiritualism you may encounter as a spiritual coach are:

- *Neo-Paganism (or simply Paganism):* Wicca, Shamanism, Native American beliefs, Druidism, etc.

- *New Age:* A wide range of beliefs influenced by eastern religions, paganism and other forms of spirituality

- *Humanism:* Secular or non-religious humanism, Non-theistic religious humanism, and Theistic religious humanism

If you would like to learn more about religion and spirituality, visit Harvard University's Pluralism Project website at **www.pluralism.org**. This site is dedicated to documenting, studying, and understanding religious diversity in America, especially with respect to non-Christian and non-Jewish religions. It features research articles, news releases, and links to hundreds of religious and spiritual resources in the U.S.

2.8.2 Christian Coaching

In an article published in *Christian Counseling Today* in 2000, life coach Christopher McCluskey characterizes the relationship between the Christian coach and the client:

> *"…the two are embarking on a journey together to understand more fully the Lord's purpose for that person's life and to see that fulfilled."*

There is a third party in this type of coaching relationship. The question that Christian coaches ask their clients is not so much "What do you want to do?" but "What do you think that God wants you to do?"

The basis of the relationship between Christian coaches and their clients is their shared faith, but that can take a variety of forms. Some coaches are traditional or fundamentalist, others are more moderate and some are liberal. This is obviously an important consideration when determining compatibility, but not the sole criterion.

The Christian Coaches Network's online referral service allows users to find a coach based on specific denomination, gender, geographic area and various personal and professional areas of expertise. You can find it at **www.christiancoaches.com/referral/search.cgi**.

In addition to personal life issues, Christian coaches also work with incorporating religious values into business—dealing fairly and equitably with employees; ethics in running a business; how to get ahead in a fiercely competitive world without crossing certain moral boundaries. There are also Christian coaches who specialize in assisting religious institutions with effective financial management. Generally, these coaches have an economics background, and most have experience in managing their own congregations.

Christian coaches sometimes train other life coaches seeking to enter the Christian tract, and give speeches and seminars at Christian colleges and universities, or before congregations and church groups. They work with members of the clergy, as well as those who want help with expanding their ministry, growing in their own personal relationship with God, or being a more effective spiritual leader to their parishioners.

There are members of the clergy who offer Christian coaching in addition to their regular jobs as pastors, ministers, etc., as well as former clergy who have transitioned into coaching full time, incorporating their religious beliefs into their coaching practices. Of course, not everyone who transitions into this branch of coaching is in the clergy, but they are individuals who are deeply involved with their respective religious institutions.

As with general life coaching, the bulk of Christian coaching tends to be done over the telephone, and the average fees are in line with what life coaches generally charge (see section 5.6 on "Setting Your Fees" later in this guide). In addition to using follow-up forms or assignments to complete, coach and client might both agree to pray for guidance about a particular issue, recite affirmations or hold devotionals.

2.8.3   Non-traditional Spirituality

Spiritual coaching may also delve into the realm of the abstruse, arcane or New Age. Shamanism, Wicca, astrology and tarot are common examples. This may work for some coaches, depending on what sort of clients they want to attract, but certain people will be turned off by this mix of spiritual forms and may look for a more conventional form of coaching. But if this is where your area of interest lies you will find a ready market for spiritual coaching based on one or more of these systems of belief.

Eastern philosophies and beliefs are often incorporated into this form of coaching. Spiritual coaching can include elements of yoga and other forms of meditation, and tie physical well-being to spiritual well-being. (This is why many spiritual coaches are doctors, chiropractors or massage therapists.)

Spiritual coaches often talk about "the flow of energy," and maintain that illness, stress, unhappiness and even physical pain are all tied to blocked flow of energy. In dealing with these issues, the coach may have the client use techniques of feng shui, the art of arranging objects to allow for maximum positive energy flow. There are many spiritual coaches who teach feng shui and report that it has been helpful to their clients.

Sufism

Some spiritual coaches are drawn to Sufism, which is a mystical-ascetic branch of Islam focused on spiritual purification and attaining oneness with God. Sufism incorporates many elements common to the "Abrahamic" religions (Judaism, Christianity, Islam), but stresses that philosophical discussions about Being and about God and Creation are not the best path to spiritual wholeness. Instead, Sufism encourages individuals to purify their hearts so that aspects of the Divine will become apparent. For a brief introduction to Sufism visit the website of the International Association of Sufism at **www.ias.org/articles/Introduction_to_ Sufism.html**.

Chakra is also employed by spiritual coaches for maximizing positive energy flow. Chakra is a form of meditation that focuses on seven energy points throughout the body, from the top of the head to the base of the spine. Each "chakra" is associated with different emotions and sensations.

2.8.4   Helping People Focus

One of the issues spiritual coaches may find themselves dealing with is helping a client find a belief system to focus on. Many people in modern western society have no firm belief system (they may consider themselves "spiritual but not religious"), but nonetheless seek some sort of spiritual fulfillment.

Others may have been brought up within a particular belief structure or as part of an organized religion like Christianity or Judaism but have become disillusioned or otherwise disaffected with the system they grew up with. They may seek a coach's guidance to help them find a belief system that works for them in their daily lives, or reintegrate their old belief system into their lives.

The coach's job will not be to try to instill his or her own personal belief system into their clients but to help them find their own paths. One way to help clients search for a form of spirituality that will work for them is through a questionnaire. Some of these are available online. The Belief System Selector at **www.selectsmart.com/religion** is a questionnaire that helps people to choose the most likely fit to their core beliefs. It also has links to resources respondents can use to find out more about the form of spirituality that most closely matches their results.

You may want to create your own questionnaire. If so, consider asking clients questions like:

- Do you currently subscribe/belong to a particular belief system?

- How is your belief system not meeting your needs?

- What do you find of value in this system?

- Do you feel that anything is missing from your life?

- What one quality about yourself do you value most highly?

- What personal qualities would you like to develop further in your life?

Questions like these will help you to understand what your client is looking for and what they would like to achieve during their spiritual coaching sessions. If they are already part of a belief system that they would like to maintain in their lives, they might only need help finding a focus or an outlet for their beliefs. Or they may need your assistance as a coach to help them integrate their beliefs into everyday lives (see the next section on workplace spirituality for more about this).

Once a client has found a spiritual focus and uncovered their core beliefs, the coach will help him or her create an action plan for finding their spiritual path. This may include helping them find resources to learn more about their spiritual issues, such as books, groups for other like-minded individuals, retreats, and so on. Just remember that a coach's role is to be a facilitator not an instructor.

Exercises commonly given to clients by spiritual coaches include maintaining a diary of thoughts and feelings to discuss during coaching sessions and creating a private "sacred space" in their home for meditation. Suggestions for creating relaxing touches to a personal meditation area include soothing music, a dimly lit space, plants, and scented candles. The area set aside for meditation should be out of the way and quiet so that the client can reflect without being disturbed by other family members, loud street noises or other distractions.

> **TIP:** If you are going to see clients in your office, you will want your workspace to reflect your coaching philosophy. A messy, cluttered or disordered office will reflect badly on you, particularly if you purport to help clients find inner harmony and balance.

2.8.5 Workplace Spirituality

Another focus, particularly if you plan to offer your services from the basis of a particular belief system such as Christian coaching, will be to help your clients integrate their already-formed beliefs into their daily lives.

For example, someone who holds deep-seated Christian values and traditions may find difficulty in rationalizing these with what they are expected to do in the workplace. Having to work on Sunday is an example of this. How will you help someone who feels that Sundays should be spent in spiritual reflection deal with the pressure of his or her manager at work insisting on Sunday as just another workday?

Other people may feel that there just isn't time enough to devote to spiritual pursuits with all the other demands on them in their secular lives. Another issue might be trying to find some sort of spiritual synchronicity with work. In other words, many people want to find meaning in the jobs they do and want to find inspiration in that.

Some businesses also have a need to develop a workplace spirituality. Many companies now feel that if they encourage personal spirituality among their employees this will foster a more harmonious and productive workplace. Spiritual coaches offer advice and training on how to effectively integrate spiritualism and the workplace.

Some companies have embraced such notions as shamanistic "spirit quests", "God squads" (people employed by companies to help employees deal with traumatic events in their lives), or even prayer groups in the workplace. A spiritual coach can help companies look at the types of programs they can offer for employees or help a corporation become a sort of spiritual entity in itself.

One book that explores the topic of workplace spirituality in-depth is *A Spiritual Audit of Corporate America,* by Ian Mitroff and Elizabeth A. Denton. In the book the authors examine how companies are harmonizing spiritual values with corporate values to create a more productive and happier workforce.

2.9   Time Management Coaching

Already a key point in many areas of life coaching, time management is the central theme of certain coaches' practices. These coaches cater to the busy, overwhelmed, harried masses, and generally find no shortage of clients. Their client list might include single parents, overworked executives, or anyone with an expanding schedule and a decreasing amount of freedom. The idea is to help the client do what needs to be done, while still finding the time to do what she wants.

This section is an overview of the major elements of time management, with suggested ways to effectively help your clients. It is adapted from the *FabJob Guide to Become a Professional Organizer*, by Grace Jasmine.

In the last 20 years, time management has been one of the most dominant self-help themes in books, articles, seminars, and websites. Many clients are frustrated because they feel they don't have enough hours in the day to accomplish the things they really need to do. They know that less important stuff is chewing up the time.

These clients may be falling behind in their work or putting in lots of late extra hours because they can't accomplish their goals during the standard work day. The phone rings too much; they are drowning in email; or they get too burned out to finish the job so they zone out in front of the television or their home computer. There is a solution to all this frustration and you can help your clients find it.

2.9.1   Find Out How Time is Spent

The first step is to help your clients understand how their time is currently being spent, so have clients log their daily routines for two weeks. A two-week period is enough for you to discover the variances in clients' current schedules. Have clients keep track of their major activities in one-hour or half-hour bites. You can use the Time Activity Log form provided on the next page.

> TIP: Don't let clients fill out their time logs at the end of the day or the end of the week, because they often will forget their hourly activities. Ask them to commit to filling in the log throughout the day.

Notice that the Time Activity Log includes evenings and weekends. This is an intentional reminder that clients have all their waking hours to accomplish their goals. In addition to the daily work schedule, they need to plan for their family time, relaxation time, and exercise routines.

Time Activity Log

	SUN	MON	TUE	WED	THU	FRI	SAT
A.M.							
12:00							
1:00							
2:00							
3:00							
4:00							
5:00							
6:00							
7:00							
8:00							
9:00							
10:00							
11:00							
P.M.							
12:00							
1:00							
2:00							
3:00							
4:00							
5:00							
6:00							
7:00							
8:00							
9:00							
10:00							
11:00							

Using the results from your clients' log sheets, fill out the Time Activity Summary below to summarize each day's events. (Feel free to change the example categories on the left hand column on the form.) Ask your clients how typical those weeks were for them. If you think that the information is skewed, ask your clients to fill in the forms for another week and try again.

What does the Time Activity Summary tell you? Perhaps it will tell you that nothing needs fixing. Look at your client's priorities and goals. Do they want to spend time with their families? How much time in a week is reasonable? Maybe they have the right amount of time allocated already and they just need advice to spend their time in more productive ways.

On the other hand, changes might be needed in your clients' schedules to make room for their priorities. Discuss the amount of time that each category demands from your clients daily. Work with clients to select target times or percentages that make more sense for them and align with their goals.

Time Activity Summary

	SUN	MON	TUE	WED	THU	FRI	SAT
Sleeping							
Commuting							
Productive Work							
Cooking/ Cleaning							
Eating							
Studying/ Homework							
Phone Calls							
Distractions							
Internet/ Video Games							
Television							
Email							
Grooming							
Family Time							
Exercise							
Social							

2.9.2   Time-Saving Tips

No one can make more than 24 hours happen in a day, but there are ways to help frustrated clients find more time in their day than they have now for the important things. In general, look for things to eliminate, ways to reschedule, and opportunities to combine activities. It is important that clients start to feel the power they have over their days. Consider the following common time management problems and suggestions and keep an expanded list of your own.

Too Much Time Commuting

Consider avoiding the worst part of rush hour or start the day by leaving for work 30 minutes earlier and going home 30 minutes earlier. A commute can be shortened dramatically by avoiding peak traffic times.

Too Much TV Time

You might suggest to clients that they consider videotaping or using TiVo to control what day and time a favorite program is watched. They can also skip through the commercials to save even more time!

Need More Quiet Time at Work

See if the client's employer allows for flex-scheduling. Many companies allow employees to work eight 9-hour days and one 8-hour day every two-week payroll period, with one additional day off. That gives the client an extra hour each day when the phones aren't ringing to concentrate on those pressing tasks that need to get done.

Need More Free Time

Many employers now offer a 4-by-10 plan, which could allow your client to put in a 40-hour week in 4 days. That gives a client a 3-day weekend every week to get those big chores done.

Too Much Time on the Phone

Does a client need to call someone who loves to talk? To avoid a gabby caller ruining your client's time management plan, suggest your client keep a piece of paper handy with conversation cues to keep on track.

Too Much Time Doing Chores

What is your client's time worth? Is it really well spent on hours of lawn care, laundry, housecleaning, or car maintenance? Evaluate what chores around the house can be done as well or better by professionals. Perhaps hiring someone to do some of the chores is worth the price if this will free the client to do those things that are more important.

2.9.3 ABC To-Do Lists

In section 3.1.3 you will find a goal setting worksheet. Using this worksheet you can help your clients turn their goals into doable, step-by-step tasks. Those smaller tasks can be used to make up your clients' to-do lists, breaking down each task into smaller tasks.

But what if you have a client who has 45 items on their to-do list? The answer is simply to put first things first. Prioritize. Have the client go through the to-do list and mark each item with an A, B, or C:

- "A" things must be done first in chronological order, or are those items that potentially will deliver the greatest benefit to the clients' lives.

- "B" things are important to do but in the larger picture they are not urgent.

- "C" things can logically happen later or are merely "nice to have" instead of "must have now."

TIP: Remember that priorities change over time. The ABC markings should be reviewed monthly to see if they still reflect the clients' goals.

Now clients actually start to control what happens in their day. Have clients use the Time Activity Log sheet provided and use it as a Weekly Planner.

Start by filling in the parts of their daily routine that are unavoidable, such as grooming, commuting, standing meetings, and scheduled classes. Everywhere else, clients can work on their to-do lists. Have them start filling in the blank time on a calendar with A-list to-do items. When those are completed, move on to the B-list items, and then eventually take on the C-list tasks.

> **TIP:** Far too often, clients remember to schedule deadlines when things are due, but not the work itself needed to complete the tasks. Remind them that scheduling working is more valuable than scheduling due-dates for when goals should be met.

Tell your clients that if they don't complete tasks as scheduled, then they must change tomorrow's schedule and put it back to deal with until completed. Keep the highest priority items on the top of the list at all times.

2.9.4   Personal Organizing Products

Coach your clients that the routine of prioritizing, planning, and performing the work is the most important element of time management. When it comes to managing time, PDAs don't have much on the old paper-based personal calendar. The important thing is that they start using some kind of organizer and stay with it.

Maintaining only one calendar is very important. If a client uses a digital handheld organizer and a desktop computer software calendar, they need to be sure that they are synchronized daily. If the family maintains another calendar at home, keep it synchronized with the personal calendar. Too many calendars with different information cause miscommunication and disorganization.

The Day Planner

There is no shortage of personal day organizer products on the market, which are all quite similar. Have your clients flip through several brands and decide what feels right for them and reflects personal taste.

Computer Calendars

Today, all the major business-oriented email software packages contain a calendar utility for scheduling appointments and reminders. If your clients have access to this software, be sure to suggest they use the application to schedule appointments with themselves or set up reminders to work on their to-do lists.

PDAs

A large assortment of affordable Personal Digital Assistants (PDAs) is on the market and your clients may choose to manage their calendars using that technology. They should allow clients to synchronize their calendars with the calendar maintained on their desktop computers, as well as having Internet access and email utilities. Note that clients should spend their money only on features they will really use. Gadgets and features eventually provide more distractions and challenges than benefits in time management.

2.9.5   Celebrating Success

Just like quitting smoking, getting out of debt, or losing weight, when clients take control of the way they use their time, it is cause for celebration. Old habits, even bad ones, are hard to break. One well-known and successful behavior modification technique is to reinforce good behavior with a reward system. Especially in the fragile, early days of learning a new routine, convince clients to commit to rewarding themselves for staying on track.

Perhaps a client should buy that new CD they have been thinking about as a reward for filling out the weekly planner for a whole month. Encourage a client to take their spouse out to a concert, a picnic, or a special dinner to reward both of them for their efforts and mutual support of each other. Advise the parents of a child who stayed with a new homework schedule for a month to find a suitable, pleasing reward.

2.10 Weight/Body Image Coaching

People are increasingly conscious of their fitness and physical appearance. While fad diets, vitamin supplements and hair growth products promise fantastic results, coaches who work with clients on weight and body image issues take a more realistic, practical approach. The emphasis is on developing a workable, long-term plan for clients to be the best that they can possibly be.

There are many different problem areas that fall under the weight/body image coaching area, many of which are often intertwined. These could include:

- Weight

- Lack of exercise

- Improper diet

- Unhealthy consumption of caffeine or alcohol

- Smoking

- Self-esteem issues

- Stress

This kind of coaching may incorporate a diet or exercise routine. As a weight or body image coach you are not a personal trainer or a dietician (unless of course you have those qualifications already). Your job will be to encourage clients to make exercise and a healthy lifestyle part of the daily routine and keep them motivated to continue with their improvements.

To do this, you will start with a short assessment of the client and his or her goals. This is much the same as in other forms of life coaching. You will have the client fill out a questionnaire or create a statement of their goals with respect to improving their body image or losing weight. Then, when the client has stated his or her goals, you will help them clarify what areas to work on first. For example, you might help the client identify how other areas of their lives are affecting their unhealthy lifestyle.

Many clients who come to coaches looking for ways to improve their self-image may also have self-esteem issues or are battling a stressful lifestyle or a stressful event in their lives such as job loss or divorce. These things can affect people in negative ways and contribute to substance abuse or an unhealthy lifestyle, including poor eating habits and not exercising.

> **TIP:** Be prepared to encourage clients to see professionals like personal trainers, nutritionists/dieticians, substance abuse counselors, or medical professionals such as their family physician or a psychotherapist when necessary.

2.10.1 Understanding Why People Overeat

Emotional eating plays a big part in the over-eating habits of many people. According to MedicineNet.com, 75% of overeating is caused by emotions. Further, in a recent research paper by the U.S. Department of Energy's Brookhaven National Laboratory, researchers revealed that they had discovered that emotional eating is similar to what a drug addict feels when craving drugs. You can read a summary of the results of this paper at **www.bnl.gov/bnlweb/pubaf/pr/PR_display.asp? prID=06-107**.

Often, feeling lonely, angry, frustrated or bored, people reach for "comfort foods" that help to assuage these feelings. Unfortunately, in these cases people may be feeding their emotions more than their bodies. They end up feeling guilty or ashamed of themselves because of overeating, and then eat more to try to bury those feelings, creating a vicious cycle of feeling bad-eating-feeling bad. You may need to help them discover what it is they are really hungry for.

Psychology Today magazine has a quiz which identifies emotional eaters on their website at **http://psychologytoday.psychtests.com/tests/ eating_disorders_access.html**.

The first step in helping clients who are emotional eaters might be to get them to keep a daily journal or log to track when and why they eat. This will help them to discover what causes them to eat. Did they eat because of a conflict or argument? Were they feeling sad or angry about something? By keeping track of their eating habits they will soon discover a pattern.

Once a pattern has been established, the next step is to create an action plan to start dealing with it. Although emotional eating is a symptom of the unhealthy eating habit, the underlying cause (anger, depression, sadness, etc.) can now be dealt with because you and your client will now know what triggers the habit. You can help your client to work out new coping strategies for dealing with stressful or emotionally difficult situations.

Obviously, these patterns of self-abuse or self-neglect also apply to other substances besides food. There may be similar emotional triggers in clients who habitually over-indulge in tobacco products, caffeine and alcohol. There are countless programs available to help people deal with habits like these. Success in all of them is often dependent on the individual knowing that someone out there supports and understands what they are going through. As a weight/body image coach your job will be to provide emotional back-up and motivation and there are a number of strategies you can employ to keep clients on the path to success.

Visualization can help to motivate clients. This technique is explored further in section 3.4.1. In visualization exercises, clients imagine themselves thin, or as a non-smoker, or getting up in the morning and going for a run or to the gym. By using this technique, they will be able to imagine the improvements and the benefits of living a healthier lifestyle.

Finding alternatives to eating when dealing with stressful or emotional situations is another coping strategy you can help the client with. Alternative activities will help to take his or her mind off eating and might include:

- Reading a good book or magazine

- Listening to music or playing an instrument

- Going for a walk

- Exercising

- Engaging in a task like housework, gardening or yard work

- Talking to a friend (perhaps their life coach)

- Writing a journal entry

- Meditation

2.10.2 The Importance of Exercise

Exercising regularly is an important component of a healthy lifestyle. Many people find that they have difficulty in trying to find time for regular exercise even though they recognize its importance. Symptomatic of this, health and fitness clubs rush to get their ads on the air and into the newspapers every January to take advantage of that all-too-common New Year's Resolution of joining a gym to get regular exercise and become healthier.

As mentioned earlier, exercising is an area of life many people find difficult to fit into their daily routines. Your job will be to help motivate people into finding or starting an exercise program that's right for them. You will also provide feedback and continuing support once they do start.

An exercise program can also be an important part of a weight loss regime. You may find yourself working with clients who have weight loss as part of their exercising goals. Or you may encounter clients who have an unrealistic image of themselves and their weight. Perhaps they are at a healthy weight already but feel that they need to be 10 or 15 pounds lighter because pop culture has told them that they need to look like a supermodel. (See below for more about clients with inappropriate body image beliefs.)

2.10.3 Set Point Theory

Set Point Theory is the idea that adult individuals have an "ideal" weight or "set point" which represents a stable weight range for any individual. This varies from person to person and is largely dependent on genetic factors and metabolism. In other words, this point is reached naturally if a person eats only when they are hungry, stops eating when they're full and exercises moderately.

Most people have a range of 10-20 pounds that represents their set point weight range. Their bodies are "set" at a certain weight somewhere within this range. This is one reason why dieting doesn't work well for some people, because when you lower your caloric intake, your body responds by slowing down your metabolism. This results in less activity in terms of converting fats to energy, so you don't actually burn fats as a result of eating less food. Conversely, when you speed up your metabolism, through exercise for example, you actually do start to burn fats to produce energy.

One consequence of dieting in set point theory, then, is that even though a person might initially begin to lose weight as a result of eating less, they will eventually reach a point where the body naturally tries to again establish the set point. This means that the dieter will reach a plateau where a balance is again reached between weight loss and food intake. At that point they will stop losing weight and may start to gain it back. Another consequence of this is that when a person goes off a weight-loss diet they crave more food. As a result, it's very easy to gain back any lost pounds and sometimes even more.

It is important to note there are other theories and research that conflict with set point theory. For example, in February, 2007, Reuters reported the results of research by Pennington Biomedical Research Center in Baton Rouge, Louisiana, that "dieting alone is just as effective as dieting plus exercise." Because even the experts disagree, and your clients are likely to have heard many conflicting ideas about weight loss, it is wise for a coach to encourage a more holistic approach in their clients.

Rather than recommending a diet program, coaches can propose an approach that recognizes the limitations of dieting and includes exercise, focusing on helping clients adopt a healthier body outlook. In other words, clients shouldn't expect to look like supermodels or bodybuilders as a result of dieting and exercise. Instead, a client can learn to accept his or her body as it is (along with its limitations) while adopting a healthy lifestyle, including eating the right foods and getting a reasonable amount of exercise.

2.10.4 Motivating Clients

People often set out to achieve their weight loss and exercise goals or the goal of quitting smoking or drinking less with the best intentions and great enthusiasm. Unfortunately along the way they may experience setbacks. Often this leads them to lose enthusiasm for what a few months or weeks earlier had been a desirable goal and they lose their motivation to continue.

One of your tasks working as a weight loss/body image coach will be to continually keep your clients motivated to achieve their difficult goals. Here are a few tips for keeping clients motivated:

Have Realistic Expectations

Weight loss can be a complex process, involving many different aspects of diet, exercise and individual metabolism. Clients should be aware that weight loss may take time. They can't expect to have "six-pack abs" in a couple of weeks of exercise, or lose 50 pounds in a month of dieting or calorie-counting. These kinds of changes take time and shouldn't be the major focus anyway. Instill in your clients the concept that they are taking charge of their health and making healthy changes in their eating and exercise habits.

Most of all, they need to respect their bodies and know that they are taking control of their own health. This is true for almost every aspect of changing unhealthy habits. Clients need to set realistic goals by using a goal-setting worksheet, for example, as described in section 3.1.3 of this guide, and work toward them.

Keep It Real

Clients may tell you that they have gained weight despite "eating very little" and "getting lots of exercise." In fact, research has found that most people, and women in particular, significantly underestimate the amount that they eat and overestimate the amount they exercise.

According to Brian Wansink, Ph.D., director of the Cornell Food and Brand Lab at Cornell University and author of *Mindless Eating: Why We Eat More Than We Think*, quoted in an article in *Runner's World*: "In general, people will underestimate the calories in a typical meal by about 20 percent, but after a tough workout, you might underestimate how much you're eating by as much as 50 percent."

To assess their eating and exercise, you can recommend to your coaching clients that they keep a food and exercise journal. Ask clients to commit to filling it in throughout the day, as they may have trouble remembering everything later on.

Understand Nobody Is Perfect

We all make mistakes. Clients will inevitably experience setbacks in one form or another. In the section on set point theory we mentioned the plateau dieters reach when they no longer appear to be losing weight. Many people become discouraged when they reach this plateau and begin to feel frustrated that their weight loss program isn't working. Some clients will go back to unhealthy habits at this point because that is their familiar coping mechanism. This inevitably leads to feelings of guilt, shame, or hopelessness. You will need to help clients understand that this is natural and encourage them to continue.

Use Rewards

Rewards can be built into short and long range goal setting. For example, a client who has successfully gone without a cigarette for three weeks can use some of the money saved by not smoking to buy a treat. Or clients who reach the first 10 pounds shed in a diet and exercise weight loss program can treat themselves to something special like a slice of cheesecake. This helps clients understand that a little bit of excess is okay from time to time. Just be sure that clients are in the proper frame of mind for appreciating that a reward is not an excuse to backslide or revert to old coping mechanisms.

Resources

The Diet & Fitness site at MSN.com which can be found at **http://health.msn.com/diet-and-fitness.aspx** has many excellent articles with research and advice from Harvard, *Psychology Today*, the Mayo Clinic, and other experts. Topics range from exploring why people overeat to overcoming weight loss setbacks. Insight for overeaters can also be found at the Cornell University Food and Brand Lab site at **www.foodpsychology.cornell.edu** and the Mindless Eating site at **www.mindlesseating.org** as well as the book *Mindless Eating: Why We Eat More Than We Think*, by Brian Wansink.

2.10.5 Clients with Inappropriate Body Image Beliefs

Just as there are people who are overweight and eat to cope, there are people at the opposite end of the spectrum who are in fact at an appropriate weight who believe they need to lose weight. Bulimia is an extreme example of this negative body image conception. This is more common in women than in men, although the number of men suffering from inappropriate body image beliefs is rising. The U.S. Department of Health and Human Services says that 90% of people with distorted body image beliefs are women.

In many ways, pop culture is to blame for this. Thinness is idealized in advertising, film and television programs. As a result, people are constantly bombarded with the message that they need to be thin to be healthy and socially acceptable. The body image coach's job is to counter ideas like these and help clients create realistic ideas about their own bodies.

A client may come to you with an initial idea about ways to achieve their idealized body image, but you find out that they are in fact showing signs of inappropriate body image. Your job will be to help them understand the roots of this belief. This may involve looking at other areas of a person's life to see what affects their self image.

Changing coping mechanisms might be central to the coaching process, whether in the area of nutrition, exercising, or any other activities or thought processes that lead to weight and body image problems.

Self-esteem is often an issue that needs to be addressed. Helping clients in establishing a social network or a relationship with a health care professional may also be needed. Again, looking at patterns of negative thoughts or emotions might be necessary in order to identify when these feelings arise and how they are coped with.

People who have a distorted body image often resort to constant dieting, exercise addiction, or other extreme behaviors. Coaches help clients to establish a realistic body image and stop focusing solely on their looks. Again, this is tied to a holistic approach of creating and maintaining a healthy lifestyle in an ongoing process.

2.11 Work/Life Balance Coaching

Work/life balance is one of the central themes of life coaching, and some coaches work exclusively on this area. There is no shortage of busy people who could potentially benefit from a little help in balancing their hectic work and home schedules. Clients might want to spend less time at work, and more time with their families, or just the opposite. Maybe part-time work or even a different job is the answer.

2.11.1 Coaching Individuals

Individuals who seek out work/life balance coaches may have problems dealing with a number of issues. These might include:

- Stress (caused by conflicts both at work and at home)

- Long working hours

- Position/responsibilities

- Living within one's means

- Burnout

- Time management

- Role conflict (i.e. one person is mother, homemaker, employee, boss, etc.)

Life coach and author Roberta Neault of Life Strategies Ltd. in Coquitlam, B.C., provides an excellent summary of the issues involved in trying to find personal work/life balance. In her article "That Elusive Work-Life Balance!" at **www.natcon.org/archive/natcon/papers/natcon_papers_2005_e5.pdf** she notes that most definitions of work/life balance "include the notions of flexibility, juggling and sustainability."

Although sometimes the warning signs of imbalance are ignored or avoided, Neault observes that "most people know when they are out of balance: they are constantly tired, feel as if their choices are limited, have minimal control, and are no longer able to effectively manage their lives. They may experience life as 'happening to them' and notice that their responses are more reactive than proactive."

Some of the issues of people seeking work/life balance coaching include:

- Feeling like they have no control over their work life

- Feeling guilty for not making enough time for hobbies, family, self

- Feeling overwhelmed or over-committed both at home and at work

- Feeling exhausted, angry or anxious all the time

Stress is probably the most common result of a work/life imbalance. People who feel that they have little control over their lives as a result of the demands of their jobs and personal lives often experience unhealthy stress levels. High stress levels can affect health in a variety of ways, such as poor eating habits, not getting enough sleep, or exhaustion. All of these can have potentially dangerous consequences for people experiencing them on a prolonged basis.

Many people seeking life coaches feel that their lives are out of control. They need someone to help them get back on track and regain a healthy balance between their working lives and their family or personal lives.

The first step in helping clients is to identify ways that their lives are out of balance. A simple questionnaire may be helpful for this. Clients provide Yes/No answers to statements.

Sample Work/Life Balance Assessment

YES	NO	
☐	☐	I often feel overwhelmed by the demands on me at home and at work
☐	☐	I frequently feel tired
☐	☐	I often find time to work on hobbies
☐	☐	I wish I could spend more time with my family
☐	☐	I find my job fulfilling
☐	☐	I took a vacation this year
☐	☐	My family gets upset with me because I work too much
☐	☐	I feel generally unsatisfied with my life
☐	☐	I feel that I am healthy
☐	☐	I frequently feel angry
☐	☐	My finances frequently worry me
☐	☐	I often think about work when I'm not working

The answers to questions like those in the sample work/life balance assessment can help you and your client understand what parts of their life are causing them the most distress. They can also help you to focus in on what in their life gives them satisfaction and help you to identify where conflicts arise. For example, if a person answers that they find their job fulfilling but also wish they could spend more time with family, then perhaps they need to find a way to work less or manage their time more effectively so that they can find the balance between a job that makes them happy and enjoying time spent with their family.

On the other hand, a person might be unhappy in their job but at the same time work long hours because they need the money to make ends meet. Financial problems are a frequent source of distress for people. Perhaps they need to refocus their efforts on cutting expenses so that they can work fewer hours. Maybe they need to think about moving and lowering their rent or mortgage costs, or getting their credit card debt under control so that they can have more disposable income available for leisure or other personal pursuits.

As with most forms of life coaching, getting clients to create a statement of short-term and long-term goals (see section 3.1.3) and then working toward those will be essential. Your first telephone coaching session with a new client might go something like this as you steer them towards creating a set of goals:

COACH: You indicated in your answers to the initial assessment quiz that you feel overwhelmed. Are there any areas in your life that are particularly overwhelming for you?

CLIENT: Well, I feel like I work constantly and never find the time for anything else. I pick the kids up from the babysitter after work, get home and make dinner, give the kids their baths and get them into bed, and then crash in front of the TV. I feel so exhausted all the time! There's just no way out of this.

COACH: How about the weekends? Do you have any hobbies you enjoy doing?

CLIENT: Weekends are just as bad. I never get anything done on weekends because I have to catch up on the housework, buy groceries, and Saturday is the kids' soccer day. I spend my weekend either in the car or doing laundry. It just never ends.

COACH: Does your husband help out?

CLIENT: He tries, but he works night shifts at the factory, so he's often sleeping when I'm at work or working when I'm home. He's always complaining that he never has time for the yard work and we almost never see each other any more. But we have to work as much as we can just to make ends meet.

COACH: Okay, I think I have a fairly clear picture about your work/life balance issues from your assessment and what we've just been talking about. You both seem to work long hours and your family life is suffering. Are there financial issues we might need to look at here, too?

CLIENT: Our mortgage is killing us for one thing. It's my fault. We shouldn't have bought the house we did, but it was the one I wanted. Plus there's the cost of the babysitter after the kids get out of school. We've also got two car payments and we maxed out our credit card for a vacation in January. We both needed to get away so badly, though! But we're still paying for it.

COACH: I completely understand. That probably was a much-needed break for you. Have you thought about moving to a cheaper house and lowering your mortgage payment as a start?

CLIENT: We have talked about it, but we haven't had much time to sit down and discuss it fully. I think we'd both be willing to do that if we just had the time to work out the details.

COACH: Maybe that should be your first goal, then. We'll work out a set of short-term and long-term goals for you. I'll email you a worksheet for that. Maybe the first short-term goal should be finding the time for both of you to sit down together and have a good look at your finances. If you could get that under control, you might not have to work so much and then you could start to find a little more time for recreation and family.

CLIENT: That sounds great! I think I might finally be seeing a light at the end of this tunnel!

As you can see from this sample dialogue between coach and client, too much time spent working can be a major drain on personal resources. On the other hand, this client has let home life create the necessity for working long hours. A cycle of debt, working to pay off the debt, and losing time for personal pursuits and family life has been created as a result.

Another symptom this client exhibits is role conflict. That is, she is feeling overwhelmed by the many roles she needs to serve: employee, wife, mother, and homemaker. The coach may need to help her find a balance between these functions such as by helping her to find ways to cope with the many demands on her time (perhaps using better time management methods).

And of course there are many other ways that personal lives and jobs collide. Another reason that a person might feel an imbalance in these two areas is job dissatisfaction. An area that might need to be looked into is job responsibilities. A client may have too many responsibilities and the demands on their time make spending more time with family impossible. In this case, if a client really wants to find a balance they may need to consider a change of position to one with less responsibility, or even a new job with fewer responsibilities but that allows them more personal time.

Sometimes people find themselves in careers they hate but that pay very well. People feel trapped and hopelessness sets in. Life becomes gray and dull. You can help them focus on the links between job satisfaction/dissatisfaction, wellness and personal fulfillment. In a case like this, some career coaching might be in order. Section 2.3 outlines what is involved in career coaching.

2.11.2 Working with Companies

Companies also have a need for work/life balance coaching. More and more companies are beginning to recognize that employees need to have time for their families as well as their jobs. Helping companies to develop work/life balance strategies for their workers is a common function of coaches offering this type of service.

Occupational pressures are the number one source of stress for people in North America. This can include anything from an unsafe work environment to clashing with coworkers, or job insecurity to overwork. According to a recent study by The American Institute of Stress (**www.stress.org**), workplace stress and burnout costs companies an estimated $300 billion annually in the U.S., and almost $12 billion for companies in Canada according to a similar study by the Conference Board of Canada (**www.conferenceboard.ca**).

Companies are starting to recognize the need to develop effective strategies for helping employees find a balance between their workplace lives and their personal lives; a strategy that ultimately saves the company money and improves productivity. The Conference Board of Canada says that worker stress and health issues arise from three main areas: the physical work environment (occupational health and safety), individual lifestyle choices and health, and the psychosocial work environment (management practices and strategies).

Probably the most important of these to companies wishing to improve workplace conditions in pursuit of work/life balance goals is the last because those are the ones they most often have a high level of control over. The control that companies have over the workplace environment includes the demands of work on employees, the way work is organized, the amount of control individuals have in their jobs, and the individual's perception of the rewards for their efforts at work.

Here are some common strategies employed by companies in the workplace to achieve their balance goals. As you read them, think about programs and services you could develop and offer to companies. You can find more information about some of these areas in section 2.4 on corporate coaching, as there is overlap between corporate coaching and many work/life balance areas affecting companies.

- Monitoring employee needs and concerns (surveys, 360° feedback, etc.)

- Training in communications, conflict resolution, problem solving, team building

- Worker feedback on improving performance

- Involvement in community activities

- Company sponsored fitness training (including fitness facility access)

- Organized sports such as basketball, volleyball, tennis, etc.

- Providing continuing education and training opportunities

- Recognizing employees for their achievements

- Embracing diversity

- Flexibility in scheduling and workplace (for example, allowing employees to work at home occasionally)

Other helpful work/life balance resources include the *Occupational Stress Inventory-Revised*, a set of three questionnaires measuring work stress, psychological strain and coping ability, available from Sigma Assessment Systems at **www.sigmaassessmentsystems.com** and *Quality of Life Questionnaire (Respondent Self-Evaluation) and User Kit*, a free resource that helps to identify problem areas in quality of life, which can be found at **www.ohsu.edu/psychiatry/research/qol.shtml.**

2.12 Other Specializations

Following is a description of other areas you may be interested in specializing in. You can read more at LifeCoachGuide.com (**www.lifecoach guide.com**), where you can search an online directory of coaches from over 20 different disciplines.

Alternative Lifestyles

Despite how far society has come in the treatment of gay, lesbian, and transgendered people, these individuals may still face many personal and professional challenges, such as rejection by family members, persecution, and low self-esteem. Coaches in this specialty generally rely on their own first-hand experiences to help their clients accept and embrace their identities. They may help a client develop a plan for "coming out," or for just dealing with everyday life.

Cultural Difference

America used to be called "the melting pot," and this expression can now be used to describe a number of countries in the world. Coaches who work with clients in this area are often multilingual, have experience living or traveling abroad, or are from a different country and understand the challenges of adjusting to cultural differences.

Their clients may be people who have just emigrated from another country, foreign business people on long-term assignments, or people who have moved to a different part of the country and have trouble "fitting in." These coaches sometimes refer to themselves as etiquette consultants.

Healthcare Professional

Coaches who work with healthcare professionals are usually doctors or nurses themselves, and many maintain a practice in addition to coaching. They understand that with mountains of paperwork, medical malpractice suits and increasing patient loads, workers in the healthcare field could use a sympathetic ear. These coaches inspire and assist healthcare professionals to successfully manage their practices.

Illness

While a long-term or serious illness does not always mean imminent death, it usually means a significant life transition. The coach can be there for the client who is coming to terms with a major disorder. Often the coach is an experienced healthcare professional, and has access to resources and information that could further benefit the client. The client does not necessarily have to be suffering from a disease; maybe just going through a normal, natural process. Examples are menopause, baldness or the decreased ability to perform certain tasks.

Mentor Coaching

Mentor coaches usually coach other life coaches in this relatively new profession. However, mentor coaches do not restrict their client list to new or aspiring life coaches. In fact, many established and practicing coaches have mentor coaches to help keep their coaching skills sharp, and provide them with objective feedback that they may not always get from their clients.

Midlife Issues

People change, they age, they go through many of the same stages, transitions and even crises. What do people do when after 20 years or so, their children finally move out of the house? What do they do when they are approaching middle age, and have a lot that they want to get off their chests? What do they do when they want to go back to school 15 years after they've graduated? They go to a life coach.

Sales/Marketing

Great salespeople are not only good at selling, they are masters at communicating, motivating and inspiring. If they can sell so effectively, they figure that they would also be good at coaching others to sell. The same is true for good marketers; they know how to get the word out, how to make others believe in their product, and they are confident that they can transfer these skills. While still allowing clients to develop their own unique plans, these coaches will also tell them what they know works and doesn't work, based on the coach's experience.

Self-Awareness

Life coaching entails helping people achieve their dreams and goals, but some clients don't even know what those dreams and goals are. So there are life coaches who dedicate their practice mainly to helping clients with self-discovery. Coaches may use a variety of tools, profiles and assessments to help clients determine their strengths, likes and dislikes, or the coaches may be more informal in their approach, asking thought-provoking questions and carefully feeding back the responses.

3. Providing Coaching Services

Just as there are many different coaching specializations, there are many different ways to coach. You may choose to coach individuals or groups, and deliver your services in-person, online, or by telephone. To give a few examples, you might offer 10 minute "laser" coaching sessions on the telephone, meet clients in person for half hour sessions, conduct full day training programs for companies, or present weekend retreats for groups of individuals. This chapter will cover each of these options, and more, and provide an introduction to coaching exercises and instruments you can use in your coaching practice.

3.1 How to Coach Individuals

Obviously, different clients have different needs, and what works for some will not work for others.

Some clients will want a coach just to be their confidante, friend, or sympathetic ear. This does not mean that the coach takes a totally passive role, but that he or she does not nag or pester clients about doing what they are supposed to do.

Other clients want coaches who will be a little more forceful, who will "get on their case," if necessary. A proactive approach to coaching works well with some clients and under some circumstances. If Jane, a habitual procrastinator, says that she is going to call a certain company about a job interview on Friday at 3:00 p.m., the life coach might call Jane at 2:50 p.m. and remind her, especially if Jane failed to do it the last couple of times.

The information in this section may help you decide what approach to take in your own coaching practice. It begins with an overview of the initial consultation and intake session, then describes what happens during coaching sessions, and explains how to help your clients achieve success. It concludes with a sample coaching session.

3.1.1   Initial Consultation and Intake Session

Initial Consultation

Coaches typically offer an initial consultation to give prospective clients an opportunity to learn more about the coach's services and what coaching can do for the client. This meeting is also an opportunity for the coach to decide if he or she wants to work with the client.

> **TIP:** Some coaches offer a free initial consultation, while others charge a fee. More information about fees is provided in section 5.6.

If both parties agree to proceed, the coach generally gives the client a personal evaluation to complete, known in life coaching as an intake form. The intake form helps clarify the client's goals and establish the focus of the coaching. You can use a client intake form such as the sample included below.

Your intake form should include contact information for the client, fees agreed to and payment method, as well as a short description by the client of what they hope to accomplish. The coaching contract should always include a disclaimer to the effect that you are not offering the client counseling or therapy (unless you are licensed to do that) and that the client agrees that you are not responsible for any actions he or she takes as a result of advice given during coaching sessions with you. (See section 5.7.3 for more about client contracts.)

Sample Client Intake Form

Client Intake Form

[Your company name] is happy to welcome you as a new client. We are excited that you chose us to help you achieve your personal goals. Please complete the following information and return it via email or fax so that we can get started.

Date: _____

Individual Client

Name _____

Corporate Client

Company Name _____

Title _____

Contact Information

Address _____

City _____

State/Prov. _____ Zip/Postal Code _____

Work/Type of Business _____

Number of Years Employed/ In Business _____

Business Phone (include area code) _____

Fax (include area code) _____

Home Phone (include area code) _____

Work Email _____

Home Email _____

Date of Birth (mm/dd/yyyy) _____

Spouse/Partner's Name (if applicable) _____

Children's Names/Ages (if applicable) _____

_____

_____

Session Day/Time/Frequency _____

Start Date:_____

Fees and Payment Option

Monthly Fee_____   Per Session _____

Check _____   Pay Pal _____

Visa/MC (card number and expiration date):

_____

Disclaimer: The Client is aware that the coaching relationship does not represent psychological counseling or any kind of therapy. The Client is also aware that coaching results can vary and are not guaranteed. The Client agrees that he/she is entering into coaching with the understanding that the Client is responsible for his/her own decisions and results. The Client also agrees to hold the Coach free from all liability for any actions or results for adverse situations created as a direct or indirect result of advice given by the Coach. (Client initials)_____

Session Contact Procedure: The Client shall contact the Coach at the agreed hour. If the Client fails to make the appointment time, the Client is still responsible for the coaching fee, unless 24 hour notice was given to reschedule the call. The Coach will make every effort to reschedule with the client.

_____   _____
Client Signature   Date

_____   _____
Coach Signature   Date

Important Issues

Please briefly outline any issues you would like to deal with and what you hope to achieve in the coaching setting:

Issue #1

_____

_____

_____

_____

Issue #2

_____

_____

_____

_____

Issue #3

_____

_____

_____

_____

Issue #4

_____

_____

_____

_____

Issue #5

_____

_____

_____

_____

Personal Profile

Please answer the following to let us get to know you a bit better:

1. I would describe myself as:

    _____

    _____

    _____

    _____

2 Others would describe me as:

    _____

    _____

    _____

    _____

3. The three things that I like most about my life/situation are:

    _____

    _____

    _____

    _____

4. If I could change three things about my life/situation, they would be:

    _____

    _____

    _____

    _____

5. My three greatest accomplishments (so far) are:

    _____

    _____

    _____

    _____

6. Some of my hobbies/interests are:

_____

_____

_____

_____

7. The one thing I would like most to accomplish (but haven't yet) is:

_____

_____

_____

_____

8. The one thing I wish I could change in the short-term is:

_____

_____

_____

_____

9. I think that the most important thing in life is:

_____

_____

_____

_____

10. I am interested in working with a life coach because:

_____

_____

_____

_____

When to Say "No"

When the call comes from someone who wants to hire you, your first impulse may be to start immediately. But before you say yes, consider whether you actually want to take on a particular client.

During the initial consultation, ask questions and listen carefully to determine what the client wants and expects. When you are just starting out, you might be eager to take on as many clients as possible, but remember that quality is better than quantity.

Most coaching deals with people on an individual basis, and compatibility is paramount. People who want you to make their decisions for them and tell them what to do are not good clients. You are there to listen, encourage and support, not to preach or instruct.

Ann Ronan of Grant Right (**www.grantright.com**), who specializes in coaching for people and organizations seeking grant funding, judges how serious prospective clients are by how quickly they fill out and return the intake form. If the intake form is returned promptly along with payment for the first month, she knows that the client is ready to begin. "If someone doesn't get back to me for a week or so, that usually tells me something," Ronan says.

Sometimes you will talk to a prospective client and just not feel right about the person. Maybe it's the client's tone of voice or manner of speaking. This is also probably a sign that the two of you will not work well together. This may sound trivial, but if you have bad vibes about the person from the beginning, you will have difficulty being an effective coach. You should not say, "There's just something that I don't like about you," but nonetheless be honest and state that you do not feel that the two of you would make a good match.

As mentioned earlier, you should also avoid people who seem depressed, have low self-esteem or are angry with the world. They would be better candidates for therapy. A client who tells you "I'm dissatisfied with my career, and I'd like to make a transition," is acceptable. One who tells you, "I'm dissatisfied with my life, and I'm thinking of ending it," is not.

Intake Session

Once you have received the completed intake form, contract, and payment for the first month, you are ready to begin coaching.

The first official session between a coach and a new client is often longer, more detailed, and more intense. Sometimes known as the intake session, it can last an hour or even two, depending on the client. This is because additional time is needed to establish what the client's goals are, how he or she will accomplish them, and what style of coaching will be the most effective. Granted, much of this information will come up during the initial consultation and in reviewing the intake form, but often only on a superficial level.

The intake session establishes the basic framework of the coaching, although that framework is understandably subject to change. For those clients who have a lot of issues to sort out, you might want to break the intake session down into two separate 45-minute or one-hour sessions. Remaining focused and alert during a two-hour conversation can be difficult.

Go over the information that the client has supplied on the intake form. Some of the responses will merit a little more elaboration. Make sure that you clearly understand the client's goals, intentions and expectations. Remember that you are not attempting to develop a psychological profile for your client, you are just trying to get a better idea of what he or she wants. You will get as much information as possible during the initial consultation; the intake form helps to fill in the gaps, so to speak.

> TIP: Life coaching often goes in its own direction. After a few weeks or a few months, clients may discover that their goals have changed. Some who originally indicated that they wanted more free time may now find that what they really want is a different job. Others concerned with their image or appearance may later decide that a closer relationship with their significant other is more important. If the life coaching helped clarify that, then both of you have been successful.

Carbon Coaching Intake Sessions

Carbon coaching intake sessions are typically a bit different from the usual life coaching intake sessions. Although the intake session will have similar goals in terms of finding out more about the client, their individual goals, and so forth, the intake may include an initial assessment of the client's lifestyle as it relates to the goal of helping to reduce global warming.

Clients may come to you not really knowing much about some of the issues surrounding global warming or about carbon coaching. Perhaps they've seen the movie *An Inconvenient Truth* and were spurred into action. As with other forms of coaching you will offer an initial consultation and assessment. This might include discussing with the client some of their goals with respect to entering into a carbon coaching relationship. You might also want to provide clients with a brochure or a link to a document on your website that explains what global warming is all about and how individuals contribute to it so they can find out more about the issues.

After your consultation session, your intake form can be sent to the client to finalize the coaching contract. This is fairly standard with life coaching in general. Next though, you will conduct an in-home consultation, for a fee, to help the client determine their carbon footprint as described in section 2.2.1. After the in-home consultation, the client may be ready to sign a contract with you for carbon coaching services on an ongoing basis. You can choose to do that on the spot or give the client a day or two to think about it, providing them with additional information about climate change if they'd like to know more.

During the intake session, be sure to explain your coaching style. Provide samples of the tests or questionnaires that you give, and ask how the client feels about them. Give examples of exercises that you do with clients, as well as any homework or fieldwork that you typically give. Real life examples of what you have done when working with other clients lend you credibility. Keep in mind other clients' privacy concerns, however, and don't mention names unless you've already gotten permission.

Find out how the client feels about certain coaching techniques that you employ. How does he feel about role-playing? How about keeping a journal? Does the client want to be held absolutely accountable for everything, or need a coach with a looser style? Does the term "homework" have a negative connotation to the client? Emphasize that you are flexible with the techniques you can use.

If you gave the client any additional assessments or evaluations to complete, the intake session is the time to go over the results with the client, to see whether the client agrees or disagrees with what they indicate. If the client disagrees, that's fine. The coach's role is not to say, "The results indicate that you need to improve this, this and that, so these areas should be the focus of our coaching."

Give the client the opportunity during the intake session to ask questions about you. Talk a little bit about your background, qualifications, experience and reasons for going into life coaching. You need to make the client feel relaxed, trusting and assured that you are both personable and competent. Let her address any lingering questions, doubts or expectations. The client needs to like you, and vice versa.

3.1.2   Conducting a Coaching Session

The standard coaching session typically lasts 30 minutes. There are coaches who conduct 45- and even 60-minute sessions, but remaining focused that long can be difficult. For coaches who conduct sessions by telephone, half-hour sessions also take into account the client's telephone charges, since many are calling long distance.

As you are talking to a client, take notes or jot down some key ideas. Keep a dossier on your clients, and refer to it prior to a scheduled session so that you have a heads-up on what you are going to discuss.

"Good afternoon, Kathy. When we spoke last, you indicated that you were going to ask your boss for a raise. How did that go?" Taking notes also helps reassure clients that you are paying attention.

For example, "We've been talking for 15 minutes so far, Walt, and you've mentioned three times the fact that your brother-in-law keeps borrowing stuff from you. Is this an issue on which you'd like to focus?" But remember to leave it up to the client to set the agenda for the session. Kathy or Walt might have something else on their minds which they feel takes precedence.

> TIP: Some coaches ask their clients for permission to record sessions, so that the coach can review them later. But people who know that they are being recorded might be leery of saying something "wrong," and many will feel uncomfortable with the request.

To help you conduct your own sessions, here are the key elements of what happens during a typical coaching session:

Asking Questions

Life coaches often talk about helping clients to close the gap between where they are and where they want to be. This is like an unofficial mission statement in life coaching. To determine what this gap is, life coaches ask their clients probing questions and let one answer lead to another question until the real issue is isolated.

A lot of what you do will be obtaining information from the client, repeating what he or she has told you, and then following up on the response with more targeted questions. This allows clients to process out loud, to verbalize their problems and issues and come up with solutions. Although you want to let clients direct the focus of the coaching, you will occasionally need to steer them in the right direction.

Few scenarios are as frightening to novice coaches as running out of questions to ask a client. Familiarizing yourself with possible questions is a good idea, but you don't want to sound like you are reading from a list. Strive for a relaxed, natural tone. Though the questions you ask are meant to elicit reflection from the client, you will sometimes receive short, even mono-syllabic responses. While each client brings unique issues that foster unique questions, below is a list of common questions which can be applied to different situations.

- What is the worst/best that could possibly happen as a result?

- How else could you have handled the situation?

- Do you know anybody else who has been in a similar situation?

- When do you think you'll be able to get started?

- What other solutions have you tried?

- How do you think that other people perceive you?

- Why does that issue bother you so much?

- What will happen if you don't do this?

- Can you come up with any more suggestions?

- On what would you like to focus today?

- Are you sure that this is what you really want?

- What steps will you take to accomplish this?

- What will your first step be?

- What is the time frame for completing this?

- What choices have you not considered?

- How do you know that this will/won't work?

- Can you summarize what we've discussed so far?

- What is most important to you here?

- Will this matter to you in one week/one month/one year/five years?

You will need to tread lightly with clients when discussing certain issues. If a client indicates strong resistance about a particular topic, you might follow up with "Why does that subject bother you so much?" or "Is there a reason that you don't want to go there?" But if the answer is still "I don't want to talk about it," respect that.

Communication Skills for Coaching

Listening

While listening seems like an easy skill to master, most of us experience challenges in at least one of the following areas involved in listening: paying attention, understanding, and remembering. You can improve your listening skills by focusing fully on someone when they are speaking. Here are some ways to do that:

- Don't be distracted by loud noises, the other person's misuse or mispronunciation of a word, or an uncomfortable room temperature, things that all can affect your listening.

- Avoid interrupting the other person. Allow the other person to finish speaking before jumping in with a comment or question.

- Keep listening to the other person, even if you think you know what they will say next. If you make assumptions, you may miss the point they're making.

- Pay attention to non-verbal signals which may provide additional information about a speaker's emotions.

- Consider the perspective of the person talking and the context of their comments. For example, a new employee may speak in much more positive terms about a company than other employees because they are excited about being hired for their new job.

- Ask questions if you need any points clarified.

- Paraphrase what the other person has said to confirm that you understood what they said correctly so as to avoid misunderstandings.

Vocabulary

In all communication situations, your vocabulary is important. You're not communicating effectively if the reader or listener doesn't understand you. Speaking over the heads of your clients using industry specific or technical terms might sound impressive but it's not effective. If you must use terms and acronyms that your client may not be familiar with, explain them as you speak.

In addition to vocabulary, there are many other verbal and vocal traits that may affect the way a life coach is perceived. People may make judgments about a coach's competence, knowledge, and trustworthiness based on his or her accent, pronunciation, grammar, use of fillers (such as "uh" and "um"), and vocal qualities such as volume, tone, pitch, and rate of speaking. To improve your vocal communication skills, ask people you respect for feedback on any areas that could be improved.

Non-Verbal Communication

Non-verbal communications skills are especially important when you are conducting in-person coaching sessions. Generally, if there is conflict between the words being spoken and the message communicated by the body, the body is more likely to be believed by the client. Controlling your non-verbal communication so that you do not inadvertently communicate negative messages is essential.

Be conscious of your body language, including your facial expressions, eye contact, posture, gestures, and other body movements. Notice when you make particular gestures out of habit or as a reaction to what's happening around you and choose to use positive body language. Negative body movement such as fidgeting and crossed arms, and negative facial expressions such as narrowed eyes and furrowing the brow, send off signals of uneasiness and a lack of confidence, both of which are unattractive qualities in a life coach.

Reading other people's non-verbal cues can help you in your work, too. Although body language can't tell you precisely what someone is thinking, it can give you clues so you can ask follow up questions, even as basic as "How do you feel about that?" If you want to improve this skill, you can find excellent advice in books such as *Reading People,* by Jo-Ellan Dimitrius and Mark C. Mazzarella, and *How to Read a Person Like a Book,* by Gerald I. Nierenberg and Henry H. Calero.

Identifying Problems

When clients are dissatisfied with their careers, relationships, or some other aspect of their lives, you want to have them spell it out. Ask them to make a list of what is wrong, so you can go over the various aspects together. Both of you can write it down, in fact. The list might read:

Things that are bothering me at work:

1. My boss is a jerk

2. My job is boring

3. My commute is long and the traffic is heavy

A coach might break down each respective issue as follows: "Saying that your boss is a jerk is pretty ambiguous. What specifically does he or she do?" In response to the client's answer, the coach might follow up with "Have you said anything about it? Is your boss someone you can approach? Does he or she treat other employees this way?"

As for the client's second complaint, the coach might respond "You say that your job is boring. Is there anything that you like about it? Are there any other tasks or responsibilities you could take on that would be more interesting? How about chances for promotion or even transfer to a different department?"

After either resolving the first two issues or agreeing to table them until next time, the coach might say, "Your commute is long and the traffic is heavy. If you left a little earlier in the morning, could you beat some of the morning rush? Is public transportation available? Can you carpool with anyone in your office?" The discussion might eventually lead to possible solutions for one, two or all three issues, or may lead to an entirely different conclusion: the client would be happier working somewhere else.

As a coach, you should be listening more than talking. While asking questions is an integral part of your role, you want to give clients room to expand on their answers. Think of yourself as a match, igniting introspection. This does not mean refraining from ever asking yes or no questions, but an open-ended approach yields more information and allows for deeper reflection by the client.

You will also need to be aware of what's not being said. What the client is leaving out could be evidence of a topic of great importance that he or she is reluctant or unable to discuss. For example, if a client never discusses or glosses over an important aspect of his or her work, this is likely a sign of a larger problem at hand. Recognizing a client's omissions is a first step; the next is to help the client verbalize the "unsaid" by asking questions about the topic, however reluctant the client might be.

Closely related to this is the necessity for a coach to try to detect why certain emotions are being displayed by a client. In their tone of voice, a client can illustrate emotions when speaking, such as anger or grief. You can also read a client's emotions in their body language—for example, they can look tense or agitated. Effectively gauging what stirs emotions in a client aids a life coach in helping a client determine root causes, and can ultimately help in turning a topic of tension into one that is manageable and productive.

Challenging Assumptions

Challenging assumptions is an important concept in life coaching and goes hand in hand with identifying problems. Often, a client's assumptions about what causes a certain problem become barriers to solving the problem. In addition, there may be hidden or unarticulated assumptions at work. Clients often assume that something will not work, "just know" that they would not be able to do something, or don't feel that they have any skill in a particular area, all of which can be based on preconceived notions and not experience.

It's important also for the coach not to succumb to the negativity that can often be expressed by the client. Life coach Jenna Avery (**www. highlysensitivesouls.com**) explains the challenges she faces in helping clients to overcome these negative preconceptions:

> "We unravel and reframe these limiting beliefs so they can make new choices that are better aligned with their sensitivity and the truth of who they really are. Once they've discovered that stronger sense of themselves, stop their negative thinking patterns, and make self-referencing choices, they are better able to set strong boundaries and have a clearer sense of direction in their lives. Knowing how to work with "gremlins" and limiting beliefs is a powerful tool for a coach to have in his or her tool belt.

Often when we begin coaching, my clients can go through periods of despair about their circumstances and their ability to change them. As a new coach, a challenge that can come up is not falling into despair with your client, but instead maintaining the wider perspective and holding the vision for the client that there is another way beyond what they can see at this time. One of my coaches once said to me, "I know without a shadow of doubt that this will work out for you, and I will remember it for you until you are able to do so for yourself." It was a profound, life-altering, experiential moment in which I was able to grasp the greater potential of what is possible. I do this for my own clients now.

I also find that it is important for me to have faith in my abilities as a coach, because sometimes clients will be so in doubt that they don't see a way out or through what we are working on, and can be afraid that we won't get there. It's important to stay tuned into the knowledge that coaching does work and to resist falling into the fear with the client."

— *Jenna Avery, Highly Sensitive Souls*

It's important for the coach not to fall into the client's patterns of thinking. Rather, it's the life coach's job to point out to the client that preconceived ideas, opinions and hearsay are not valid reasons to avoid certain actions, and that these invalidated issues are holding them back from progressing in some areas. The idea here is to encourage clients to be flexible, to help them to understand that there are several ways to approach every problem and situation, and unless one makes an attempt they'll never know if it works or not.

Start by identifying the obvious, known assumptions. Make a list of these and then try to come up with other assumptions that may be at work. For example, let's revisit the sample work/life balance coaching session in section 2.11.1. You might remember that the client expressed a wish to have more free time and not feel exhausted all the time. The explicit assumptions are that she and her husband work too much and have a variety of family activities that take up too much of their time, leaving them feeling exhausted.

However, there are some implicit assumptions that are made in this example, too. These unarticulated assumptions are drawn out by the coach by asking questions like "What issues make you feel overwhelmed?", "Does your husband help you?", and finally, and most revealing, "Are there any financial issues we need to look at?" Rather than just accepting the client's negative assumptions that change is impossible, the coach makes assumptions that go deeper than just "Why are you feeling overwhelmed?" and as a result is able to come up with the hidden issues that are in fact the root causes of this client's work/ life imbalance.

This technique works for almost any area of life or business. By challenging clients' assumptions about different areas in their lives, coaches help clients to overcome their self-imposed limitations. For example, coach Roberta Rosen sometimes sends clients on informational interviews to find out about potential jobs that the clients assume they couldn't do or wouldn't like, as well as sending them on informational interviews for jobs that they assume they would like.

When coaching, if you find that your experience with the particular subject directly contradicts the client's assumption, offer your feedback. Be clear that you are not trying to sway the client to your line of thinking, but let them know that you personally have not found the client's assumption to be the case, and provide examples.

3.1.3   Helping Clients Set Goals

Why and How to Set Goals

We've all heard that when you fail to plan, you plan to fail. Life coaches can help people give form and structure to their desires. Talk is cheap, goes the saying, but when clients put their thoughts on paper, read them aloud and see them every day, they become more focused, more serious. People who say "I want to be happy/rich/successful, etc." are not being clear enough. Coaches help them break down generic, unformed ideas into concrete plans. Plans are further subdivided into steps. After all, climbing one step at a time is far more practical than leaping up an entire staircase.

On the next few pages you will find two versions of a Goal-Setting Worksheet created by FabJob to help your clients identify the steps they need to take to achieve their goals.

Goal-Setting Worksheet

Statement of goal:

_____

_____

_____

Priority: _____   Term of goal: ❏ Short-term (within 3 months)
                                     ❏ Medium-term (within 3 years)
                                     ❏ Long-term (over 3 years)

Life area: _____   Target date: _____

Obstacles: Solutions:

_____   _____

_____   _____

_____   _____

_____   _____

Action steps to achieve it:	Target date for step:	Reward for completing step:
_____	_____	_____
_____	_____	_____
_____	_____	_____
_____	_____	_____
_____	_____	_____
_____	_____	_____
_____	_____	_____
_____	_____	_____
_____	_____	_____

Is it worth it to me?   ❏ Yes   ❏ No

What achieving this goal will mean to me:

_____

_____

_____

Goal-Setting Worksheet with Instructions

Putting your goals in writing can help you make your dreams a reality.

Statement of Goal

Must be specific, measurable, stated positively and simply. Think big.

_____

_____

Priority

How does this goal rank compared
to your other goals (#1, #2, #3, etc.)? _____

Term of Goal
- ❏ Short-term (within 3 months)
- ❏ Medium-term (within 3 years)
- ❏ Long-term (over 3 years)

Life Area
- ❏ Career
- ❏ Financial
- ❏ Physical
- ❏ Mental
- ❏ Emotional
- ❏ Spiritual
- ❏ Family and Friends
- ❏ Community/Environment

Target Date

This goal will be accomplished by: _____

Obstacles

What currently and potentially stands between you and this goal? Include both tangible and intangible obstacles such as lack of money, time, support, or education, fear, etc.

_____

_____

_____

Solutions

How will you overcome the obstacles? Include both tangible and intangible resources you can use to help you pursue your goal, such as self-confidence, support from other people, education, time, money, etc.

_____

_____

_____

Action Steps to Achieve It

Break your goal down into smaller tasks. Remember to include steps for handling obstacles. List a target date for each step (it may help you to work backwards from your target goal date). And remember to reward yourself after completing each step in order to positively reinforce your behavior.

Step #1

Description: _____

Target date: _____

Reward for completion: _____

Step #2

Description: _____

Target date: _____

Reward for completion: _____

Step #3

Description: _____

Target date: _____

Reward for completion: _____

Step #4

Description: _____

Target date: _____

Reward for completion: _____

Step #5

Description: _____

Target date: _____

Reward for completion: _____

Step #6

Description: _____

Target date: _____

Reward for completion: _____

Step #7

Description: _____

Target date: _____

Reward for completion: _____

Step #8

Description: _____

Target date: _____

Reward for completion: _____

Step #9

Description: _____

Target date: _____

Reward for completion: _____

Step #10

Description: _____

Target date: _____

Reward for completion: _____

Is it worth it?

Are you really willing to do what it takes to achieve this goal?

❑ Yes   ❑ No

What will achieving this goal mean to you?

How will achieving this goal benefit you? Include any benefits for your family, the other people in your life, and the community.

_____

_____

_____

_____

_____

_____

_____

_____

Evaluating Clients' Goals

Always remember that the client's goals, not the coach's, are what matters. Your clients need to decide what they want and how they are going to get it.

Once a client begins goal-setting, you will often find that a client will list many goals. The two of you need to prioritize which one you will tackle first. Two or three small goals may be handled simultaneously, particularly if they are closely related. For example, a client who wants to both lose weight and feel better about his or her appearance can likely combine the two goals. But if a client has goals such as getting married, starting a new career, and buying a new house, trying to work on all three at the same time would likely be overwhelming.

Prioritizing goals and letting one accomplishment lead to new aspirations is a good way to keep clients coming back. You and the client establish a goal, and set a timeframe to meet it. The subsequent success can open up new opportunities, and lead the client to investigate new possibilities he or she never even imagined before. In addition, once a client has achieved a major milestone or even taken successful steps to accomplish smaller goals, you can ask "What else would you like to accomplish?"

> TIP: Remember to make the question open-ended. Asking "What else would you like to do?" is more effective than "Is there anything else that you would like to do?"

Some clients may need a little help in clarifying their goals. Of course, there is a thin line between helping a client clarify goals and telling him or her what to do. Here is where you might refer back to the original evaluation that you had the client complete after the initial consultation:

> "Bruce, in your evaluation, you indicated that you were most comfortable with creative endeavors. You said that you dislike boring, repetitive tasks, and that you hate sitting still for long periods of time. Why don't we try to come up with some possible jobs for you that would take that into account?"

A client's statement of goals should be specific, measurable, stated positively and simply. Any single goal should be ranked against all other goals according to how important it is to the individual. The goal should be identified as either short- or long-term. That is, determine whether the goal is something that is able to be or needs to be accomplished within a relatively short time, such as a few weeks or months, or if it is something that will take longer to achieve, perhaps because it is dependent on achieving other goals first.

In the sample session in section 2.11.1, for example, the client's overall goal is to find a work/life balance. In order to achieve that, she indicated that one of her long-term goals was to reduce her family's amount of debt by selling their house and purchasing a cheaper one with a lower mortgage. The short-term goal that preceded this was to sit down with her husband to discuss their financial situation and options for getting themselves out of debt. A number of other steps are tied to achieving goals like these. For example, once the goals have been established, they must each be assigned a target date, which will be the date the goal will be accomplished. Then, obstacles to success must be identified. In other words, what obstacles currently and potentially stand between the client and a particular goal?

After setting a time to completion and identifying any obstacles to completion, you and your client must vet solutions to overcome any identified obstacles. Include both tangible and intangible resources clients can use to help pursue the goals, such as support from other people, education, time, money and so on.

Achievement of the larger goal step can be further broken down into smaller steps. These action steps break the major goal down into smaller tasks and define target dates (possibly working backwards from the ultimate date) to complete each step. The client should be encouraged to reward themselves after the accomplishment of each step in order to positively reinforce the process of achieving their goals.

Also make sure that clients take into account the feasibility of their goals, and that they are not setting themselves up for failure. This is why establishing a series of small goals, enumerated in a plan of action, is essential. Big dreams are not unattainable, but looking at each frame individually helps to focus on the big picture more effectively. Without saying "That's a bad idea" or "I can't see you doing that," you sometimes need to ask the client if he or she is being realistic.

Setting timeframes for clients' goals is also important. When a client decides on a list of goals or a specific goal, have them decide which goals come first, and when these goals need to be met. Establishing deadlines can be very motivating, and lend more immediacy to a project. Both coach and client need to realize, however, that deadlines don't have to be set in stone. Prepare for unforeseen circumstances and setbacks that may occur. After two or three months of working on a particular goal, the client may realize that he or she needs more time, or even that the goal is nearly accomplished.

Maybe after getting halfway through a project, the realization comes that it was not the right project. Then comes the point at which the coach helps the client determine what the right project is, followed by how and when the client will complete it.

Goal-Setting Example

Take an example of a client who wants to publish a novel. Call him George. George has written a number of short stories and had some luck in submitting them to magazines, so he is confident in his literary ability. The idea of just sitting down, writing a novel and sending it to a publisher overwhelms George, but he doesn't want to give up, so he enlists the services of a life coach who is a published author.

George and his coach decide to first focus on writing the novel, then determining where to submit the finished product. The process of writing the novel is broken down into smaller steps, for example:

- Writing a plot summary

- Listing the main characters

- Developing a background for the main characters

- Determining the length of the novel

- Making an outline of the chapters

- Coming up with a title

George may already have a basic idea of the plot, the protagonist or the setting, but needs to develop them a little more. Depending on how much time he can or is willing to allot, George may take two weeks or a month to complete the steps on his list. George's coach has him write down his list and post it by his desk rather than just make a mental note. The coach also keeps the list on file and reviews it before and after each weekly session.

After the initial five steps have been completed, George moves on to actually writing the novel. The consensus might be either that George spends a certain number of hours per week writing, or commits to finishing one chapter per week, which he in turn sends to his coach. By having George send him what he has written every week, the coach can comment on the manuscript in progress and hold George accountable for completing the steps in his plan of action. George's plan might also incorporate other aspects of writing, such as researching or joining a writers' group.

> **TIP:** If after reading the first draft the coach feels that the work is inferior, he would be doing George a disservice by not being honest with him. Maybe George needs to enroll in a creative writing course, or maybe he needs to re-examine his career choice.

After finishing the first draft, George's next step is to rewrite. He reads through his manuscript, makes a list of what he likes and does not like, then establishes a timetable for making whatever changes he feels are necessary. After another month, he sends his coach the final draft, and asks him for a critique.

George and his coach then discuss finding a publisher. Does George want to go the route of self-publishing? Will he consider a print on demand company? Are there any contests for authors of first books? Does he prefer to go the traditional route? Say that he chooses the last option. His coach then has him come up with another list of possible publishers, agents, or potential contacts who might be able to help. Each week, George agrees to call "x" number of people on that list. Without a coach to guide and inspire him, George might be just another person who spends more time daydreaming about being a published author than he does working on it.

A client who wants to write a novel is just one example, but the concepts can be applied to any endeavor. If instead George wanted to find a new job, his coach would have him make different lists that would in turn lead to different plans. What does George like to do? What kinds of jobs would allow him to do that? In what geographical area would he like to work? Would he prefer a large, medium or small company?

Based on the preceding criteria, George's coach could help him come up with a list of companies, and George would contact a certain number each week. Again, without a coach to guide and inspire him, George might stay in an unrewarding job because he doesn't know how to leave it and find one he would enjoy more.

3.1.4   Helping Clients Achieve Success

Keep the Focus on the Goals

Remember that you are not in charge; the client is. But the role of the coach is not totally passive. Without being heavy-handed, you can tactfully and effectively help clients reaffirm their goals. Let them use you as a sounding board occasionally, even to complain, gripe or moan for a while, just to blow off steam. We all have bad days or bad weeks, and venting one's frustrations is cathartic. But there comes a point at which you have to say, "Fine. You are unhappy about this. What are you going to do about it?"

At times, you will need to gently steer the conversation back to the issue at hand if the client starts to digress. For example:

COACH: How did your apartment hunting go this week?

JENNIFER: I found six that I might be interested in, and I went to see three of them. Two were one-bedroom, the last one was an efficiency. I don't really think that I want another efficiency, though. I'm complaining enough now that my apartment is too small. My friend moved into an efficiency from his one-bedroom apartment, and he wound up having to spend an extra $200 a month on renting a storage room. I can't see myself doing that. I want to have access to all of my stuff when I need it. One time my friend was going to go swimming, and he found out that his swimming trunks were in the storage rental place, which was about 20 minutes from his apartment!

COACH: So it sounds like you want to concentrate on one-bedroom apartments.

Occasionally you may have clients who commit to take certain steps or actions toward a particular goal, but don't follow through. We all have unproductive weeks, but if you notice a pattern of proclaimed commitment followed by inaction, ask the client to consider re-evaluating his or her goals:

> "Julie, for the last three weeks, you've been saying that you'll write at least two more chapters of your doctoral thesis, but every time that we've spoken, you haven't worked on it at all. Are you sure that you want to go for your Ph.D.?"

Make Clients Aware

A good life coach makes clients aware of thought processes and be-havioral patterns that may be hindering progress. People often resist change, and while they may say that they want to accomplish some-thing or develop more effective habits, they may unconsciously cling to old ones because "The devil they know is better than the devil they don't know." A good life coach asks the client "What's holding you back, and why?"

For example: "Jack, you keep saying that you're going to wake up a half-hour earlier on Tuesdays and Thursdays so that you can exercise before work, but for the past two weeks, you have forgotten to set your alarm. Why do you think that is?" In some cases, the coach might even call Jack one morning at whatever time he says that he wants to wake up!

Often, clients need to determine if they are doing anything that is coun-terproductive. Asking "What else should I be doing?" is not always enough; clients have to ask "What am I doing wrong?" With the help of the coach, the client must learn what needs to be unlearned.

Don't be too shy about making clients aware of bad habits, or behaviors that manage to sabotage their progress. For example, maybe Lucy says that she would like to get along better with her co-workers. She admits that often she reacts when she should respond, or is too quick to lose her temper. At work one morning, a colleague makes a remark which she finds to be condescending. She tells her coach, "I suppose I could have just let it go, but I told him off." The coach might respond, "Well, if you could have just let it go, why didn't you?" Simply point out that the client says that she wants one thing, but keeps doing things that basically throw a monkey wrench into her plans.

In addition to periodically reiterating what the client tells you during the coaching session, it's a good idea to summarize afterwards. Go over main points, repeating the client's stated goals and objectives. This lets the client know that you are listening, and allows him or her to clear up any misunderstanding on your part.

Accentuate the Positive

Have the client focus on what is going right with his or her life. Ask the client how he or she can apply what is going right to remedy what is going wrong. Problems need to be acknowledged, but the focus of the coaching should not be gripe sessions. A good coach listens carefully, asks powerful questions, and holds clients accountable. If the client has agreed to pursue some course of action before the next session and take steps to forward the accomplishment of certain goals, ask, "Did you do what we discussed, and how did it go? If you didn't do it, what happened that prevented you?"

Clients may sometimes need an ego boost, particularly when they don't feel that things are going their way. Keep notes on your clients, the assignments that they complete, and the steps that they have taken to achieve their goals. Periodic progress reports give them an idea of how far they have come, and help reinforce their commitment to continued success: "Mary, you say that you're having a bad month, but let me remind you that you have consistently been doing all of the things on your weekly list," or, "When we started coaching three months ago, Hank, you expressed concern with your appearance. I understand that you're a little upset because you went off your diet last week, but you're still seven pounds less than you were when we started."

Suggest that clients reward themselves for the successful completion of goals on a weekly or monthly basis. The satisfaction of a job well done helps, but sometimes a little extra incentive is good.

Suppose that Mary wants to open her own business, and, after a couple of sessions with her coach, has drawn up a list of initial steps to take:

- Decide on a location

- Make an appointment with her accountant

- Come up with a list of estimated expenses

During the week, Mary does everything that she has committed to do. So on Saturday she can go see that movie that she wanted to see, or dine at that new restaurant that she wanted to try or buy something for herself.

To reach their goals, clients need to combine positive affirmations with decisive action. Either one separately is insufficient. Simply wishing that they had a better job, more money or a more fulfilling life won't make it so. Similarly, a lot of people work very hard for a long time and have little to show for it.

As a life coach, think of yourself as the client's cheerleader. You sincerely believe that your clients are whole, capable, intelligent and decent human beings capable of finding and doing whatever will best help them accomplish their goals. If you don't sincerely believe in them, then you wouldn't have agreed to work with them. Make sure that they know that, and give them positive reinforcement when they need it.

Though life coaching is primarily concerned with the present and how it will shape the client's future, coaches sometimes ask clients to look at their past successes for inspiration, as well as possible insights in resolving current conflicts or situations. Coaches can ask "Have you ever been faced with something similar?" This doesn't imply identical circumstances, but in most cases, the client can find some sort of common denominators in previous problems that were successfully resolved, and perhaps apply parts of the solution to the issue at hand.

Take a Break

Be aware that clients may need to take time off from coaching for personal reasons. Difficult or stressful life events may arise in their lives or they may just need a break to re-evaluate what they want to get out of life coaching. You may even suggest this to a client if you know the client is having a hard time or notice a drop in the client's motivation. You can be most effective as a life coach when the client is feeling good, inspired and motivated.

A week's hiatus can give the client a chance to step back and objectively assess his or her current situation, deal with whatever non-coaching issues are interfering, or just rest and return to the coaching process with more energy and determination. The result may be that the client is not ready at this time in his or her life to continue with the coaching. If that is the case, you would both be better off finding out earlier rather than having the client later ask for a refund, or leave with a bad impression about life coaching.

Occasionally clients will not be able to keep scheduled appointments, either because something urgent came up, or they simply forgot. When a client makes a habit of missing sessions, you may have to re-evaluate the coaching relationship.

3.1.5   A Sample Coaching Session

Here is a sample dialogue between a coach and a client:

COACH: So, how did your week go?

CLIENT: Fine, I guess.

COACH: If I recall correctly, you had decided to clean your garage, go over all of your old receipts and paperwork and throw out anything older than six months, and finish reading the book that you started in January.

CLIENT: Finished the book. I just sat down first thing Saturday morning and read straight through. It was about 6:00 when I finally finished, though, but I'm glad I did. As for the paperwork, well, I went through about half of that, and decided to finish the rest later. Later never came, though. I just couldn't get into it. It's just not a lot of fun.

COACH: No, I guess not. How about the garage?

CLIENT: Ugh! I don't even want to think about it! I have to do it later, I guess, but I don't even want to think about it now. I started, sort of. But there's so much. I just took a look all around me and got bewildered.

COACH: I suppose it is a rather daunting task. Is there any way that you could break it down?

CLIENT: Let me see. Starting next week, I could sweep the floor one day, then pick up all of the tools and put them back in the tool shed the following day. After that, I could take all those newspapers to the recycling center.

COACH: How about all of that paperwork?

CLIENT: Maybe I'll scan all of the old stuff before I throw away the hard copies. You never know when you might need something. But I'm half done, already. The other half should be really easy.

COACH: You think so?

CLIENT: I know so. Today is Monday, and since it's already 8:00 p.m., I doubt that I'll have time today, and tomorrow night is my bowling league. So that leaves Wednesday.

COACH: So what happens Wednesday?

CLIENT: I get home from work at about five-thirty. By the time I finish dinner it's about six. I eat fast. So I should be able to do it by… nine. Wow. That's a long time.

COACH: Could you somehow break that down, as well?

CLIENT: I could also put in just a certain amount of time organizing my paperwork each night until I finish, sort of like what I'm going to do with the garage. I'll break it down over two days, so it doesn't seem so long and boring. I'll spend an hour each night.

COACH: One hour?

CLIENT: No, maybe an hour and a half. Ninety minutes.

COACH: Great. So Wednesday and Thursday, you organize your paperwork from 6:30 till 8:00 p.m. Do you think that'll be enough time to finish?

CLIENT: Yeah, should be. Then I'll stay in Friday night and work on cleaning out the garage. I'll put away all of the tools, then sweep the floor. Saturday I'll take the newspapers to the recycling center. Then I'm done.

COACH: Just speaking from personal experience, I've found that if you pick up the little things lying around in your life, you have more time, room and energy for the big things. Do you remember that when we first started two months ago, you were saying that you wanted to be certified in Lotus? I had you make a list of the top ten things that you wanted by the end of the year, and that was number one on the list.

CLIENT: Yeah, I remember. I keep meaning to get around to it. That sounds like a pretty lame excuse, doesn't it?

COACH: My only reason for bringing it up is that after you pick up the little things in your life—the garage, the paper-work—what big things do you want to focus on? Is Lotus certification still on the list?

CLIENT: Yes, it is.

COACH: How much time are you willing to spend on it next week?

CLIENT: I still have Saturday and Sunday open. I'll come up with a plan for how I'm going to get my Lotus certification.

COACH: What kind of plan?

CLIENT: I'll outline the steps, like we've done before with oth-er things, and list which topics I'm going to study and when, and maybe even come up with a tentative date that I'm going to take the test. I'll email it to you.

COACH: All right, then. It's June right now. Let me ask you this: if you really put your mind to it, how long do you think it would be before you're ready to take the test?

CLIENT: That's a good question.

COACH: Well, let's hear a good answer.

Disclaimers

Our litigious society demands that we pay attention to certain "unpleasant" issues. As a coach, your role is to be a confidante, not an advisor or legal counselor. You are there to listen, to respond and to ask questions, not to tell the client what he or she should do. Ultimately, the client decides what he or she wants to accomplish, and is subsequently responsible for any consequences arising from actions undertaken.

A word of advice about advice: Sometimes a client will ask your opinion on something or would like to know what you did in a similar situation. Don't play games by constantly responding "Well, what do YOU think that you should do?" When asked for your opinion on a matter, qualify that you are giving just that. You might say, "If I were in your position, I'd consider this," or, "I would go with the red wine if you're serving pasta," but don't say, "This is what you should do."

3.1.6   Laser Coaching

Some coaches offer laser coaching in addition to their regular sessions. Laser coaching is, in effect, a la carte coaching delivered over the telephone. The term "laser" refers to the highly focused and concentrated nature of the technique similar to the intensity and focus of light produced by a laser. Laser coaching calls generally last five to fifteen minutes, although they can last longer than this, and work well for clients with tight schedules who prefer to focus on one issue or problem at a time. Some examples might be:

- An executive who has to make a difficult decision to lay off an employee

- A writer who must decide where to submit an article that he or she has written

- A housewife who wants to take a couple of business courses

- A student trying to come up with the best way to study for a major exam

Techniques of Laser Coaching

Get to the Heart of the Issue

The most important part of laser coaching is that you get to the heart of the issue as quickly as possible. Techniques for doing this include keeping clients focused on what is the real issue, listening and interacting closely with what clients are saying, identifying strengths and weaknesses in their arguments, and trying to see the issues from their points of view.

The central difficulty in laser coaching is keeping clients focused by not letting them wander from the main problems they want to deal with. Laura Meyer, who specializes in divorce recovery coaching, advises that "laser only works if you are following the right track with the client, otherwise you can get lost and not remember what the client wanted to be coached on in the first place. This happened to me in the very beginning until I fine-tuned the skill."

This means that if clients start to tell a story, for example, bring them back to the main issue politely but firmly. Help them find a truth about their situation. In other words, this is where you will need to help them focus quickly on the strengths or weaknesses in what they are telling you they want so that they can recognize where the benefits lie for them.

As spiritual coach Marguerite Manning explains:

> "I always think of it as being just as simplistic as that old Henny Youngman joke; you know, a man says to his doctor "Hey Doc, it hurts when I do this" and the doctor replies, "Well, then, don't do that." Only with laser coaching, you get your client to come to the same conclusion all by himself. If you have an opportunity to work with a laser coach firsthand, it's the best way to understand it. It's also a great tool to have in your self-analysis tool belt. (I speak from experience on that one)."

Maintain Objectivity

Manning characterizes laser coaching as somewhat like guiding the client "through a maze from the higher vantage point of objectivity." Most of the time, the conclusion is already obvious to the coach, but not so to the client. Your job as a life coach in the laser coaching process is to help clients see the truth of their circumstances and then help them to find a solution. The coach's job is to get clients to reach the same or similar conclusion about their situations that you've already reached as their coach.

To do this, keep in mind these 3 basic steps recommended by Manning:

1. Touch your client by doing whatever is necessary to establish trust

2. Intrude as a partner by validating his pain/issues

3. Laser in on his solution to the problem by taking an opposite position, pointing out the truth as you see it, exaggerating their truth and emphasizing their inconsistencies and not letting them get away with blame, excuses or denial.

Dos and Don'ts of Laser Coaching

Other important dos and don'ts recommended by success coach KC Christensen-Lang include:

- Do let the client know up front that you will use this method and explain the benefits.

- Do let them know you are there to keep them focused.

- Do encourage them by explaining that coaching is all about action and taking them from where they are today, to where they want to go. Laser coaching allows this exciting process to happen.

- Do remind them "How would you say this or explain this in a laser method?" or "How can you make or see this point in a laser way?" They will immediately shorten their version and get to the heart of the problem.

- Don't let them ramble on too long.

- Don't use it when they need to vent; it is important to listen and let them pour out their heart on occasion, but laser coaching helps the client move forward quicker and get more out of their sessions.

Getting Experience

Most coaches who employ laser coaching recommend that you find an experienced mentor (see section 4.1.4 for more about finding a mentor) who is familiar with the techniques. Marguerite Manning notes that laser coaching is "best learned by role-playing with an experienced coach. If you plan to employ laser coaching, you should find a coach you can work with and gain a bit of experience before using it. Eventually, you will develop your own style as well."

If you would like to experience laser coaching firsthand, Tom (T. J.) Jones, director of Career Planning University, has designed a program called A Coach in Your Pocket, which combines features of e-coaching and laser coaching. Monthly subscription to this service starts at about $20. A Coach in Your Pocket gives clients weekly email support, and is an inexpensive way for them to determine if coaching would be beneficial for them. "If you email us a question, we'll email you an answer back, or some ideas how to handle it," Jones explains. "Options are also available for personal one-on-one telecoaching."

Although many coaches use laser coaching because of its ability to help clients narrow their focus and gain insight into the larger problems, not all coaches offer this service due to its focus on short-term solutions to short-term problems. Spiritual coach Marlee LeDai explains her preference for longer-term coaching methods in this way: "I work much more on an organic level. It takes time for things to grow. It takes a lot of courage and nutrients for the client to dig deep and come up with authentic solutions. Laser coaching bypasses all this in favor of short-term solutions."

If you choose to use laser coaching in your practice, you should definitely try to find someone to help you master the technique. All of the experts we contacted stressed the importance of finding a mentor experienced in laser coaching to teach you how to use it effectively.

3.2 Coaching Groups

Coaches who work with groups may either present short programs such as corporate trainings (covered in section 2.4.2) or workshops and retreats (covered in section 3.3.5) or do ongoing group coaching which is the focus of this section. Group coaching can be an extremely effective style of coaching.

In group coaching, members of the group can help support and encourage each other, much the same way that a life coach would support and encourage them on an individual basis. As a life coach, you are there to moderate the group, keep them on track, and steer the discussion away from any issues that really don't belong in coaching. Group coaching focuses on achieving the goals of individuals within the group as well as those of the group as a whole.

One of our experts describes her experience coaching groups in a workshop setting:

> "What happens in a workshop depends on the attitudes and mix of individuals; you can never predict the benefits and results. I've seen it be the whole gamut from where the entire class becomes best friends, getting oodles out of the material and stay in contact for years...all the way down to where really only one participant stays fully engaged and feels lonely, but follows through. But for all those who do engage, the benefits range from at one end, grasping a single concept that leads to the next steps one by one, to having a life changing experience altogether."
>
> — Marlee LeDai, GoGirl Coach

Group coaching also can be a cost-effective alternative for individuals who might not otherwise be able to afford individual coaching. Group coaching enables you to lower your fees for individuals taking group sessions. This enables more clients who otherwise could not afford coaching to experience it, and also gives you the chance to work with more people. Clients who try group coaching first might eventually decide to go for one-on-one sessions.

3.2.1   Presenting a Group Coaching Session

While 30 or 45 minutes per week with an individual client may be ideal, one-hour sessions are more practical with a group. The members can take turns working on their goals, issues and situations. If you coach a group of ten people, for example, spend about 5 minutes per session on one client, rotating so that everyone eventually has a turn. The coaching will have to be a little more focused and concentrated, as this leaves little time for "small talk" between coach and client. Once you and the group members become accustomed to this, your group sessions should go quite smoothly.

Debra Jackson, a life coach from Lake Oswego, Oregon, describes how she introduced life coaching to a small group. She started by trying to explain to them the concept of life coaching, but quickly realized that teaching by example was much more effective. She asked a particularly inquisitive member of the group to agree to a mini-coaching session. The woman at first declined, so Jackson simply asked her if there was something that she wanted to change about her life, or something that she would like to be doing that she wasn't currently doing. After an initial hesitation the woman opened up, speaking freely of a number of different goals and desires that she had. After asking the woman to narrow her focus to one issue, Jackson gave a very effective presentation to the four women present about how life coaching worked.

This approach can also be tailored to larger groups. Break them down into units of three to five (depending on the number of people) and have them each come up with a list of changes that they would like to make or goals that they would like to accomplish, and take turns reading them. After giving them a half hour or so to come up with their lists, take a few minutes talking to each group individually and see how they did. The following section will give you more ideas for exercises you can use with clients.

Support groups of many kinds are popping up everywhere, particularly in large metropolitan areas. Moderating a support group is a good opportunity for a coach to market him or herself, as well as possibly obtain additional individual clients and get referrals. Limit group size to about ten to 12 members, and meet in a public place for one hour per week. For the first session, have each person start with a brief introduction. See below for an example of an in-person group session.

Example: Coaching A Weight Loss Group

Make the first group coaching session somewhat informal and introductory. Schedule one hour for this "group intake session." Greet everyone at the door and introduce yourself. Give everyone time to assemble, and provide some refreshments such as juices and a vegetable tray or some other healthy snack (you don't have to provide this for every session). This will give clients a bit of time to relax and mingle a bit and set them at ease before the session work really begins.

Once everyone has arrived or within a specific time period, perhaps 5-10 minutes after the scheduled starting time, introduce yourself more fully. Tell them about your background, what led you to weight loss coaching, and how you plan to help them. Let them know that you've "been there, done that." Don't use language like "I'm going to do this for you," or "I can promise you this," "I guarantee you," and especially not "I'm going to help you lose 10 pounds in two weeks." You're not, and that's not what you're expected to do.

Do tell them that you are going to assist them to do whatever they want in terms of their weight loss goals. Tell them that they are here to support and encourage each other, and even to offer constructive criticism when necessary. Explain to the members that you are sympathetic to their situation and that you are providing a shame- and guilt-free environment where everyone can feel comfortable and share their common experiences.

After your introduction, give the group members five or ten minutes to mingle. Tell each person to introduce him or herself to at least two other members. Have them give their names, shake hands if they want to, and offer one or two sentences about themselves.

For the first session, you might want to give them a brief questionnaire or evaluation. Also have them fill out a card with their names, addresses and contact information. They should include a brief statement about what brought them to the group, and what they hope to achieve. Ask that they also bring a resume to the first meeting. Collect this information and review it later.

In many respects, you will work with a group in much the same ways that you work with individual clients. Group members might start by telling the group why they decided to give weight loss coaching a try, perhaps using the information cards they've filled out as a guide. Once everyone has contributed to this part of the session, you can work on goal-setting.

First, provide everyone with an individual goal-setting worksheet such as those in section 3.1.3. Some people in the group in this early phase of the coaching may not have a clear idea of the kinds of goals they want to achieve. If you find this is the case, then a brainstorming session might help people to focus on their goals. Remember to keep goals specific, measurable, stated positively and simply as mentioned previously. Once goals have been set they should be prioritized.

Make a list of the group's individual goals. You should quickly see that there are a number of goals in common to most group members. These can be prioritized according to how easily or quickly they can be achieved. From there have the group come up with suggestions for how these common goals can be achieved.

You may not have time for all of this individual and group goal-setting in one session. If not, try to get at least the individual goal-setting activities finished by the end of the first session, so that you can build on that for the next session.

For subsequent sessions, you will want to explore with the group ways to achieve the goals they have agreed are mutually important. These might include:

- Finding ways to cope with emotional eating

- Finding online or print resources for balanced nutritional and dietary information

- Finding resources for exercising such as gyms, personal trainers, online sources, etc.

Taking the first example, emotional eating, the group might explore together all the many reasons why they turn to food to cope with a variety of events in their lives. Again, you'll probably find that individuals in the group share many of the same coping mechanisms. Many in the group may begin to recognize themselves in what others in the group are saying. From there, the group can share any individual triumphs, no matter how small, they have experienced and that have helped them to stop their emotional eating habits.

Keep in mind that some individuals may not be ready to share their experiences with the rest of the group. This may create suspicion among others in the group, but you need to assure everyone that participation, while highly encouraged, is always voluntary. Let them know, though, that the coaching will not be as effective if not everyone participates. Reiterate that everyone's contribution is valued and respected.

One of the important aspects of group coaching is that, as people discover various resources on their own, they can share them with the group and add them to the pool of resources that everyone can benefit from. It's also important to challenge, though always in balance with supportiveness, strategies that may not benefit everyone and why that is so.

After the group coaching session, follow up with a recap of the session by an email (or phone call for anyone who doesn't have email) to each individual in the group so that everyone will remember what was explored and accomplished during the session.

3.2.2   Group Coaching Considerations

Stanley J. Lieberman, an attorney and life coach in Exton, Pennsylvania, offers the following advice for facilitating group coaching:

> Group members may be reluctant to share too much information with others in the group… [so] include a confidentiality clause in the coaching contract when working with groups. This clause simply advises all participants that what is said during the sessions is not for public dissemination. Indicate what types of issues will and will not be discussed.

> A group size of between five and ten works best. With fewer than that, participants don't get a wide variety of viewpoints and perspectives, and with more than that, time constraints can pose a problem. Prior to the first group session, the coach should have one individual coaching session with each of the members, to debrief them, so to speak.

> Group sessions can be conducted over the telephone via conference call, or in person. If geographically feasible, the first group meeting should be conducted in person, because clients like to associate a face with a name. After the initial meeting, the coach and the clients can decide if they would like to continue face-to-face or simply have telephone coaching. As a practical matter, face-to-face sessions have a higher fee because of the coach's travel time and time away from his or her office.

Consider using email in addition to your group coaching sessions. After a group meeting, send an email to the members, reiterating what was discussed, on whose goals you focused, and what is scheduled for the following session. For example:

> "This week, we talked about Joe's goal of buying a new Porsche, Glenda's plan for moving out of her parents' house and Brandon's search for a good computer-programming training school. Joe agreed that he would decide on the model and color that he wanted; Glenda planned on searching the classified ads for the next week under "Roommates wanted," and Brandon was going to ask the four programmers he knew at work if they could recommend a particular school…"

Send an occasional coaching evaluation or follow-up questionnaire (see section 3.5.1 for a sample post-session evaluation form) to gauge the responses of the members. This is particularly helpful in group coaching, when you may not have as much time to devote to each individual's feelings and responses. If a client doesn't have email or access to a computer, you can call him or her instead. Be willing to go the extra distance.

Some people may not wish to exchange contact information with strangers. Find out from each person individually whether he or she is comfortable with this. If someone is uncomfortable, you can maintain all of the contact information, and notify group members about upcoming sessions, changes in session times, cancellations, etc.

3.3 Ways to Deliver Coaching Services

When we asked our experts about their preferred method of delivering services to clients, the answer was overwhelmingly by telephone. However, there are a number of different methods for delivering your services to clients besides using the telephone, including face-to-face (in person) meetings, email, chat room or messenger-type programs, teleclasses, and seminars and retreats. You can use any combination of any of these methods in your coaching practice.

What is important is that however you deliver your coaching services to clients the delivery method is flexible and convenient for them. Weight/body image coach Sophie Pachella told us, "I have clients I've never met in person, and clients I see face-to-face weekly. I enjoy the personalized aspect of a face-to-face meeting, and also the accessibility and convenience of the phone and Internet. Both have their advantages, and even local clients opt for a little of both." You'll probably find that you will use a bit of everything at first until you find a delivery system that works best for you.

Using phone, email or Internet delivery allows for a great deal of flexibility in scheduling sessions with clients. If you live in a large metropolitan area, it's sometimes easier to contact clients by electronic means rather than fighting traffic to make a long trip to meet someone face-to-face across town. Electronic delivery of services also allows you to reach clients you might never have had otherwise. As Sophie Pachella mentions, "I have a client in British Columbia who I would never be able to work with if I didn't conduct teleconferences."

In the following sections we'll look at a few of the most common ways of delivering services to clients. We'll also give you a brief overview of the advantages and disadvantages of each. After reading these sections, you should have a good idea of the methods that you might want to try in the beginning.

3.3.1   In Person Coaching

Coaching in person traditionally has been the most common delivery method for coaching services, although the life coaches we interviewed use in-person coaching only a small percent of the time. However, this is still a widely used method and you will probably use it at some point in your career, especially in coaching corporate clients.

Conducting in-person coaching is usually done in the coach's office (whether a home office or an office outside the home) or at the client's residence, although a weight loss coach might meet a client at a facility such as a gym and a corporate or executive coach would probably meet in the client's place of business. You should decide when you start if you plan to offer in-person coaching and plan for it. If you will offer in-person coaching, check with your clients whether they would prefer a session in your office or in their home, but be sure to have your office ready beforehand in case they'd prefer to meet at your office.

If you plan to conduct in-person coaching sessions from your place of business you will need either a home office or an established office somewhere else. In either case, you will need to set up your office with all the furnishings and equipment you will need to do business. For example, you will likely need a sofa or loveseat, a few comfortable chairs, a desk, computer, fax, and so on. (See section 5.4 for more about setting up your office space.)

If you plan to offer services to executives and corporations, you will most often meet with clients at their offices. However, you should be prepared to take along with you everything you will need in order to conduct the coaching session. While your first meeting with clients (individual or corporate) will probably be an initial consultation and intake session (see section 3.1.1) subsequent meetings will require you to have on hand any coaching instruments such as assessment tools with you. For this, you should have a briefcase or a portfolio case, and a few lidded boxes to carry your materials with you.

Advantages and Disadvantages

One of the major advantages to in-person coaching is that you will be able to "read" clients' reactions to your coaching much easier than you would by phone or other remote means. Face-to-face coaching helps you to better gauge clients' moods or feelings about the issues they are bringing to you and lets you judge their reactions to your suggestions. In most ways, it is a much more personal style of coaching.

In-person coaching is also ideal for clients who may not be comfortable being coached by someone they've never met. They may be looking for a coach nearby who offers this service and would otherwise not choose a coach who only offered coaching by telephone or other electronic means.

Coaches who coach in person normally charge a higher fee for this service. One of the reasons for this is the cost of setting up and maintaining an office in which to see clients. Also, in-person coaching is generally a bit more time-consuming than other forms of coaching. (See section 5.6 for more about how to set your fees.)

One of the disadvantages to in-person coaching is that sessions may not be as productive as telephone coaching sessions because of the personal interactions that take place. In addition, as mentioned above, personal meetings with clients can take up a bit more of your time. Relationship coach Laura Meyer told us she does only about 5% of her coaching in person and finds that she's not always able to get right down to business with her face-to-face clients. She notes that these sessions "always run longer and have too much idle chitchat."

Another disadvantage is that there is less flexibility than with other means of coaching delivery. Most of our coaches responded that they felt their client base would be much more limited if they offered only in-person services. In addition, scheduling conflicts are heightened when coaching only in an office or in-home setting.

3.3.2   Telephone Coaching

Telephone coaching is a popular method of coaching for both coaches and clients. Some of the advantages for clients in choosing telephone coaching include:

- no travel expenses

- not limited by geographic location

- no parking issues

- no childcare problems

- flexibility of scheduling appointments

Telephone coaching also allows for laser coaching, which lets clients work on urgent, single issues in short sessions over the phone (see section 3.1.6).

Of course, one of the disadvantages for clients in choosing a coach who offers mainly telephone coaching is the potential for long-distance charges to quickly add up. Many coaches offer email coaching as a part of or in addition to the monthly coaching fee to offset this.

Some coaches conduct sessions on their cell phones, but cell phone conversations are not always private as they can be intercepted by someone who has a scanner. Another word of caution about coaching via cell phone: don't do this when either you or the client is driving. Not only does this hinder the ability to drive safely, but hinders the effectiveness of the coaching, as well. Coaching requires active involvement and concentration by both parties, much more so than a typical cell phone conversation about what to pick up at the store for dinner or what time a movie starts. Also, coaching while driving precludes the possibility of taking notes and writing down key points.

As an alternative to one-on-one telephone coaching many coaches offer teleclasses or conference call coaching (see section 3.3.4).

3.3.3   E-Coaching (Cyber Coaching)

Email

Coaching via email is becoming popular, particularly where long distance telephone charges are a concern. Once or twice a week, the client emails the coach with whatever issues, concerns or questions that he or she has, and the coach responds with answers, observations or suggestions.

Email coaching may also be used as an adjunct to telephone coaching. Many coaches offer this service "free" as part of the monthly coaching sessions fee allowing their clients daily or unlimited emails. Although the element of real time is lost in this venue, coaches who do this say it is just as effective.

Online Chats and Messaging

The advent of online chat rooms and instant messaging has made live online communication much easier. While anonymous individuals congregate in cyberspace to swap opinions on everything from current events to philosophy to pop music, this technology has found some more practical applications, among them, life coaching.

Both America Online (**www.aim.com**) and Yahoo! (**http://messenger. yahoo.com**) offer free instant messaging, which you do not need to be a subscriber to use. Microsoft's Messenger comes built into the operating system, so that's another alternative. These instant messaging programs also make online group sessions possible, too.

Advantages and Disadvantages

E-coaching (or cyber-coaching as it's often called) can be a cost-effective alternative to long-distance telephone calls. Instead of communicating via a weekly telephone chat, coach and client can agree to be online at a certain day and time. This works well if clients are deaf or hearing-impaired, too.

Another advantage of e-coaching is the convenience. There is no need to coordinate chat schedules and parties have more time to think about what they want to say. This can be a real advantage, too, if the coaching takes place between two widely separated time zones.

One drawback with chats and messaging is the extra time that it takes to have an online conversation. Even the fastest typists speak much quicker than they type, and what can be accomplished in 30 minutes over the telephone may require twice as much time over the Internet. If you choose to offer e-coaching, you should still speak with clients on the phone for the first couple of sessions, if possible.

A drawback to coaching by email (and this is also true of chats and messaging to some extent) is that it can sometimes be difficult to tell exactly what the client's message is intended to convey. They may be trying to express their dry sense of humor but you might be reading it as sarcasm or despondency. In addition, poor grammar and spelling, or the use of abbreviations like those often used in text messaging, can make it difficult for you to understand exactly what a client is trying to tell you.

Other problems you might encounter include viruses being transmitted by email and security issues such as hackers intercepting emails (and chats). Try to save any highly confidential issues for telephone or in-person sessions. In addition, privacy can become an issue if other individuals besides your client have access to the client's computer, so be sure to discuss these issues with clients to be sure these problems will not arise.

3.3.4 Teleclasses

Most coaching consists of one-on-one, 30-minute weekly sessions between coach and client. However, some coaches have expanded their practice through "teleclasses," where they can speak to a group of people in a conference call format. 800 number conferencing services provide "bridge lines" so that multiple clients can call in to take part in the same conference call. Examples of possible teleclass topics are:

- Improving self-confidence

- Reducing stress

- Budgeting

- Being assertive

- Choosing the right career

- Communicating effectively with your partner

- Finding your life's mission

- Finding your carbon footprint

Jill Chongva, who provides entrepreneur coaching services through her company Virtual Assistant Diva (**www.vadiva.com**), believes that tele-classes are very effective in introducing potential clients to coaching:

> "By offering a free teleclass, potential clients are introduced to my coaching style and outlook in a way that my website or brochures can't communicate. They are able to experience the coaching process first hand, and see if my style would mesh with their own to determine if they want to enter into a partnership with me. The teleclass also offers a degree of anonymity that participants would not enjoy in traditional workshops or lectures. This allows open and honest interactions where participants can share and I can communicate in a way that other mediums don't provide."

Conducting Teleclasses

According to Anna Kanary, a corporate teleleader trainer in British Columbia, Canada and a certified teleleader with Teleclass International, teleclass leaders must keep four points in mind:

- Different students have different styles of learning and processing information. These styles include visual, tactile, verbal and auditory. The teleclass leader should incorporate all of these elements into a teleclass, if possible. One way to facilitate visual processing, for example, would be to have students take notes, make lists or draw a simple chart during the teleclass.

- Encourage students to participate. The teleclass leader needs to encourage people to speak up, ask questions, give feedback, etc. "Lurkers" (to borrow a term referring to people in Internet chat rooms who never type anything) hinder effective teleclasses.

- Don't be too pushy in trying to sell your products or services, and don't engage in shameless self-promotion. Even a free teleclass, which your first few will likely be, should provide valuable content. Too often, "free" is associated with "cheap" or "worthless." Don't fall victim to this.

- The class should have structure. Too many people talking at once, background noise or other distractions, or excessive time spent on introductions and small talk all detract from your teleclass. Encourage people to phone in on time, and conduct your class in an orderly and organized manner.

You should keep your hands free when facilitating a teleclass. This will allow you to concentrate better, and take notes on what the students are saying, just as you would take notes while talking to a client during a regular coaching session.

Teleclasses usually last an hour at a time—longer than a typical half-hour coaching session—and using a handset for that long will make your arm tired or give you a neck cramp. Wearing a headset is better than putting the telephone on speaker, because the latter still allows background noise, and often, your voice will sound far away. Request that participants in your teleclass not use a speakerphone either.

At the conclusion of your teleclass, thank all of your participants, and ask them permission to follow up with an email. You might send them additional information on your services, reiterate what you covered during the hour, or ask them to fill out a short survey or questionnaire. Some coaches who conduct teleclasses will even offer discounts for previous students who sign up for future classes. You typically will already have students' emails from when they registered for your class, but ask if you are not sure.

Preparing for Teleclasses

Make an outline of the teleclass that you will be leading, so that you can keep in mind all of your key points, and refer back to the outline if you get stuck. Reading from your outline verbatim is not practical, as you never know what is going to come up during a teleclass. Your outline should have short, succinct points upon which you can expand during the actual teleclass.

Prior to a teleclass, most coaches will email participants a reminder of the upcoming session, and include a brief overview of what will be covered, the telephone number and PIN (Personal Identification Number) that callers should use and a primer for teleclass protocol. The latter basically states that participants should call in on time, use a land line instead of a cell phone, try to keep background noise to a minimum and identify themselves when they speak.

Like teachers in conventional classrooms, coaches also may email notes or handouts about the teleclass, depending on how much information that they will be covering. But don't overwhelm your students with dozens of pages that they have to print out, study and remember.

Some teleclasses actually become "telecourses" and last two or three sessions, with each session generally scheduled a week apart. Keeping participants coming back two and three times can be difficult, so if you plan on extended teleclasses, make sure that you have enough important information to cover, and always leave your students hungry for more information at the end of the hour. Something like, "Next week, I'm going to get into this…"

Finding Teleclass Hosting

Telephone Bridge Services (**www.telephonebridgeservices.com**) and Teleclass.com (**www.teleclass.net**) offer dozens of new classes and seminars every week on a variety of personal and business topics. The cost ranges from $25 to $150 for a one-hour session, but many are offered free of charge. Sign up for some of the free classes to get a sample of the different topics. Be aware that long-distance charges may apply, though.

In order to conduct teleclasses on either of these websites, you must first become a certified teleclass leader, or "teleleader," which requires a specific number of training hours and can cost a few hundred dollars, depending on which service you use.

However, FreeConference (**www.freeconference.com**) offers conference calling services for companies and private individuals. By opening a free account, you can schedule conference calls for up 50 to 100 participants, and give each caller a private access code. Another option gives you a variety of conference controls, including a presentation mode feature so that callers can hear you, but can't speak. The latter works best with large groups. If you want to hold an interactive, question-and-answer session, limit group size to eight to ten callers.

Try conducting a few free teleclasses first, to gain exposure for yourself, then you can start to charge. In addition to credit card and PayPal (see section 5.7 for information about these payment methods), offer prospective students the opportunity to pay by check. Some may not have credit cards, or may not want to pay with them, or they just might feel uncomfortable with online transactions.

Advantages and Disadvantages

One of the main advantages to offering teleclasses is that you can reach a large number of people very quickly. This is, in fact, a two-fold advantage for the coach. First, the teleclass format is cost-effective, since you coach many people in one session instead of one person at a time over many sessions, reducing both your time spent coaching and your telephone costs (it is also cost-effective for participants). Second, those who participate initially in a group session may also be interested in one-on-one coaching, increasing your clientele.

Teleclasses can also be a good marketing tool, although as suggested above, you don't want to overdo it and appear to be trying too hard to push your other products and services. Still, you can let participants know that you offer more than just teleclasses. Further, this is an excellent way to market your services to corporate clients, since the teleclass can be tailored to a specific corporation's needs and delivered simultaneously to any branch offices they might have around the country.

One disadvantage to conducting teleclasses is the time invested in preparing them. Often you can spend hours preparing for a teleclass, particularly if you have never conducted one before or it is a new class that you're developing. However, once you have prepared the material you can use it again and again.

Another disadvantage is that participation from those calling in cannot be guaranteed. Sometimes you need to work hard to keep everyone engaged. An additional disadvantage is that you might find it hard to determine the benefits and results of the class if you don't follow up with a post-session evaluation of some kind such as emailing participants.

The main disadvantage for clients is that conference calls are less personal and more "public" since multiple clients are discussing similar issues at the same time.

3.3.5   Workshops and Retreats

Another popular method of bringing coaching services to clients is through workshops (or seminars) and retreats. Workshops usually take place where large numbers of people can be brought together in one room, such as a hotel's convention center, an auditorium, or other large venue. Retreats are usually scheduled in quieter or more out-of-the-way locations so that clients participating in the retreat can get away from their usual routines for a few days of introspection and personal growth. Although coaches also offer workshops in the teleclass format explored above, in this section we'll look at workshops and retreats that take place in person with clients.

In many ways, both workshops and retreats are similar to group coaching. Section 3.2 looked at the dynamics of group coaching and how to conduct a group session as well as considerations for facilitating group coaching. In this section we'll look at the logistics of coaching groups of people as a unique method for delivering services to clients. In other words, we'll examine why you might want to host a retreat or workshop and how to prepare for this form of coaching.

The Purpose of Workshops

Workshops are used to get a lot of information to a lot of people in a short amount of time. Sometimes multipart seminars are scheduled to give clients a break in between these mass information sessions. A workshop event could take place over a couple of days as well.

A workshop or seminar can be a good way to get your services to people who might not otherwise have used coaching services. A workshop or seminar can get people excited about the idea of coaching. As weight loss/body image coach Sophie Pachella (**www.eatstrong.com**) explains:

> "I think seminars are most useful for folks who would never otherwise hire a nutritionist privately, for those who wish they could but can't afford it, for those on the fence, or for those who are just curious. In other words, people I wouldn't usually see. It allows them to listen without "committing", to ask questions, or to just listen to other people's questions if they're shy. Usually, people really open up and get on a roll. Questions are always flooding in and we always run out of time."

One of the most important aspects of workshops for participants is that they are focused on shared experiences with others who are also participating. For example, women often have the experience of trying to juggle working, raising their children, looking after the household and so on, and can easily find common ground with other participants in a work/life balance workshop, like the Working Mothers' Workshops offered by life coach Amber Rosenberg (**www.workingmotherscoach. com/workshops**).

You can offer workshops to any group of people who might have a common interest or set of experiences that they want to deal with through coaching. Coach Marlee LeDai offers workshops for writers, people experiencing marriage or relationship meltdown, and she has another in development for people sharing the common experience of caring for elderly parents suffering from Alzheimer's Disease and dementia. If you find that many clients come to you with similar issues, you can easily develop a workshop out of one of them to deliver coaching services to a large number of people.

Even if you coach mainly by telephone, many coaches offer workshops in a teleclass or teleseminar format. However, chances are that a lot of people in your geographic area may have similar issues and just aren't aware of your coaching services. You can tailor your teleseminar to a venue-based workshop or seminar to bring your workshops to these local clients. Workshops are a great way to market your services to potential clients in your area. (See Chapter 6 for more about marketing.)

The Purpose of Retreats

Retreats are a little different from workshops in that they usually take place in an isolated, tranquil location in order to help participants to focus on whatever issue is the theme of the retreat. Examples of retreat locations include a resort on the beach, a spa facility, a monastery, and so on. By moving the program to an isolated location, you help your clients get away from the everyday distractions that might otherwise keep them from focusing solely on the coaching. This allows them to become completely immersed in the coaching experience.

Like workshops, retreats generally focus on a single area of personal growth or development for the group. Themes for retreats include couples retreats, spiritual growth and enrichment, weight loss, etc.

To get a better idea of the retreats and retreat locations offered by a wide variety of coaches, visit the Retreat Finder website **www.retreatfinder. com**. Many of the retreats featured at this website focus on spirituality and health and wellness, but you can offer a retreat on any theme so long as the people involved would benefit by separating themselves from the demands of their usual everyday routine.

Planning a Workshop or Retreat

Developing a Theme and Curriculum

Your theme for a workshop or retreat ideally should develop naturally as an outgrowth of your coaching practice. Every one of the coaches we interviewed told us that in their coaching niches they found similar issues cropping up over and over. As a result, you can develop your theme as an outgrowth of the issues you most often coach. Marlee Le-Dai explains her workshop development process:

> "My curriculum is always around issues that I focus on in my coaching: midlife issues, writing, and eldercare. When a coach cares deeply about her clients and about the people in her niche, working up a curriculum is as natural as breathing. My workshops are not contrived, but sprout organically from my passions and my deep commitment to encouraging women in life's most profound transitions."

Sophie Pachella offers a variety of seminars that represent some of the themes she explores with her individual clients. Her seminars are based on popular themes that she frequently sees in her regular coaching sessions. In explaining how her seminars are received by participants, she told us:

> "Everyone, even the skeptics, loves to discuss nutrition and how it affects health, performance, testosterone in men (!), hormone fluctuations in women, and so many other things. Once people realize I'm not an ogre pushing carrot sticks and cottage cheese, you can see their postures relax and an expression on their face which suggests 'okay, I can do this.'"

Your workshop curriculum is basically an outline of what you hope to achieve, a breakdown of the topics you will cover, how you will deliver the material, and a timeline for the event. Essentially, this will be in the form of a syllabus or lesson plan similar to those you might see in a college course, although these can take a variety of forms. The important thing is that you set out clearly what you to hope to help clients accomplish and how you intend to accomplish it.

First, decide what your outcomes for clients during the event will be. For example, if you are a time-management coach, your outcomes might include having clients know how to use a PDA or day timer effectively, learning to identify how their time is being used ineffectively, and so on. Create a written statement of these outcomes on your syllabus.

Next, outline the knowledge or skills you would like clients to walk away with when they are finished the workshop or retreat. This might include nutritional and exercise information for weight loss/body image clients, what goes into writing an effective resume for career coach clients, organizational tips for time-management clients, etc. Create a statement of the knowledge or skills goals in the syllabus.

Finally, you might include a list of the desired attitude changes you hope to see in clients. This can be followed up with some simple exercises such as those outlined in section 3.4 for clients to do individually or in groups. You can then evaluate how successfully the knowledge they have gained has produced the desired outcomes of the workshop or retreat.

Once you've completed the syllabus, you can provide it to clients after they've signed up for the workshop or retreat. You can also use it to provide an outline of the event, which you can then use to promote it on your website. (See section 6.2.3 for more about marketing ideas for your website.)

Below, you will find a sample syllabus similar to what you might use in a workshop or retreat. The "outcomes" and "knowledge" sections in the sample are very broad and general topics, and any one of them easily could be broken down further to create an entire workshop. Ideally, your workshop or retreat should be very focused on just a few specific issues.

Sample Workshop Syllabus

Host: Everything Balances Life Coaching Services

Date: October 17, 2009

Location: Conference Room C, Libra Hotel

Facilitator: Ima Coach

Welcome to Everything Balances' "Managing Your Midlife Crisis" workshop.

Many people become discouraged (or even depressed) with the thought of getting older and they start to lose touch with the things that once gave them pleasure. Many also begin to feel that they've done nothing but work for years and that their jobs have taken over their lives.

In this exciting one-day experience, you will learn how to enjoy life in a more balanced and positive way. You'll discover new ways to view your work and your play and become a happier YOU, and you'll discover new tools to help you to prepare yourself for the issues you'll encounter in the years ahead.

[Outcomes] Participants will:

- Appreciate that leisure is as important in life as work
- Find their ideal work/life balance
- Be able to integrate their own sense of spirituality into everyday living
- Discover their ideal career direction
- Look ahead to retirement without fear

[Knowledge] Participants will discover:

- Tips for managing their time more effectively
- The root causes of many of their work/life balance issues
- Tips for integrating spirituality into their daily lives
- Their ideal career and how to achieve the most from it
- How to plan effectively for the many issues they will face before, during and after retirement
- The power of sharing experiences with others

Activities

- Meet others facing similar issues
- An overview of issues common to the "Midlife Crisis" (you're not alone!)
- Individual goal-setting activities
- Journaling activities
- Guest speaker: Bea Neader (professional organizer)
- Group discussions
- One-on-one session with Ima Coach
- Dialoguing exercises
- Relaxation and focusing exercises
- Retirement planning tips

Finding a Venue

In many cases, the venue you choose will be close to where you live, particularly if you are hosting a workshop. For retreats, you might want to be a bit more creative in terms of finding the ideal location for the kind of retreat you want to host. You wouldn't want to host a spiritual or couples retreat in a distracting place like Las Vegas, for example.

How to Find a Local Venue

You probably have a wide range of venues available for you to host a workshop. Your choice of a venue will depend upon a variety of factors such as the size of your group, the activities you're planning, the tone of the workshop, etc. Take these factors into consideration as you choose the location for your event.

Venues you might consider include:

- Hotel conference rooms

- Schools (auditoriums or classrooms)

- Restaurants

- Library meeting rooms

- Sportsplex

If you're not sure how to find a venue or who to contact, a good place to start is your local Chamber of Commerce. Your local Chamber will have a website listing all its members and their services offered along with contact information for each. To find your local Chamber website you can search the national directory at **www.chamberofcommerce. com** by typing in the name of your city. In Canada, the web address is **www.chamber.ca/article.asp?id=286**.

To find resources like schools and libraries or other government facilities you can rent, try the Blue Pages in your local phone directory. There you will find listings for your local Board of Education offices, city parks department, library listings and so on.

How to Find a Retreat Venue

Finding a location for a retreat can be a bit more challenging that finding local venues, but also a lot more interesting and fun. Again, it's important to consider what you're trying to achieve and how you will achieve it, just as with workshops, so be sure to find a location that works for you. Some good places to host a retreat are:

- Guest ranches

- Spas

- Resorts

- Monasteries

- Country inns or bed-and-breakfasts

- Cruise ships

Keep in mind that some of these locations can be expensive and your clientele will have to be comfortable paying the extra costs involved. Make sure that you are providing a truly valuable event for clients so that they feel they are getting their money's worth.

Depending on the retreat venue, you can try approaching the facility's management or owners to see if they might be able to offer a discount for a group booking. Most small to medium sized facilities usually are willing to do this, especially if your group will attend during a non-peak season. Larger facilities are less flexible but most do offer group discounts, especially for larger groups.

To find possible retreat venues you can try the Official Travel Guide's website at **www.officialtravelguide.com**. This site has a searchable directory of websites for visitor's bureaus, hotels, and meeting facilities around the world. You can search by location, hotel chain, or find a facility using the parameters for your requirements you input into their search engine. Another resource to try is the Retreat Finder website mentioned earlier, which has a "Rent a Facility" page where you can input your needs to find a matching facility. (The direct link is **www.retreatfinder. com/Facility_Basic.asp**.)

Other Considerations

Hosting a retreat in some exotic locale is a little more involved than hosting a local workshop as you can imagine. Therefore, this might not be the best choice early on in your coaching practice unless you already have experience as an event planner or something similar.

Instead, you might want to first try out a workshop. A good way to do this is to offer a small-scale workshop as a teleclass so you can get a feel for it. When you're comfortable with the format you can then try a workshop at a local venue and eventually try a retreat if that is something you'd like to work toward.

Remember that your workshop is not a lecture. Although you will probably provide a short speech that outlines the workshop objectives, you will not monopolize the event. Instead, your role is to act as a facilitator to the group just as you would in a group coaching session and much as you would during regular one-on-one coaching sessions for individuals.

Section 5.6 has more information about setting fees for workshops and retreats, and provides additional information on how to lower your costs for hosting these events.

3.4 Coaching Tools

Coaching tools include exercises and instruments. In this section, you will learn about exercises and instruments which you can choose to incorporate into your coaching practice.

Exercises are activities that the client does during the session or between sessions. This chapter has already covered the exercises that most clients do in coaching – setting goals and responding to questions.

Coaching instruments include assessments (questionnaires or tests) that you can have your clients do to give them greater insights into their behaviors and attitudes. An example of an instrument is the goal-setting worksheet included in section 3.1.3.

TIP: Instruments can be useful discovery tools for the coach and the client, but don't place too much emphasis on them. Not every client will want or need to complete a questionnaire. Such clients may come to a life coach because they want support and encouragement, not clarification.

3.4.1   Sample Exercises for Individuals

Role-Playing

Role-playing can help clients practice how they would act in real situations. If they are nervous about a job interview, a potential conflict with a difficult co-worker or even a conversation with a spouse, role-playing provides an opportunity for rehearsal. As a coach, you can play the human resources recruiter, the difficult co-worker or the spouse. Clients need not worry about making mistakes or saying the wrong thing. It's only practice.

Occasionally, you may want to ask the client to put himself or herself in your position. Maybe Rhonda is truly stumped regarding a course of action, or is pressuring you to come up with possible solutions to a problem. Her responses to your questions seem to be "I don't know" or "I can't think of anything." Ask her to pretend to be the coach. What questions would she have for her client? What exercises might she give? How would she handle the session? By coming up with questions that Rhonda believes you might ask her, she will indirectly be asking herself what she should do, and possibly coming up with the answer.

List-making

Life coaches are big on lists. Keeping lists reminds clients of their goals and desired outcomes. The lists should be posted where clients will be able to look at them frequently. Some lists will change periodically, others will remain constant until a particular goal is achieved. Here are some possibilities:

- Coaches inspire their clients to dream big, and one way that they do this is by having them make a list of everything that they would do if they knew that they could not fail. This exercise focuses on the positive and stimulates the imagination. Maybe from looking over the list the client will realize that he or she can do some, most or even all of those things.

- Ask clients to make a list of things that they are going to do every week. The items on the list might be focused on attaining a particular outcome, or they might be of a more general nature.

- Ask clients to write down the three things that they desire most, and to read the list each night before they go to bed.

- Ask the client to list the three or five or even ten greatest accomplishments for the month. What goals were successfully completed? What steps were taken to ensure the success of future endeavors? This reinforces the positive nature of life coaching, inspires the client and clarifies purpose.

Rating Satisfaction Levels

One possible exercise to help clients clarify goals is to have them rate their satisfaction with five major areas in their life—work, relationships, finances, health and leisure—on a scale of one to ten. Then take each area individually, starting with the one that scored the lowest.

Take Elizabeth as an example. Elizabeth rates her relationships at four, which she decides is unsatisfactory. After careful analysis and discussion, she discovers that she never has time to date or socialize because she works 60 hours per week. No wonder she is lonely! But it never really occurred to her before, because she never had a coach to walk her through the process of self-analysis.

Alternately, Elizabeth might rate her leisure at ten and her finances at four. She has a very active social life, and spends a lot of time dining out, attending concerts and going shopping. She also spends a lot of money doing all of these activities, and with the help of her coach, comes to the conclusion that if she wants to bring her finances up to a six or seven, she might have to lower her leisure to a nine or eight. Balance.

How about Bill? His relationships and leisure are tied at five, so he might choose to work on one, the other, or both concurrently. Or maybe his health is more important to him at the moment, despite the fact that he rated it a seven. He decides that before undertaking any improvements in other areas of his life, he wants to bring his health up to ten. So after a couple of coaching sessions, he commits to exercising 30 minutes three times per week, cutting down to one cup of coffee per day and going to bed by 10:00 p.m. every night.

Prioritizing

Life coaches help people prioritize, organize and execute. The path to fulfillment is often strewn with tiny obstacles, tasks or bothersome little chores that block the way like so many small rocks under bare feet. Sometimes clients need to pick them up or sweep them out of the way before proceeding. They could be errands that need to be run, telephone calls that need to be made, bills that need to be paid, whatever.

Ask clients who feel that their lives are cluttered with all of this "small stuff" to make a list of these annoying chores or obligations, and commit to taking care of as many as they can. In her tape series "Dare To Live Your Dream," author and motivational speaker Barbara Sher (**www.barbarasher.com**) sums it up like this: "If you don't let go of the peripherals, you aren't going to be able to focus on the central thing."

So clients can donate to charity that pile of clothing that they have been planning to have altered for the past year and a half; they can sell that motorcycle that has been sitting in the garage for five years because they never had time to ride it; they can give away that guitar that they have been intending to learn to play since 1999.

People sometimes also need to eliminate projects that have been smoldering on the back burner for so long. This is not the same as removing the small stuff cluttering the path to fulfillment.

Unpleasant though it may be, clients may have to selectively abandon some projects which, after careful consideration, they honestly admit to themselves that they have no intention of starting, let alone finishing. A well-nurtured dream is an inspiration, but a half-finished one is nothing more than an energy drain, and a depressing reminder of what never was. Encourage your clients to take a long, hard look at what is really important.

Some projects are worth dusting off and reviving, to be sure, but some are not, and identifying those that need to be discarded is as important as identifying those that are truly meaningful. Often people find themselves enamored with the concept of doing something, more so than they are with truly doing it. A good life coach helps them realize the difference.

Visualization and Affirmation

Most of your clients will likely have heard of visualization and affirmation, which have been popular techniques for personal development for decades. However, your clients may not actually be using these techniques which, based on the individual, may be worth trying.

To use visualization, tell your clients to visualize what they would like to obtain or accomplish. While you are talking to them on the telephone, tell them to close their eyes and form a mental picture of their accomplished goal. Clients who want to lose weight should picture themselves as slim. Those who are seeking a promotion or a better job should imagine that they are sitting behind the desk in their new office.

Walk them through the process the first few times until they have the idea. You are not trying to be a hypnotist, just putting them in a positive frame of mind. There is a distinct difference between envisioning desired outcomes and merely daydreaming or wishful thinking. The former is an active mental process requiring sustained concentration, not some fleeting fantasy.

While visualizations focus on using the power of vision to create success, affirmations – making positive statements – focus on the power of words. One way clients can use affirmations is to write positive, inspiring notes to themselves to serve as reminders of what they want to accomplish:

"You're on your way to the perfect job."

"Better balance = more free time."

"I am in to win."

They can use index cards, adhesive notes or even regular 8 1/2" x 11" paper. Tell them to post them on their dashboard, in the corner of their computer screen, on their desk at work, on the bathroom mirror at home, or on the fridge. They might keep one in their wallet or pocketbook and glance at it from time to time.

Affirmations can be used in a variety of other ways as well, depending on your client. For example, you might coach your clients to use positive statements in any of the following ways:

- Repeat them silently in your mind before an important event such as a business meeting where you'll be making a presentation.

- Say them aloud as you look yourself in the mirror.

- Make a recording and play it back to yourself as you fall asleep at night.

- Write them over and over again in a journal.

Client Homework

Since you may deal with your clients over the phone rather than in person, you will have to trust them to do their part by completing various exercises. You could have clients email their "homework" to you, which might prompt the more lackadaisical to act, or you could even email them little reminders.

You can also have clients keep a journal to monitor their progress, and to track what is and is not working for them. They can evaluate on a weekly basis certain moods, conditions or situations. If they wish to share their journal writings with you, fine. If they prefer to keep them private, that is fine, too.

3.4.2   Instruments for Individuals

While you can create your own instruments, many coaches prefer to buy instruments that have been created by experts. In this section we'll look at a variety of popular and useful assessment instruments often used by life coaches.

Myers-Briggs Type Indicator

The Myers-Briggs Type Indicator ® (MBTI) test is the world's most popular personality assessment. "An understanding of MBTI is critical," says John Fox, Life and Marketing Coach with 3Ethics Coaching. MBTI identifies 16 personality types based on the following four dimensions of personality:

Extraversion (E)	vs.	Introversion (I)
Sensing (S)	vs.	Intuition (N)
Thinking (T)	vs.	Feeling (F)
Judging (J)	vs.	Perceiving (P)

You can find more information about obtaining MBTI instruments and other official MBTI products at **https://www.cpp.com/products/index.aspx**. You must be qualified in order to purchase and administer the MBTI® instruments. According to the website of CPP, Inc. (formerly Consulting Psychologists Press), which publishes the MBTI instruments:

> "Qualification is granted to those who (1) have successfully completed a qualifying program ... and passed a common exam OR (2) hold a bachelor's degree and have successfully completed a course in the interpretation of psychological tests and measurements."

For information about qualification or certification (an optional accreditation program) visit **https://www.cpp.com/pdfs/MBTI_Certification_R4_Online.pdf**. Before spending hundreds of dollars for MBTI training, you can learn more about this instrument online. An excellent site is offered by Paul D. Tieger and Barbara Barron, authors of a number of bestselling books on Personality Type, at **www.personalitytype.com**. Their Personality Type Quiz based on MBTI can be found at **www.personalitytype.com/career_quiz**.

DiSC

The DiSC Assessment is based on a model developed in 1926 by Harvard psychologist William Moulton Marston. Simply put, Marston cites four factors which categorize human personality and behavior: Dominance, Influence, Steadiness and Compliance. Within those categories, there are different types of D's, I's, S's and C's, and overlap is not uncommon.

In the years since its inception, DiSC has been tailored to fit specific situations—business, personal, relationship, problem-solving, conflict resolution, attitudes, etc. Corporations use DiSC in both the training and screening of employees. Life coaches may give DiSC to clients who might need help in clarifying their goals and values. Since no certification is required to administer the DiSC profile and it contains fewer questions, some coaches prefer it to Myers-Briggs. The DiSC profile is available from Inscape Publishing (see below).

Inscape Publishing

In addition to the DiSC Assessment, Inscape Publishing has developed instruments on a variety of other topics such as time management, leadership, coping and stress. For example, here is the company's description of the Coping & Stress Profile:

> "The Coping & Stress Profile is a unique learning instrument that assesses and connects stress and coping in four life areas: Personal, Work, Couple and Family. It reveals how stress in one life area can impact other areas. Conversely, coping resources in one area can be used to effectively manage stress in another area. The Coping & Stress Profile research shows that people who develop and use four key 'Relationship Coping Resources' — Communication, Problem Solving, Flexibility and Closeness — manage stress far more effectively in all life areas than people who rely only on individual coping resources, like diet and exercise. Use this profile to identify individual stressors, coping strengths and to develop relationship coping resources for greater balance and personal satisfaction."

You can buy Inscape products for around $20 per instrument per client. Inscape products are sold through distributors. For example, you can buy a DiSC Facilitator's Kit at **www.internalchange.com/disc_profile_store/mall/ProductPage2.asp** or find a variety of Inscape instruments at **www.rebeccamorgan.com/carlson.html**. If you wish to become a distributor yourself, you can find information at the Inscape Publishing website at **www.inscapepublishing.com**.

Other Resources

Queendom (**www.queendom.com**) features hundreds of free online tests, quizzes and evaluations, covering everything from intelligence to personality to career aptitude to romantic tendencies. You can peruse their extensive inventory and take a few tests online to get some ideas, but do not plagiarize any copyrighted content. The licensing fees start at about $200, depending on whether you want to incorporate one into your website or adapt one as an intake form to give to new clients. They also develop customized tests for businesses and individuals. You may consider this a worthwhile investment.

Amby.com links to many different websites offering free personality tests and profiles at **http://amby.com/go_ghoti/on-line_tests.html**. Again, be aware of any licensing requirements before giving any of the tests to your clients. Also use your judgment as a test you find online may not have any scientific basis, however it may spark discussion with your client, and may be something to investigate.

3.4.3   Exercises and Instruments for Groups

Just as you can use coaching instruments with individuals, you can distribute instruments to groups you are working with, followed by a group discussion.

One principle of training and coaching groups is that lecturing is not an effective way of working with most groups. Instead, effective coaches who are leading training programs typically have trainees participate in a variety of activities such as group discussions, role plays, brainstorming, games, completing questionnaires, and watching videos.

However, avoid having too many games in a training session or you risk having participants feel the training is a waste of time. This is because an important principle of adult learning theory is that adults need to be shown why something is relevant. As a coach-trainer, you will need to explain how the material you are teaching can be applied to their life.

To illustrate, which of the following do you think would be the most effective exercise for an employee training session on conflict resolution?

> EXERCISE #1:
> Participants break into groups of three. You then give them a make-believe scenario about a conflict between a teenager who has been skipping classes and her parents. Participants discuss and try to resolve the situation by "role playing" (acting) the parts of the teenager and parents.
>
> EXERCISE #2:
> You ask participants to think of a situation where they personally have experienced conflict. They then break into pairs and you give them several questions so they can discuss what they experienced. For those who prefer not to discuss a personal situation, you can suggest they discuss a conflict they have observed. As part of the discussion, or as a separate activity, you have participants role play what they would say if they experienced a similar situation in future.

In the first exercise, participants are unlikely to see any direct application to their work. In the second exercise, participants can discuss and find ways of dealing with situations they have actually experienced or are likely to experience in the future.

The following two examples are from Terri Levine, founder of the coach training school ComprehensiveCoachingU.com. These sample exercises focus on listening and interpersonal skills, and are designed for teams of two or three:

"Have a conversation with the person on your right for five minutes. Use your best tuning-in skills as they describe what things they enjoy and are brilliant at. Simply listen. Then, after the five minutes are up, tell them what you heard UNDERNEATH the words—the feelings, the intentions, the emotions."

The second example involves three people, one of whom acts as a moderator while one person explains further what he or she likes about work or what is going well and the other takes the opposite position. While remaining neutral, the moderator has to get the two to come to some sort of agreement.

You can learn additional techniques for teaching adults through continuing education classes and organizations such as the American Society for Training and Development (**www.astd.org**). There are also many books available with training exercises, such as the popular series *Games Trainers Play*, by John W. Newstrom and Edward E. Scammell.

If you don't want to create your own training programs, you can buy programs that have already been developed on subjects such as communications, change, creativity, customer relations, diversity, leadership, management, sales, stress management, teamwork, and other topics. Inscape Publishing, mentioned above as a source of instruments for individual coaching, also offers Facilitator's Kits containing a fully-scripted seminar, and transparency masters and reproducible handouts. Facilitator's Kits cost about $600, and can be purchased through a distributor like **www.rebeccamorgan.com/carlson.html**.

3.5 Evaluating the Coaching

One of the best ways to evaluate your coaching is with a coaching evaluation form, which might look like one of the forms included in this section. Evaluation forms can be emailed to clients as text documents for convenience and returned by them in the same way.

3.5.1 Evaluating Individual Progress

Periodically, ask your clients how you are doing as their coach. Encourage them to be honest, even blunt. Maybe there is something that you are not doing that they would like you to do, or even something that you are doing that they would like you not to do.

Sample Coaching Evaluation Form

Date:

Name of Client:

Name of Coach:

1. What I have liked best about the coaching:

    _____

    _____

2. What I have liked least about the coaching:

    _____

    _____

3. We have made progress in the following:

    _____

    _____

4. We still need to work on the following:

    _____

    _____

5. I feel that my three greatest strengths are:

    _____

    _____

6. I feel that my three greatest weaknesses are:

    _____

    _____

7. Additional comments, suggestions, etc.:

    _____

    _____

    _____

Sample Post-Session Evaluation Form

Date:

Name of Client:

Name of Coach:

1. I would rate today's coaching session:

   1   2   3   4   5   6   7   8   9   10
   (poor)   (great)

2. For the upcoming week, I have committed to do the following:

   _____

   _____

   _____

3. I think that the main points of today's coaching session were:

   _____

   _____

   _____

4. I wish that we had spent more time talking about:

   _____

   _____

   _____

5. I wish that we had spent less time talking about:

   _____

   _____

   _____

6. Additional, comments, questions, suggestions, etc.:

   _____

   _____

   _____

Post-Session Evaluations

Periodically ask clients to fill out an impromptu evaluation of the most recent coaching session. This post-session form not only gets the client thinking about what just transpired, but gives you the opportunity to see where you stand and reinforces the focus of the session. Unlike the evaluation that deals with the overall effectiveness of the coaching, this one focuses on the most recent interaction between you and the client.

You might want to do this once a month, or once every other month. Ask the clients if they can complete and return the post-session evaluation within a day, so that everything is still fresh in their minds. A sample Post-Session Evaluation Form is included on the previous page.

3.5.2 Evaluating Group Programs

You can evaluate any type of group program (support group, workshop, retreat, or corporate training program) by distributing an evaluation form to all participants. A sample evaluation for a corporate training program appears on the facing page. You can develop a similar form for other types of group programs.

In addition to asking for feedback to help you improve your programs, you can use evaluation forms for marketing purposes as well. At the bottom of evaluation forms, especially for events such as workshops or retreats, you can include a place where participants can provide their email address to subscribe to your newsletter or ask for permission to use their comments in your future marketing. For example, include a line such as:

May we quote you? Yes! ☐

Feedback About Corporate Training Programs

Many corporate human resources departments will have systems in place for evaluating training programs and services. However, in some cases they may ask you to carry out or assist them in doing an evaluation. In addition to distributing evaluation forms (either or both immediately after the training or a month later), your evaluation might be done through methods such as: interviewing trainees or their supervisors, interviewing customers, and measuring results.

Sample Training Evaluation Form

(NAME OF COMPANY) (NAME OF PROGRAM) TRAINING
PARTICIPANT EVALUATION OF THE PROGRAM

Conducted by (Your Name)
(Date)

1. Do you feel this program was helpful and/or useful to you?

2. What topics did you find:

   Most important?

   Least important?

3. Did you find the course leader to be prepared and effective in her presentation?

4. Did you find the course materials valuable?

5. What are the major skills or methods learned in this program that you will be able to transfer back on the job?

6. As a result of any change in your thinking, new ideas, or planned actions, please estimate the increase in your personal effectiveness.

7. Please indicate the rating that best reflects your overall evaluation of this program.

   Excellent _____   Good _____   Fair _____   Poor _____

8. Any other comments?

Thank you for your feedback.
Please give your completed form to:

For example, if you held a training program with the aim of reducing complaints about the company's customer service, you could measure the company's number of complaints both before and after the training. Of course, to do a good analysis you would need to examine other factors besides the training that might have affected the number of complaints.

Getting Testimonials from Corporate Clients

The following advice is offered by Marg Archibald in the *FabJob Guide to Become a Business Consultant*.

Once the project is complete, take the time to gather quotes from your clients. Testimonials from happy clients can be used in future sales presentations, in proposals, or in promotional materials such as brochures, letters, and your website.

Throughout and after a project, clients may spontaneously express that they are pleased with your work, impressed with your skill and grateful for the results you are achieving. You may not have a pen in your hand at the moment but remember the essence of what has been said. Get it down on paper at the earliest chance you have, quoting as accurately as possible.

Do not be shy about asking if you could make use of these comments. Tell your clients how much their praise means to you and the ways it can be helpful in letting others know about your work. Everyone is busy so make it easy for your clients. Jot down their praise, print it on plain paper at your office, and present it to them for approval in person, or by fax or email. With corporate clients, ask to have it photocopied onto their letterhead and have them sign it. Many clients who are pleased with your work will be happy to give you a testimonial.

4. Ways to Learn Life Coaching

Unlike many other professions, no specific educational credentials are required to become a life coach. According to the *Occupational Outlook Handbook* published by the U.S. Bureau of Labor Statistics, counselors or therapists must be licensed to practice in all but two states, and a master's degree generally is needed to become licensed. There are no such requirements for life coaches.

However, that does not necessarily mean that it's easy for someone with no credentials to become a life coach. Those who are most likely to succeed in life coaching have educational qualifications, work experience, or expertise in a specific field that they bring to their coaching practice. Clients who have specific needs will often look for a coach who has a background in and has helped other clients with similar issues.

You probably already have an area of expertise that qualifies you to become a life coach. In this chapter, you will discover a variety of ways to further develop the skills, knowledge, and credentials that can help you attract clients and achieve success in this career.

4.1 Learning From Other Coaches

For many of the life coach experts we contacted, the career path to coaching was similar. They had each worked for a number of years in another industry. After attending a coaching seminar or individual coaching sessions, they realized how much the experience had made an impact on them, and as a result they wanted to share that experience with others. Then they sought out a coaching certification program, worked with a mentor and became coaches themselves.

4.1.1 Coaching Certification

As the field of life coaching has steadily grown, so has the number of coaching schools, organizations and professional associations. Most of them offer certification. The rise in organizations and associations offering coaching certification is partly due to a desire for more official recognition for the field, as well as to establish a network of resources and support for like-minded individuals. In addition, as more and more coaching specialties have appeared, organizations have appeared aimed solely at the needs of professionals interested in those specialties.

As you start your career as a life coach you should consider whether or not to pursue some sort of coaching accreditation. You may find that it helps clients to trust your abilities and gives you more credibility when you're first starting out. Life coach Laura Meyer advises, "There are all sorts of individuals out there who are calling themselves life coaches; everyone from consultants to therapists to just general business people, and it muddies the water. The certification and educational process helps you distinguish yourself from these people and also gives you a solid foundation on which to build your business."

While giving you credibility is certainly an important element, a coaching certification program can also offer a number of other benefits. As executive and career coach Marilyn O'Hearne told us: "The biggest takeaway for me from the training was going from seeing myself as someone passionate about coaching with transferable skills to knowing: I am a coach! I also learned a great deal about marketing, the Internet, and shifted from a practice to a business model and have a whole new circle of warm, open, bright international colleagues who exchange referrals and ideas."

Mentor coach Barbra Sundquist (**www.BecomeACertifiedCoach.com**) provides excellent free resources about coaching certification. In her audio recording *Straight Talk on Coach Certification* (available from her website), she notes that "there are several good reasons for getting certified. Not only does getting certified demonstrate commitment to a professional standard, it increases your confidence. And your coaching will improve. Even if you are a good coach, there will be things you will learn through the certification process that will make you an even better coach."

Below are some coaching organizations you might want to consider if you decide on accreditation. The first one listed, the International Coach Federation, is the leading accreditation body for the coaching profession. After the ICF information is an alphabetical list of organizations for all types of coaches, followed by information about several organizations which provide training in specific coaching specializations, and finally a list of other organizations of interest to coaches. Visit their websites to see if one of them is right for you.

International Coach Federation

Website: **www.coachfederation.org**

The International Coach Federation is the largest non-profit association for professional coaches worldwide. Headquartered in Lexington, KY, the ICF has chapters in over 95 countries and more than 17,000 members. Former U.S. President Jimmy Carter was the keynote speaker at the ICF's seventh annual international conference in Atlanta, Georgia, in October 2002. The ICF does not offer coach training per se, but is basically an oversight board, accrediting programs that meet certain criteria. You might want to look for a certification program offering official ICF recognition. You can find a list of accredited programs at their website.

Basic ICF membership is $195 (U.S.) per year for U.S. and Canadian residents. Their website provides a wealth of information for members, including links to related articles, a free coach referral system which lists member coaches, and other coaching resources. Watch for the annual international conferences scheduled for Orlando, Florida (2009), Forth Worth, Texas (2010), and Las Vega, Nevada (2011). You can also subscribe to their free newsletter, Coaching World, or simply read the archived issues, which are posted on their website every month.

Coachville

Website: **www.coachville.com**

Established in 2001, Coachville boasts more than 30,000 members in 175+ countries. Like ICF, they are committed to establishing professional standards for coaches worldwide, and serving as a support network for members. Coachville courses are accredited by the ICF.

Coachville hosts seminars and events, and also offers online coaching courses, some through their School of Coaching and Graduate School of Coaching. They have their own set of standards and proficiencies, and consequently their own certification process. Members have access to resources such as e-books, newsletters, marketing tips and coaching techniques. Coachville also has a referral service which lists 5,000 members, and includes photographs and detailed descriptions. Basic membership is free.

European Coaching Institute

Website: **www.europeancoachinginstitute.org**

This coaching organization has been accrediting members since 2000. Based in the U.K. the ECI has representatives worldwide, including the U.S., Canada, the U.K., Ireland, and Australia. Memberships are also available to those living in Europe, the Middle East, Asia, Africa and South America.

ECI has a clear statement of its standards and ethics that members must uphold, backed by a complaint process that ensures the professionalism of all of its member coaches. There are six levels of accreditation for individual coaches, depending on your level of training. They also provide accreditation for coaching training programs, classes and workshops. You can also join ECI as an Associate Member if you have coach training but don't want to pursue full accreditation.

Membership benefits include discounted entry at local events, conferences, and the European Conference, as well as a number of business-related benefits such as discounted liability insurance, business advice, and a members' coaching forum, to name a few. You can also find a list of coach training programs accredited by the ECI on their website. (Click on the "Coach Training" link in the menu.)

International Association of Coaching

Website: **www.certifiedcoach.org**

The International Association of Coaching was established in 2003 by Thomas Leonard (mentioned in section 1.2 of this guide), with a declared mission to "advance coaching to the highest standards of universal excellence." Since that time membership has increased to more than 12,000 professional coaches. Members of the IAC are expected to adhere to a strict code of ethical and professional behavior.

You don't need to be a graduate of any specific coaching program to join, but becoming an accredited IAC member assumes you are already working as a coach. Accreditation from this organization involves successfully completing the IAC's Coaching Masteries program. This involves a 9-part testing procedure to show that you understand the 15 Proficiencies of the program, and then submitting recordings of your own coaching sessions for evaluation by the IAC accreditation board. You can actually try the first part of the proficiencies testing for free on their website (look under "Certification").

Benefits of becoming an IAC member include discounted liability insurance (available only in the U.S.); a directory listing on the IAC website with your name, qualifications and a link to your website; networking opportunities with other members; discounted assessment tools, etc.

International Coach Academy

Website: **www.icoachacademy.com**

The International Coach Academy offers an ICF certified online training program that you can complete at your own pace. The academy has online communities of practice in the areas of life coaching, business coaching, career coaching, executive coaching, or spiritual coaching.

The Certified Professional Coach Training Program is a 120 hour program and includes: coaching courses, your own peer coach for a minimum of three months, business development training, a coaching practicum, and networking opportunities with coaches from around the world. You can apply for Master Certified Coach, Professional Certifided Coach, or Associate Certified Coach credentials.

The program cost is $4,350 for a single payment or $4,824 if paid over 12 months.Twice a week they sponsor a free, one hour seminar on life coaching. Participants call a telephone bridge line and have the chance to have all their questions about coaching answered. They have a monthly limit of 15 participants, and spaces fill up fast.

Career Coach Institute

Website: **www.careercoachinstitute.com**

As the name implies, Career Coach Institute specializes in career coaching. Though not all of their courses are strictly business-oriented, they also work with corporations to develop training programs. In addition, they offer courses in retirement coaching. CCI boasts that its students can obtain the first level of career coaching certification—Associate Certified Career Coach—in as few as four to six weeks. For $2,000, you will receive CCI's complete self-study program, including a textbook, several CDs containing lectures and coaching demonstrations, and a membership to CCI's Virtual Learning Community.

CCI also offers higher-level certification programs with more advanced course materials. The Professional Certified Career Coach program course is a continuation of the Associate certification and costs $3,395. The Master Certified Career Coach program is available only to those who have completed the Professional program and involves live instruction and participation in coaching sessions. The basic Certified Retirement Course costs $2,500.

Relationship Coaching Institute

Website: **www.relationshipcoachinginstitute.com**

The Relationship Coaching Institute advertises itself as the premier international training school for relationship coaches. On their website they offer free introductory audio programs, varying in length from 43 minutes to over an hour, which explore details about the various aspects of relationship coaching.

Included are an introduction to the subject, as well as the basics of coaching singles, coaching couples, and building your practice. The recordings play in Macromedia Flash Player so if you don't have that installed use the link provided on their website to download this free multimedia software. RCI also offers in-depth relationship coach training. Note that this program does not provide basic coaching training and therefore is not certified by ICF, but can be used as an adjunct to ICF certification.

Retirement Coach Institute

Website: **www.retirementcoachinstitute.com**

The Retirement Coach Institute was founded in 2003 and trains and certifies coaches in 35 countries. Its stated mission is to "transform the workplace and its workers as they enter retirement." Their goal is to help train coaches to teach others how to live authentic lives they will love. They offer four different certification programs for individual coaches as well as corporate coaching programs. RCI training is recognized by the International Coach Federation.

They offer a Certified Retirement Coach Premium package that includes a Retirement Coaching Kit and a 12-week live Teleclass Series. This course also includes Practice Development Coaching, consisting of 12 sessions of practice coaching with one of RCI's staff coaches to give you firsthand experience in retirement coaching. You can also choose to take just the teleclass series (i.e. coach certification without the practice coaching sessions) or opt for the home study certification program. Costs for these courses are $4,497 for the Premium package, $3,497 for the teleclass only option, and $1,997 for the home study program. Payments for these programs can also be made in monthly installments. Contact them at 866-226-2244 or enroll online at **www.retirementcoach institute.com/enroll-now.html**.

Other Organizations

Many other coaching organizations exist, as well as organizations not specifically dedicated to coaching but with relevant resources.

- *American Society for Training and Development*
  www.astd.org/content/education/certificatePrograms/coaching/

- *Association of Career Professionals International*
  www.iacmp.org

- *The Carbon Coach*
  www.carboncoach.com/61_contact.html

- *Comprehensive Coaching U*
  www.comprehensivecoachingu.com

- *The Hudson Institute*
  www.hudsoninstitute.com

- *The Institute for Life Coach Training*
  www.lifecoachtraining.com

- *The Newfield Network*
  www.newfieldnetwork.com

- *Philadelphia Area Coaches Alliance (PACA)*
  www.philadelphiacoaches.org

- *Professional Coaches and Mentors Association*
  http://pcmaonline.com

- *Retirement Coach Institute*
  www.retirementcoachinstitute.com/index.html

- *Spencer Institute*
  www.spencerinstitute.com

- *Success Unlimited Network (SUN)*
  www.successunlimitednet.com

4.1.2   Attending Coaching Events

There is no shortage of coaching conferences and events. The International Coach Federation and other coaching organizations hold international, regional and affiliate conferences with various presenters and usually a keynote speaker who is well-known within the coaching field. These conferences range in cost from under a hundred dollars to a few thousand dollars. Membership is usually not required for attendance, though non-members pay slightly more. Occasionally there is a prerequisite that attendees be enrolled in a coach training school.

Most events are two to four days in duration, and are divided into seminars on different aspects of coaching—marketing, niches, trends, individual styles, incorporating technology, etc. Some conferences feature coaching demonstrations and round-table discussions. Others focus on a certain theme, such as ethics in coaching, building your business, or Internet resources. Conferences can also be dedicated to specific branches of coaching, such as business coaching or spiritual coaching.

Unless finances are of no concern to you, you would do well to attend conferences where the individual seminars are included in the cost of registration.

> TIP: For tax purposes, save receipts from attending these confer-
> ences. They are legitimate business expenses.

You can find a list of upcoming events by visiting the International Coach Federation website at **www.coachfederation.org**. Click on "Conferences and Events" at the top of the page.

A lot of the coaching conferences mention in their publicity information that they are seeking presenters. Try approaching them with a proposal for a seminar, speech or workshop that you would like to give. Not all of the presenters are even life coaches; they just know something that they feel would be appropriate.

Peer Resources of Victoria, Canada, provides training, consulting and mentoring resources for businesses and individuals. They have a large number of coaching resources, including a thorough listing of conferences worldwide. You can see their list of Coaching Conferences at **www.peer. ca/coachevents.html**.

4.1.3   Information Interviews

An information interview is defined as a brief meeting with someone who is working in a career you are interested in learning about. The goal of the information interview is to collect information that will allow you to make informed decisions about your career as a life coach. The personal and professional benefits of an information interview are numerous:

- Help expand your professional network

- Increase your confidence

- Gain access to the most up-to-date career information

- Identify your strengths and weaknesses

- Get a look at a life coaching practice from the inside

To arrange information interviews, start with your network of contacts including family and friends to ask if they know anyone working in life coaching or possibly have used the services of a life coach and could help you connect. If possible, go beyond getting a name and telephone number. Ask if they would get in touch with people they know in the industry to see if you can contact them to ask a few questions.

If no one in your network knows anyone who works in coaching, you can try to arrange meetings by making cold calls. Do some research to come up with a list of local life coaches who practice in your area of interest or specialization. The more research you do prior to an interview, the more efficient it will be and the better impression you will leave.

You can find coaches that belong to the International Coach Federation by visiting **www.coachfederation.org** (click on "Find a Credentialed Coach", follow the links through to the "Coach Referral Service" page then do a search for a coach in your area of interest: corporate, small business, personal, career and speakers coaching). To find other small coaching firms, consult your Yellow Pages under "Coaching" or your local Chamber of Commerce for firms in your area.

Once you have selected some local coaches, it becomes a matter of picking up the phone and calling. Large and small firms will often have receptionists or administrative assistants answering the phones. They can be a valuable source of contact information. Ideally, you want to reach a senior person and directly ask them for a meeting. Although you are conducting an "information interview," it is usually better to avoid using that term when you first call. Many professionals assume someone who wants to set up an information interview is actually looking for a job, not simply looking to learn about the profession. So they may decline to meet with you if they do not have any current job openings.

Instead, it may be better to say that you are doing research and politely ask if you can arrange to meet with them for 20 minutes to learn about the career. People are much more likely to agree to a meeting if they know it won't take too much time. However, others in the business say that it's not unreasonable to suggest a lunch-hour meeting. It's important to remember that while some people are generous with their time and encouraging to newcomers, others may simply be too busy to meet with everyone who wants career advice. If someone you contact says they don't have time for a meeting, politely ask if they know anyone who might be available to talk with you.

If someone agrees to a meeting, arrive on time and come prepared with a list of questions such as the following:

- How did you get started in coaching?

- What do you wish you had known when you were first getting into coaching?

- What are typical duties in your job?

- Based on a quick review of my experience to date, what training or experience do you think I should pursue next?

- What advice do you have for someone just getting started in coaching?

If you have agreed to meet for a limited time, such as 20 minutes, let the coach know when the time limit is up, say you know they're busy, and offer to leave. If they are willing to continue that's fine, but don't stay longer without permission. Thank them for their time and any referrals they were able to provide. After the meeting, send a thank you note to the person you met with and, if someone referred you, thank that person as well.

> TIP: Ideally, an information interview should be a face-to-face meeting, but if this can't be arranged a telephone interview still has benefits. You may even get valuable advice from someone who isn't available to talk but is willing to answer questions by email.

4.1.4   Finding a Mentor

Almost every life coach we interviewed stressed the importance of finding a mentor coach as a way of learning coaching. A mentor is someone who has experienced the same challenges you will be facing as a beginning life coach. They have learned their lessons the hard way, and are willing to save you time and effort by showing you how to do things right the first time.

A mentor is also someone who is willing to give you personal training and advice either for free, for money or for an exchange of services. Informal networking is a great way to start off building relationships with people who can help you along in your career. While developing these relationships, you will likely come across some people who are extra friendly, extra helpful, or just someone you click with right away. These people are likely candidates for being willing to take the relationship to a more personal level and become a mentor to you.

> **TIP:** Ideally your mentor will be working successfully as a coach themselves, so that they can share with you the "how to" instead of just the "how not to."

While books and certification programs for life coaches will get you so far, the great thing about a mentor is that their advice is up-to-the-minute, personalized to your situation, and interactive—as in "you ask, they tell." And if you play your cards right, you could have a person to turn to for help making career-related decisions for years to come.

How to Approach a Potential Mentor

If you don't identify a suitable mentor in your early networking, you may need to start looking more aggressively. An excellent way to connect with professional coaches is to visit them where they work, if possible. Many coaches offer one on one in-person coaching and they may be willing to allow you to sit in on a few sessions with them (with their clients' permission of course) to see how they conduct a coaching session. Probably the best way to find a coach mentor is to hire a coach yourself, explaining that you are thinking of starting your own practice, and experience the coaching process firsthand.

Especially when you are planning on starting a business, it's actually to your advantage to approach a mentor who is not in the same town as you so that they know you won't be competing for the same clients. Also, being more wide-ranging in your choice gives you the opportunity to look for true experts in the field, as opposed to connecting solely on the basis of who is located nearby.

To make the most of your relationship, look for a mentor who, as much as possible, shares your intended coaching specialty (Chapter 2 outlines the various coaching specialties you might choose from), your values, and your way of doing business. If you can't find all this in one person, you may want to approach more than one mentor to round out the advice you receive. Once you have identified one or a few potential mentors, approach them with a written letter or email of introduction. Or you can use these same notes as conversation points when you meet with them for coffee or lunch.

Explain why you selected them as a potential mentor. This may be their success within the coaching specialty you are interested in or it may be that you admire their skills. Whatever your reason, let your potential mentor know why you chose them from among all the professionals in North America or your region.

Make a specific request. Rather than just saying you want them to be your mentor, explain what you are asking for. Do you want to talk with them on the telephone once a week for 20 minutes? Do you want to meet with them once a month over lunch? Do you want to communicate with them on a weekly basis by email? Also, be open to their offer of an alternative method of contact, since you are the one asking for a favor. Some people shy away from mentoring because they fear it will take too much time or energy. Assure your potential mentor this isn't the case.

Offer something in return. While some professional mentors charge a fee for mentoring (see below), others will provide the service at no charge. However, there may be many demands on their time, so think about what you can offer back to them. A free lunch is a start, but it's better to volunteer your services or share information. Maybe you are a great writer and can offer to write your mentor's next brochure or newsletter, for example. If they are located reasonably close to you, you could propose an unpaid internship where you would help out in your mentor's office on a part-time basis at no charge to them. This can be a win-win for both of you—they benefit from your help while you learn from their experience.

Mentoring for a Fee

If it's not possible to connect with a mentor in person, you can look for suitable professionals on the Internet using a search engine like Google or an association directory (see section 4.1.1 and section 4.1.2 for links to various coaching organizations) or in the Yellow Pages under "coaching."

You may find it faster for you to look for someone who is already working as a mentor rather than approach people who may be unfamiliar or unreceptive to the idea. Again, this comes down to which you have more of: time or money. In the case where you are paying a mentor, you need to make sure you are getting value for your money. Ask lots of questions up front about their specialty and what their availability will be like, and ask if you can speak to other people they have mentored to ensure they were satisfied with the results.

> **TIP:** Your mentor should be currently working as a life coach or else they may be out of touch with today's market. If you have any doubts, keep shopping around until you find someone who has the right credentials and reliability.

Many coaching associations, such as Mentor Coaches International (**www.mentorcoach.com**), offer mentoring programs for novice coaches or those thinking about becoming coaches. Most of the programs include a combination of coaching and mentoring. In other words, you will be coached by a professional life coach and get a feel for the skills and techniques used by successful coaches, and you will also be guided as you and your coaching practice grow.

For personal one-on-one training you should expect to pay the going rate for expert consultants. According to Steve Mitten (**www.acoach4u. com**), a former president of the International Coach Federation, many coach mentoring programs cost between $500 and $750 dollars per month with a 6-month to 1-year commitment.

If you decide to make this kind of investment in a mentoring program be sure to find one that includes at least some of the following features:

- Coaching experience from both the coach and the client perspective

- Ways to identify your ideal clients based on your coaching specialty

- Ways to market your coaching business effectively

- Ways to generate additional income

- Business principles related to offering coaching services

- Time and resource management techniques for your coaching practice

Some mentor coaches specialize in just one aspect of mentor coaching, such as marketing or certification. For example, Mentor Coach Barbra Sundquist (**www.BecomeACertifiedCoach.com**), a former certifying examiner for the International Association of Coaching (IAC), specializes in helping coaches develop masterful coaching skills with a view to certification.

You can find a list of coaches offering mentoring services in the Coach U directory at **www.findacoach.com** (click on "Find a Coach"). Many of the coaches listed on the Coach U directory also offer a complimentary first session.

Another resource for finding a mentor coach is the International Coach Federation website (**www.coachfederation.org**). They offer a search function that lets you choose a coach using a number of different criteria such as your specialty area, coaches whose professional experience matches your interests, etc.

From the site's homepage, choose "Find a Coach", then, under "Find a Coach" on the next page, choose the "ICF's Coach Referral Service" link. On the next page, you'll need to click on the "I agree to the above" link in order to continue. Finally, on the "Coach Referral Service" page, choose the type of coaching that matches your specialty area (Corporate, Small Business, Personal or Career). The direct link to the Coach Referral Service page is **http://www.coachfederation.org/find-a-coach/ find-a-coach-now/coach-referral-service-search**.

4.2 Get Coaching Experience

"I hear and I forget. I see and I remember. I do and I understand."

    – Confucius

4.2.1   Be a Coaching Client

To coach effectively, you want to experience what it is like to be coached. One way to do this is by hiring a coach. You could even work with a number of different coaches over a period of time, to get a feel for different styles. You might also volunteer to be a client for other aspiring coaches. As part of their training requirements, students at some of the life coaching schools are required to work with a certain number of clients for a certain number of hours on a pro bono (free of charge) basis. Contact some of these institutions and volunteer to help out some of the students with this requirement.

You might tell them that you are interested in becoming a life coach, but would like to find out first hand what it entails. You can be their "guinea pig" and act as a coaching client. Taking a half hour out of your schedule twice a week is not an unreasonable commitment, and will benefit you and the coaches.

4.2.2   Coach Friends and Family

One way to get hands-on coaching experience is to offer your services free of charge to friends and family members. For example, when a friend or family member wants to use your coaching services, try to treat them the way you would treat a "real" client. Schedule a meeting with them and go through every stage of the coaching process (Chapter 3 explains how to do each of the following):

- Conduct an intake session

- Do an initial consultation

- Gather information about the client (issues, personal profile)

- Conduct a coaching session

- Identify client goals

- Evaluate client goals

- Evaluate client progress

- Evaluate the coaching process

A key part of the evaluating the coaching process is getting client feedback. Every time you do coaching for someone – even a friend or a family member with a different last name from yours – ask for a letter of recommendation. To avoid misunderstandings, it's also a good idea to prepare a client intake form (like the one in section 3.1.1) and contract (like that in section 5.7.3) even if you're working with family members. (Let them know you need the practice.)

4.2.3   Volunteer with Non-Profit Organizations

Another way you can get practical experience is by volunteering your services to local non-profit organizations and community associations. You'll get the benefit of helping a worthy cause while you hone your skills, plus volunteering can be an excellent way to make contacts which could lead to future employment opportunities.

Assuming your goal is to get coaching experience, you should leave non-coaching tasks (such as walking dogs for the humane society or making decorations for parties) to other volunteers. Instead, volunteer to work with non-profit organizations that offer some sort of life skills or life coaching services to their constituents.

Another option may be to offer your services as a coach on a pro bono basis (i.e. free of charge). For example, a local health center might be open to a weight loss coaching program or your local government might be interested in some carbon coaching ideas to help make the delivery of municipal services more environmentally friendly. Whatever your specialty chances are there is an organization in your area that would be willing to use your services.

The best approach to offering your services is to try to arrange a meeting with the executive director of the non-profit organization. You would gather information about the organization's needs and present a proposal to provide life coaching services. If this can't be arranged, call and get your message to the most senior people you can. Ask them what's the best way for you to send the proposal.

In some cases, volunteer organizations look for life coaches through advertising or RFPs. Below is a volunteer opportunity recently posted on **www.volunteersolutions.org** seeking the help of life coaches:

Mentor/Life Coach

Description: Life coaches and mentors are needed to provide guidance, support and friendship to an adult or youth enrolled in our training programs. Mentors and life coaches and trainees meet regularly. We're in search of fun, supportive and professional individuals who enjoy working with people. Orientation, training and ongoing support provided.

While ads for such volunteer positions may be rare, and you must have coaching expertise and skills in order to volunteer, this illustrates the types of services you could provide to help local service providers in need. You might propose something similar to a non-profit organization in your community. Do a search on the Volunteer Solutions website mentioned above using the terms "life skills", "life coach", or "human services" to find other similar ads.

You can find help in locating your community's non-profit groups through the Internet. GuideStar is a searchable database of more than 1.5 million IRS-recognized non-profit organizations in the United States. Visit **www.guidestar.org** then click on "Advanced Search" to search by your city or state. CharityVillage has a similar database of Canadian non-profits at **www.charityvillage.com** (after you click on "Enter", click on "Links to NPOs"). You might also contact your local Volunteer Center or Chamber of Commerce. Both of these organizations usually run a volunteer matching program and can help provide the information you need to get involved.

Whatever volunteer opportunities you choose to take advantage of, make sure to ask for referrals and testimonials, and get permission to use satisfied clients as references.

4.3 Other Learning Resources

In the recent attempts to regulate coaching through lengthy, costly training programs and official designations and certifications, some have lost sight of what coaching is. Life and work experience, combined with a desire and an ability to encourage and inspire others, is what makes effective coaches, not a bunch of abbreviations or letters after your name.

This is not to say that formal coach training is a waste of time or money. There are many excellent programs and courses which can acquaint you with the strategies and practices of successful coaches, and enable you to network with a large number of other professionals and stay connected to the profession. But there is no reason why you cannot use what you already know to get started. In this section we'll look at a few resources that will help you get a feel for the coaching industry and get some insights into what others are doing.

4.3.1 Newsletters

Read the many free coaching newsletters online. These are excellent sources for networking, sharing information and communicating with like-minded individuals. Some of these newsletters include:

- *Coach U Community News*
  www.coachinc.com/CoachU/Newsletter

- *The IAC Voice*
  www.certifiedcoach.org/news/voice.html

- *The Business of Coaching*
  www.thebusinessofcoaching.com/tboc_resources.html

- *Work Yourself Happy*
  www.comprehensivecoachingu.com/newsletter.html

Another good resource is the newsletter and blogs page at Peer Resources, a website mentioned in section 4.1.2. They have an extensive listing of coaching newsletters and blogs written by life coaches, many of which are aimed at the life coaching professional. You can look into them further at the Peer Resources website. Visit **www.mentors.ca/coach freebies.html**.

4.3.2 Books

There are many good books that you can read to expand your knowledge of coaching, and develop a solid foundation for building your new career. If you would like to read these books, we have included links to Amazon.com in the e-book version of this guide (see the CD-ROM if you are reading the print book).

Dale Carnegie was one of the best life coaches who ever lived. The former salesman became an accomplished writer and lecturer, and traveled around the country giving seminars and teaching public speaking. His classics, *How to Win Friends and Influence People* and *How to Stop Worrying and Start Living*, have sold millions of copies and been translated into several languages.

Likewise, a contemporary of Carnegie, Claude M. Bristol, whose best-selling *The Magic of Believing* showed how confidence, persistence and conviction can bring great rewards and happiness. Neither man ever had any formal life coach training. Today there are many motivational speakers, self-improvement specialists and self-help gurus who basically coach others.

- *How to Win Friends and Influence People*
  by Dale Carnegie

- *How to Stop Worrying and Start Living*
  by Dale Carnegie

- *The Magic of Believing*
  by Claude M. Bristol

Following are some other books that many coaches find valuable, including books on how to coach plus a selection of books on how to achieve success in life.

- *Coach U's Essential Coaching Tools*
  by Coach U, Inc.

  This book includes client-centered assessments, forms and checklists. In addition, it provides information about marketing your coaching business and suggestions for business development.

- *The Handbook of Coaching: A Comprehensive Resource Guide For Managers, Executives, Consultants and HR*
  by Frederic M. Hudson

  Hudson asserts that the demand for coaching was spawned by the tremendous social and cultural changes of the past few decades. In a scientific, methodical way, he explores the origins, applications and direction of coaching.

- *Life Coaching: A Manual For Helping Professionals*
  by David B. Ellis

  In clear, concise language, Ellis lays out the foundations of life coaching, building smoothly upon the basic concepts and even offering solutions for dealing with sensitive issues.

- *Co-Active Coaching: New Skills for Coaching People Toward Success in Work and Life*
  by Laura Whitworth, Karen Kimsey-House, Henry Kimsey-House and Phil Sandahl

  Written by three prominent coaches, this book explores the collaborative relationship between coaches and clients that is necessary for the attainment of clients' goals.

- *Take Time for Your Life: A Personal Coach's Seven Step Program for Creating the Life You Want*
  by Cheryl Richardson

  Through real life examples from her personal and professional life, best-selling author Cheryl Richardson walks readers through a candid process of self-discovery and empowerment.

- *Creative Visualization: Use the Power of Your Imagination to Create What You Want in Your Life*
  by Shakti Gawain

  Gawain's book about realizing and reaching an ideal existence skillfully blends spirituality and practicality.

- *How to Get Your Point Across in 30 Seconds or Less*
  by Milo O. Frank

  If you want to quickly and effectively let people know about the benefits of coaching (or any other subject), this book might prove very useful.

- *Take Yourself to the Top*
  by Laura Berman Fortgang

  Fortgang clearly understands the challenges that many professionals face, but at the same time, holds readers responsible for taking charge and changing what they don't like about their lives or careers.

- *Chop Wood, Carry Water: A Guide to Finding Spiritual Fulfillment in Everyday Life*
  by Rick Fields, Peggy Taylor and Rex Weyler

  This book combines aspects of psychology and philosophy for a holistic approach to enlightenment. The title comes from the writings of an ancient Zen master, and the pages are peppered with inspirational quotes as relevant today as when they were first spoken.

- *What Color is Your Parachute?*
  by Richard Nelson Bolles

  The quintessential tome for job seekers and career changers, this book has been updated annually since its first publication in 1970. Whether you want to be a life coach or a librarian, Bolles provides fresh insights on finding your ideal position.

4.3.3   Chat Groups   *Meet Up Groups*

Online chat groups and discussion forums can be great ways to network with other coaches, find referrals, and receive answers to questions. Many of the coaching organizations feature such resources. The various blogging websites (see section 6.2.3 for more about setting up a blog on your website) have categories for coaching, and you can usually create your own category if you can't find one that meets your needs.

America Online (**http://peopleconnection.aol.com**) and Yahoo! (**http://groups.yahoo.com**) also have several chat groups for coaches. Use each site's built-in search engine to search for subjects you're interested in. Be sure to check the activity level (how often and when messages have been posted), since some groups are more popular and long-lasting than others.

5. Starting Your Own Business

The good news is that life coaching is an inexpensive and relatively simple business to start. You can start small, and grow your business to a level you are comfortable with. You might even be able to work from the comfort of your own home if you do your coaching by telephone or email. Still, there are some basic steps to follow, some potential pitfalls to avoid, and some decisions to make before you get started.

5.1 Starting Full-Time or Part-Time

If you are currently employed, some of the questions you may need to consider are:

- Should I quit my job and start my coaching business on a full-time basis?

- Should I remain at my current job and start a coaching business on the side?

- Would my employer let me keep my job on a part-time basis so I could be available to meet with clients during business hours and have a secure source of income while I'm getting my business off the ground?

- If I leave my job to start my own coaching business can I rely on my current employer to become one of my clients?

While some of your choices will depend on external factors such as whether or not your employer allows employees to moonlight, other choices will be yours to make.

Other Start-Up Decisions

Whether or not you are currently employed, there are many other decisions you will face when starting your business. For example:

- Should I have a coaching specialization or offer general life coaching services?

- Should I incorporate?

- Should I work with one or more partners?

- Where should I set up my office?

- What should I name my company?

- What systems do I need to set up (e.g. for invoicing)?

- How much should I invest in start-up costs?

- Should I hire support staff?

- What types of insurance should I get?

- What fees should I charge?

This chapter is designed to help you make these and other decisions you will face in starting your business. (The next chapter will help you decide how to market your business to attract clients.) It begins with creating a business plan and continues with an overview of other factors you'll need to consider in starting your own business.

Throughout the chapter you will also find many helpful resources for further information. If you could use more help with all areas of starting a business, the following are excellent sources of information:

- *Small Business Administration*
  The SBA offers help with business start-ups and has a variety of programs and services for the small business owner. There is at least one SBA office in every state in the United States. Call the Answer Desk at 1-800-U-ASK-SBA (827-5722) or visit **www.sba.gov**.

- *SCORE*
  A non-profit organization, SCORE has over 10,000 volunteers who provide counseling and mentoring to new business start-ups. They also offer business tips on their website. Call 1-800-634-0245 or visit **www.score.org**.

- *Canadian Business Service Centres*
  You will find a wide range of information at this site, including a step-by-step guide to walk you through starting your new business. Visit **www.cbsc.org/osbw**.

- *Nolo.com*
  Nolo is a publisher of plain English legal information. Their website also offers free advice on a variety of other small business matters. At their website at **www.nolo.com** and click on the "Business & Human Resources" tab.

5.2   Creating a Business Plan

Business planning involves putting on paper all the plans you have for your business. This seems like a tall order, and it is, but once you have completed this step you will feel a tremendous sense of accomplishment. Developing a written business plan for your coaching practice helps you maintain your focus. This requires a lot of reflection and self-evaluation, but once you have something written down, you will have better direction. As a coach, you will have your clients do the same thing with their life and career goals, so get used to walking the talk.

Besides, if you are seeking financing for your business from a bank or other lender, they will expect to see a business plan that shows you have a viable business idea with an excellent chance for success. Even if you don't need financing, putting ideas on paper will give you the "road map" of where you want to go with your business and how you are going to get there.

A business plan can also help you avoid costly surprises. If you are considering whether to leave a secure job to start your own business, a business plan can help you determine the resources you will need to start your business and decide when the timing is best for you to get started. While you are working on your business plan, you may start to question some of your previous ideas. You may come up with ideas that are even better, or decide to make some changes to ensure you have a greater chance of success.

Many successful business owners have never written a formal, or even informal, business plan. However, having a business plan, even an informal one, in which you set out your business strategy, your mission plan, and lay out the steps you will take to accomplish your goals, can add confidence and credibility to your effort.

After reading this chapter, and the next one on finding clients, you will be able to start creating your own business plan. It is a document you will probably read repeatedly as you start to operate your business. In the meantime, this section will give you an introduction to business planning, walk you through key components of a business plan, and conclude with a variety of resources to help you create your own business plan, including links to further information, business planning software, and free business plan templates.

While the format of a business plan can vary, one good approach is to divide the body of your business plan into the following sections:

- A description of your business

- Your marketing plan

- Your financial plan

- Your management plan

In addition, your plan should include the following items:

- A cover sheet

- A table of contents

- An executive summary

- Mission statement

- Financial projections

- Supporting documents

Description of Your Business

A description of your business is just that—a description of the business you plan to start and operate. The key is to include information about your business so that everyone who reads your business plan will know you're on to something viable.

You'll need to state in this section that, as a life coach, you'll be operating a service business. Include specifics about the services you'll provide and who you will provide it for. For example, if you will focus on retirement coaching, include information about what areas are involved, and point out why your services are important. See the box below for advice on choosing a specialization.

In this section of your business plan you can also discuss the coaching industry generally and give details about how your business will operate. You can include:

- Your legal structure. Will you have a sole proprietorship, for instance, or incorporate? (You'll learn more about legal structures in section 5.3.1)

- Your business hours. As a life coach, you will most likely need to have flexible hours to accommodate the schedules of your clients.

Choosing a Coaching Specialization

In deciding what kind of coach you want to be, consider your life and work experience. If you started and ran your own small business, you might want to market yourself to entrepreneurs. If you come from a management background, you probably have a lot of insight into this side of the corporate world. Maybe you taught creative writing on the high school or college level, and are eager to assist burgeoning novelists, or you worked for a dating service and know a good deal about compatibility and relationships.

Even if you were not always successful in your previous endeavors, you have probably learned a lot from your mistakes. We all bring something to the table. Ask yourself the following questions:

- Which three personality traits best describe me?

- What are my hobbies?

- What do I spend most of my time doing?

- What are my three greatest accomplishments in life?

- What are my three greatest accomplishments during the past year?

- What are three areas in which I have significant knowledge or expertise?

- With which types of people am I most comfortable associating?

- What was the best job that I ever had?

- In which area of my life do I know the most people?

You do not need to assume that you must have a particular niche. In branching out into various specialties, you do not want to overlook your primary mission: helping clients to achieve desired outcomes and lead a more fulfilling life. This could take the form of a better job, a loving relationship, more free time to travel, being prepared for retirement, or any number of other things. The basic skill set of coaching transcends the various specialties.

Coaches do not necessarily need to have the same expertise or background as their clients. The coach's expertise is in inspiring clients to use their unique skills and abilities to achieve whatever success the clients desire. This can be applied to any area of life.

But if you plan only to work from 10:00 a.m. until 2:00 p.m. three days a week, you should make that clear.

- Your business location. Will you work from home or rent an office? Identify the planned location of your business, the type of space you'll have, and why it's conducive to your business.

- Your suppliers. If you will need services and products, such as coaching instruments, where will you obtain them?

You can also touch on points you will address in other parts of the business plan. Conclude the description of your business by clearly identifying your goals and objectives and supporting them with information and knowledge you've acquired about being a life coach. It's here that you're explaining exactly why you're starting this business and what you hope to accomplish with it.

Your own company description will be unique to your coaching business. You'll find business plan models you can follow in the resources listed at the end of this section.

Your Marketing Plan

Following are key elements of a typical marketing plan. You will find additional information to help you plan your marketing in Chapter 6 of this book.

Clients

The most important elements of a good marketing plan are defining your market and knowing your customers. Knowing your customers is important because it allows you to tailor your services to accommodate those clients.

You don't want to limit yourself to a market that is too narrow—that can limit the scope of your business once it's underway. For example, if you are a relationship coach, you'll have many more prospective clients if you target "single women" rather than "single mothers over age 40." And targeting all "singles" will give you an even larger market. Quantify your market and use your marketing plan to paint a picture of a wide and ready market that needs your coaching services.

Competition

Businesses – yours included – compete for customers, market share, publicity and so forth. It's smart to know who your competitors are and exactly what they're doing. In order to provide services that are different and better, you need to look carefully at your competitors' products and services, how they're promoting them, and who's buying them.

Pricing

You'll learn more about setting fees in section 5.6, but for now be aware that you should address it, at least briefly, in your business plan. This section should consider factors such as competitive pricing, costs of labor and materials, overhead and so forth.

Marketing Strategy

You'll need to think about how you'll advertise and promote your business. Have a budget in mind, or at least set percentages of your income that you'll invest back into marketing the business.

Your Financial Plan

Financial management is crucial to running a successful business. Your business plan should describe both your start-up costs and your operating costs. The start-up budget includes all the costs necessary to get your business up and running. Operating costs are ongoing expenses, such as advertising, utilities, rent and so forth.

Remember to include the following items in your budgets. Notice that some expenses overlap on the startup and operating budgets. More information about start-up expenses is provided in section 5.4.2.

Start-up Budget

Legal and professional fees, licenses and permits, equipment, supplies, stationery, marketing expenses.

Operating Budget

Make a budget for your first three to six months of operation, including expenses such as: personnel (even if it's only your own salary), insurance, rent, marketing expenses, legal and accounting fees, supplies, utilities, printing, membership dues, subscriptions, and taxes.

Your financial management plan also should address the accounting system you plan to use. Many small business owners conduct their own accounting, using software such as Quicken (**http://quicken.intuit.com**) or QuickBooks (**http://quickbooks.intuit.com**), while others hire someone to set up a system.

Your Management Plan

No matter how large your business is, managing it requires organization and leadership. Your management plan will therefore address issues such as:

- Your background and business experience and how they'll be beneficial to your coaching business.

- The members of your management team (even if you'll be the only member).

- Assistance you expect to receive (this can be financial help, coaching, professional advice, or other forms of aid).

- The duties for which you and any employee or employees will be responsible.

- Plans for hiring employees, either now or in the future.

- A general overview of how your business will be run.

The Extras

In addition to these major areas, your business plan should include the extras mentioned earlier. You can find more information about these extras in the resources that follow.

A Cover Sheet

This identifies your business and explains the purpose of the business plan. Be sure to include your name, the name of the business and the name of any partners, if applicable; your address, phone number, e-mail address and other pertinent information.

Table of Contents

This goes just under your cover sheet and tells what's included in your business plan. Use major headings and subheadings to identify the contents.

Executive Summary

Basically, this is a thumbnail sketch of your business plan. It should summarize everything you've included in the main body of the plan.

Mission Statement

This summarizes your company's goals and purpose. A mission statement can be as simple as Disney's "To make people happy" and can include a list of bullet points about how you plan to accomplish that mission. Here are a few resources to help you create a mission statement for your coaching business:

- *How to Create a Mission Statement*
  www.how-to.com/Operations/mission-statement.htm

- *Mission Statement Builder*
  www.franklincovey.com/msb/

- *Online Mission Statement Builder*
  www.nightingale.com/mission_select.aspx

- *Preparing Your Mission Statement*
  www.businessplans.org/Mission.html

Financial Projections

This is an estimate of how much money you'll need to start your business, and how much you expect to earn. Remember to support your projections with explanations.

Supporting Documents

If you will be seeking start-up funding, you'll be expected to include financial information. This may include your personal (and business, if applicable) tax returns for the past three years, and a copy of a lease agreement if you will rent office space.

Resources

There are a number of excellent resources available to help you write your business plan. The following are among the best:

- *SCORE*
  Offers an outstanding free business plan template, available in Word or PDF formats. They also offer an online workshop on how to "Develop a Business Plan" and many other resources. Visit the home page at **www.score.org** and click on "Business Tools" or go directly to **www.score.org/business_toolbox.html**.

- *Small Business Administration: Business Plan Basics*
  The Small Business Administration has links to sample business plans, a business plan workshop, an interactive business planner and more. Go to **www.sba.gov/smallbusinessplanner**. Under #1, click "Write a Business Plan."

- *Online Small Business Workshop*
  The Government of Canada's Online Small Business Workshop offers detailed information about every step of business planning. Go to **www.cbsc.org/osbw** and click on "Preparing a Business Plan" or you can find links for each province by going directly to **www.bsa.canadabusiness.ca/gol/bsa/site.nsf/en/su04938.html**. Other Canadian resources include: Canada Business Interactive Business Planner (free registration required) at **www.canadabusiness.ca/ibp/en** and BDC (Canada) Business Plan Template at **www.bdc.ca/en/business_tools/business_plan/default.htm**.

- *Business Plan Pro Software*
  If you want help creating a professional business plan, another option is to buy business planning software. The standard version of Business Plan Pro is available for $99.95; the premier version is $199. Both are available at **www.paloalto.com** and offer a step-by-step guide to creating a business plan, as well as 500 samples.

5.3 Legal Matters

5.3.1 Choosing a Business Legal Structure

Like all entrepreneurs, life coaches are faced with the decision of how to legally structure their business operation. Your business structure affects your taxes and your liability (responsibility) for any debts of the business. Which structure you choose will also have an impact on how much it costs to start and run your coaching business. The sole proprietorship is the least costly way to go into business, but it doesn't afford some of the legal protections of a corporate structure.

In this section we will look at the advantages and disadvantages of each for businesses, including the characteristics and benefits of various legal forms a business may take.

Sole Proprietorship

A sole proprietorship is any business operated by one single individual without any formal structure or registration requirements. A sole proprietorship is the simplest and least expensive business legal structure when you are starting out. It is also the easiest because it requires less paperwork and you can report your business income on your personal tax return. One drawback to this type of business is that you are personally liable for any debts of the business.

In other words, without going through any formal processes, you can begin your coaching business simply by getting the word out that you're in business. However, there are usually business licenses and permits required by local municipalities in order for you to conduct business. The costs of these licenses are usually minimal, but be sure to check with your local municipal licensing office.

Here are some of the advantages and disadvantages of starting your coaching business under the sole proprietorship model:

Advantages

- Easy to start
- Low start-up costs

- Flexible and informal

- Business losses can often be deducted from personal income for tax purposes

Disadvantages

- Unlimited personal liability: the sole proprietor can be held personally responsible for debts and judgments placed against the business. This means that all personal income and assets, not just those of the business, can be seized to recoup losses or pay damages.

- All business income earned must be reported and is taxed as personal income.

- More difficult to raise capital for the business

Partnerships

Another business structure that some coaches choose over sole proprietorship or incorporation is the partnership.

A partnership is precisely as its name implies, a business venture entered into by two or more people with the intent to carry on business and earn profits. Partnerships can be beneficial for coaches as the workload and finances can be shared, and partners with differing areas of expertise can increase business opportunities.

You must register your partnership with a corporate registry. This does not mean that you must incorporate, only that you are making a formal declaration of entering into business with another person or persons. Be sure to consult your local business registry and a lawyer specializing in business registry. The primary purpose for doing this is for each partner to protect himself or herself concerning issues such as sharing profits, liability and dissolving the partnership equitably.

Below are some of the advantages and disadvantages to partnerships:

Advantages

- More initial equity for start-up costs

- Broader areas of expertise can lead to increased opportunities

- Lower start-up costs than incorporation

- Some tax advantages

Disadvantages

- All partners are equally liable for the other's mistakes with the same liability as a sole proprietorship

- Profits and losses must be shared

- The business must be dissolved and reorganized when a partner leaves

---

Working With a Partner

A good partnership requires a bit of planning if it is to run smoothly. You may want to have an attorney set up a legal partnership, spelling out what each partner contributes to and takes out of the business.

Beyond any legal issues, before going into business with a partner you should spend many hours talking about how you will work together, including:

- what each of you will be responsible for

- how you will make decisions on a day-to-day basis

- what percentage of the business each of you will own

- how you see the business developing in the future

- what you expect from each other

During your discussions you can learn if there are any areas where you need to compromise. You can avoid future misunderstandings by putting the points you have agreed on into a written "partnership agreement" that covers any possibility you can think of (including one of you leaving the business in the future).

Incorporation

Incorporation of a business means that a separate, legal corporate entity has been created for the purpose of conducting business. Like an individual, corporations can be taxed, sued, can enter contractual agreements and are liable for their debts. Corporations are characterized by shareholders, a board of directors and various company officers. As such, ownership interests can be freely transferred.

Creating a corporation requires filing of numerous documents to legalize your coaching business, as well as formally naming a president, shareholders, and director(s), all of whom can be a single person as set out in the company charter. As the rules and forms required for incorporation vary from state to state and province to province, it's best to consult your local business licensing office or a local lawyer specializing in incorporation.

While it is probably best to seek legal expertise when incorporating, if you have the expertise and knowledge, you can incorporate your own business or use one of the many online resources that specialize in these matters. Here are a few websites offering such services, often for only a couple of hundred dollars:

- *BizFilings*
  www.bizfilings.com

- *The Company Corporation*
  www.incorporate.com

- *Intuit—My Corporation.com*
  http://mycorporation.intuit.com

- *Form-a-Corp, Inc.*
  www.form-a-corp.com

Here are some of the advantages and disadvantages to incorporating your coaching firm.

Advantages

- Protect personal assets and income from liability by separating your business income and assets from your personal.

- Corporations get greater tax breaks and incentives

- Ownership can be sold or transferred if the owner wishes to retire or leave the business

- Banks and other lending institutions tend to have more faith in incorporated businesses so raising capital is easier

Disadvantages

- Increased start-up costs

- Substantial increase in paperwork

- Your business losses cannot be offset against your personal income

- Corporations are more closely regulated

An S Corporation is similar to the corporation in most ways, but with some tax advantages. The corporation can pass its earnings and profits on as dividends to the shareholder(s). However, as an employee of the corporation you do have to pay yourself a wage that meets the government's reasonable standards of compensation just as if you were paying someone else to do your job.

Limited Liability Company

A Limited Liability Company is a newer type of business legal structure in the U.S. It is a combination of a sole proprietorship (where there is only one member of the LLC) or partnership and a corporation, and is considered to have some of the best attributes of each, including limited personal liability.

An LLC business structure gives you the benefits of a partnership or S corporation while providing personal asset protection like a corporation. Similar to incorporating, there will be substantial paperwork involved in establishing this business structure. LLCs have flexible tax options, but are usually taxed like a partnership.

Here are some of the advantages and disadvantages of LLCs:

Advantages

- Limited liability similar to a corporation

- Tax advantages similar to a corporation

- Can be started with one (except in Massachusetts) or more members like a sole proprietorship or partnership

Disadvantages

- More costly to start than a sole proprietorship or partnership

- Consensus among members may become an issue

- LLC dissolves if any member leaves

In the end, choosing a business legal structure for your coaching practice is a personal choice, and the advantages and disadvantages should be considered thoroughly. Many coaches begin their independent venture as a sole proprietorship because of the low costs, and incorporate as the business grows and the engagements become larger and more complex.

For more on business structures take a look at the resources available at FindLaw.com (**http://smallbusiness.findlaw.com/business-structures**) or the excellent advice offered at the Quicken website (**http://quicken. intuit.com/small-business-finance/home-business.jsp**).

For some additional government resources to help you decide which structure to choose, try the Small Business Administration in the U.S. and Canada Business Services for Entrepreneurs in Canada.

- *U.S. Small Business Administration*
  Click on "Choose a Structure"
  www.sba.gov/smallbusinessplanner/index.html

- *Canada Business Services for Entrepreneurs*
  Click on "English" then on "Starting a Business" and choose
  the "Forms of Business Organization" Fact Sheet
  www.canadabusiness.ca

5.3.2 Choosing a Business Name

Your business name needs to do several things. It must:

- Describe what you do

- Be easy to pronounce

- Attract customers

- Be unique

- Be available

Should You Use Your Own Name?

Like most entrepreneurs, life coaches have the choice of either using their own name as part of the business name or choosing a relevant yet "catchy" name for the business. But there are a few things to consider when deciding how to present and market your coaching practice.

Using your own name for the business, which most often includes your surname such as Smith Life Coaching, is one way to establish yourself as a leader in the field and get your name out at the same time. The drawback to using your surname as part of your business identity, particularly when starting out, is that it probably will be unfamiliar to those searching for coaching services, prompting these potential clients to go with larger, more established coaches.

Many life coaching practices use in their business name some element of the types of services they offer. For example, a business name such as Inner Vision Life Coaching might be more appealing to someone seeking a spiritual coach than simply Smith Life Coaching.

Trademarks and Name Registration

Although choosing a business name for your coaching practice is entirely up to you, there is one essential consideration: your business name should not resemble the name of another similar business offering similar services. For one thing, prospective clients may confuse the other business with yours and go with your competitor's services instead of yours. In addition, if you do use a name too similar to another business that was in business first they will have grounds for legal action against you.

Most start-up businesses do not bother to trademark their names because it can be costly and time-consuming. However, if your company name is truly unique, you might want to consider it. You can do it yourself, or hire a lawyer to do it for you.

In most jurisdictions, if you operate under anything other than your own name, you are required to file for a fictitious name. It's usually just a short form to fill out and a small filing fee that you pay to your state or provincial government. You can find links to the appropriate government departments for filing your name at **www.sba.gov/hotlist/businessnames. html**.

Before registering a fictitious name, you will need to make sure it does not belong to anyone else. You certainly wouldn't want to spend your initial investment money, only to find out you couldn't legally operate under a name you had chosen because someone else owns the rights to it. So do some research on the names you like. A trademark database lists all registered and trademarked business names.

In the U.S., the essential place to start is with the U.S. Patent and Trademark Office. You can hire a company to do a name search for you, or conduct a free search yourself at the USPTO's website. The web address for finding out more about trademarks at the USPTO is **www.uspto. gov/main/trademarks.htm**.

In Canada, the default database for name searches is the Newly Upgraded Automated Name Search (NUANS) at **www.nuans.com**. There is a $20 charge for each NUANS search. You can also hire a company such as Arvic Search Services (**www.arvic.com**) or **www.biznamesearch. com** to help you with name searches, trademarks and incorporating your business for a fee. Check online for "corporate registry services" to find other companies.

For more advice on trademarks and other matters to consider before choosing a business name, visit **www.nolo.com** (click on the "Business & Human Resources" tab, then on "Starting A Business," then on "Naming Your Business").

5.3.3   Licensing, Tax and Insurance

Licensing

State Laws and Regulations

Coaching is still in the incipient stages and has not been subjected to much regulation. Although coaches are not allowed to call themselves counselors or advisors, they do not have too many restrictions placed on them.

However, the issue came under some scrutiny in the state of Colorado, due to a complaint filed in 2002 against a life coach accused of practicing unlicensed psychotherapy. The state considered drafting legislation concerning life coaching, but has not done so yet. Still, if you live in Colorado or plan to work with clients there, contact the Mental Health Licensing Section of the Colorado Department of Regulatory Agencies to make sure that you do not run afoul of any regulations.

The Colorado Mental Health Licensing Section advises (at **www.dora. state.co.us/mental-health/trends.htm**) that "Persons who are considering personal coaching as a career, or an addition to an already established career, are advised to seek counsel from an attorney with experience in mental health practice issues or consultation from a trained mental health professional." This is good advice no matter where you live.

Local Business Licenses

You may be required to get a business license from your municipality. In addition, if you want to work from home, you'll need to check local zoning laws to ensure you can operate a business from your home. Check the website of your municipality. Most have a business licensing section where they outline the regulations for starting a home-based or other small business. If nothing else, you can find contact information to look into the issue further.

You may also be required to have a county or state license so be sure to check with regulatory agencies in your area to determine what you'll need. The following resources may be helpful:

- The U.S. Small Business Administration has helpful information about state and federal licensing requirements. Visit **www.sba.gov/smallbusinessplanner**. Under #2, click on "Get Licenses and Permits."

- For a list of websites with licensing requirements state by state go to the SBA's page on "Where to Obtain Business Licenses" at **www.sba.gov/hotlist/license.html**.

- For information about licensing and regulations for coaching in Canada, check out the "Regulations for Consultants" at the Canadian Government's Canada Business Services for Entrepreneurs site at **www.cbsc.org**. Click on "English" then under "Topics" choose "Starting a Business" and scroll down to "Starting a Consulting Business." Choose "Regulations" in the "Topics" menu.

Tax Information

In addition to filing your income taxes for the business, you will also need to comply with other tax requirements. It's always best to understand your specific taxing obligations from the beginning, as tax collectors often follow the guiding principle: "ignorance of the law is no excuse". Therefore, you should research what tax rules will apply to your small business.

Your state or local government will almost certainly require you to collect sales tax on all taxable services and products sold to your clients. This usually involves applying for a tax resale number at your local taxpayer field office. Many state governments now allow online applications for resale numbers through their official websites. The tax resale number may also be called a sales tax permit or a sales and use tax permit.

After securing your resale number, you can start charging sales tax on all taxable transactions you make—using the tax rate assigned to the area where the services are being performed. As your sales grow larger, keep all collected sales tax in a separate bank account, so that the money will be easily accessible when taxes are due. Based on the estimated sales of your business, you will be asked to pay these taxes monthly, quarterly, or yearly. In Canada, you also will need to have a Goods & Services Tax (GST) account number and collect and remit this tax.

If you hire employees or operate as a corporation or partnership, you will need to apply for a federal tax identification number, also known as an employer identification number or EIN. Similar to a social security number, this identification number is assigned to businesses by the Internal Revenue Service for the purposes of filing business taxes and reporting employment taxes. To make sure that you understand all the federal tax requirements, you may find it helpful to take a small business tax workshop.

The Internal Revenue Service has a link on their website where you can download forms and order publications by mail on topics such as record keeping, selecting a tax year (fiscal or calendar), copyright and patent issues. You may still choose to hire an accountant or an attorney, but a familiarity with the basics of self-employment is helpful.

- *Internal Revenue Service Small Business/Self-Employed*
  www.irs.gov/businesses/small/index.html

- *Starting a Business*
  www.irs.gov/businesses/small/article/0,,id=99336,00.html

For Canadian citizens, the Canada Revenue Agency offers similar information geared to entrepreneurs and small business owners.

- *Canada Revenue Agency*
  www.cra-arc.gc.ca/tx/bsnss/menu-eng.html

- *Canada Revenue Agency*
  (Small businesses and self-employed individuals)
  www.cra-arc.gc.ca/tx/ndvdls/sgmnts/slf/menu-eng.html

Canada Business Service Centres has an online small business workshop at **www.canadabusiness.ca** that thoroughly covers issues related to starting a small business. Not all of the information will apply to every situation, but you can review the list of topics and click on the ones you want.

Insurance

All businesses need insurance. The amount of insurance you decide on is entirely up to you, but as a businessperson you should at least consider some form of liability insurance. Since life coaches generally are not therapists or other licensed human services professionals, you are not subject to malpractice suits, however, there are other liability issues to consider.

Liability Insurance

Regardless of the business structure you choose, some type of professional liability or Errors and Omissions (E & O) insurance is a good idea. There is always the possibility that something will go wrong that a client feels you are responsible for, even if it is out of your control.

This type of insurance may be useful if problems come up because you neglected to do something, thinking the client was going to do it. For example, as a corporate coach, you neglect to distribute a new company policy document to the company's employees that resulted from programs you introduced to the company, thinking that management was responsible for doing this. As a result, the company experiences serious financial losses and it holds you responsible for its losses. In this event, you might find E & O insurance valuable.

Property Insurance

If you conduct your coaching business out of your home, your homeowner's policy may not necessarily cover you for losses related to your coaching practice (i.e. property or liability). Make sure that you are familiar with your homeowner's policy and what losses or liabilities it covers.

If your business office is located somewhere other than your home, you will likely need coverage for any fire, damages or thefts that occur at your place of business. If your office is the source of a fire or other event that causes damage to other nearby businesses, you will likely be liable for those, too. Be sure to look into having thorough insurance protection for your place of business to cover any such possibilities.

Business Interruption Insurance

You may also need business interruption insurance. In the event that your property or equipment is damaged or destroyed, this type of insurance covers ongoing expenses such as rent or taxes until you get your business up and running again. Some policies offer riders, which can provide a few thousand dollars worth of protection for a slight additional cost. Depending on your situation, this may or may not be sufficient.

Life Insurance

If your family depends on your income, you may want to consider life insurance or disability insurance. Other types of personal insurance include health insurance or dental insurance (if you're not covered under a spouse's plan). Most people have some form of life insurance, but many do not have disability insurance, even if someone else employs them. It is an important form of insurance to consider, however, when you are solely responsible for your income.

Automobile Insurance

Also be sure to ask an agent about your auto insurance if you'll be using your personal vehicle on company business. If you're liable for damages in an accident that occurs while you're conducting business, your business could be at risk. Ask about special coverage that protects your business in those types of circumstances.

Insurance Plans

The Insurance Information Institute has good advice for business owners in professional practice. You can find out more about property and liability insurance policies that are available to you at their website (see the link below). You also should check out the National Association for the Self-Employed which offers reasonably priced insurance plans for self-employed people. State Farm has a program available specifically for home-based businesses.

Anyone who is self-employed can find several types of relatively affordable insurance, as well as other small-business assistance, from membership organizations including:

- *Insurance Information Institute*
  www.iii.org/smallbusiness/specific/professional/

- *National Association for the Self-Employed*
  www.nase.org

- *National Association for Female Executives*
  www.nafe.com

- *State Farm: Business in the Home*
  www.statefarm.ca/ca/insuranc/business/businhme.htm

Canadians have most of their health care expenses covered by their provincial governments. For expenses that are not covered (such as dental care, eyeglasses, prescription drugs, etc.) self-employed professionals may get tax benefits from setting up their own private health care plan. Puhl Employee Benefits (**www.puhlemployeebenefits.com**) is an example of the type of financial planning company that can help you set up your own private health care plan.

Finally, be sure to include any business insurance coverage that you decide to purchase in your start-up expenses. Insurance costs are a legitimate start-up expense and you will be able to use these costs as an expense deduction for business tax purposes. Any business insurance costs on an ongoing basis are also deductible.

5.4 Setting Up Your Business

5.4.1 Office Location

The first thing you will need is a place to work. Your choices include working from home or renting space.

Working From Home

Many coaches do the majority of their coaching over the telephone. Sessions can be conducted while the coach or client are in the office, at home, on the beach or in a hotel room. A lot of former commuters have traded the daily trek to the office for the comfort and convenience of working at home.

However, even with the freedom that coaching gives you, you will still need office space in which to take care of the daily tasks of running a business. These tasks can include answering telephone calls and emails, bookkeeping, scheduling, etc. So you will need a space that can allow you privacy and enough room to equip an office with all the essentials needed to effectively run your business.

A spare bedroom or space in the basement can be easily converted into a functional, even attractive office. Wherever you choose to set up your office, be sure that it is a space that is off limits to your family, since client confidentiality is essential. In addition to this, you want a quiet space where you can coach, as well as do your paperwork without interruptions from family. Also, having a spot that is set aside from your living areas in this way will allow you to close the door at the end of your workday and walk away from the office.

There are a few tax breaks you can take advantage of if you have a home office, too. You can deduct from your income taxes a percent of your mortgage payment and property taxes (or rent) and a share of utilities and maintenance costs. There are various methods to make those calculations, but by far the easiest – and most acceptable to the tax authorities in both the U.S. and Canada is to use an entire room, and to use it for no other purpose.

In the U.S., IRS Publication 587 has information on how to compute the calculation and file the deduction. You can download this information by visiting the IRS website and searching for the publication numbers from the search engine on the front page. The Canada Revenue Agency has similar online services. (See section 5.3.3 earlier in this chapter for more about your business tax obligations and links to the IRS and Canada Revenue Agency.)

Renting Space

While a home office works well for many life coaches, others prefer to rent a separate space. A separate space can create a better impression if you plan to have clients visit you. Some corporate coaches have offices, as do coaches who train other coaches or those who have hired employees. Others just feel more professional if they have somewhere other than a designated room in their house to go every day.

Some coaches conduct group sessions, where a number of clients meet with the coach on a weekly or bi-weekly basis to discuss the goals that they have set for themselves, and share the progress they have made or setbacks they have encountered. If you are coaching a group through a corporate client, they will supply the meeting space. If you are working with individual clients, you will need to find a suitable meeting space.

Office Space

Remember that you don't absolutely have to rent office space to be a coach. One of the main reasons people become coaches is to give themselves more freedom and flexibility, and spending several hundred dollars a month for office rental, plus additional time and travel expenses, may be defeating the purpose.

If you do decide to rent office space, try to secure a short-term lease — six months or even month to month. Don't get locked into a one or two-year lease before your business is firmly established. Also, you might consider renting office furniture and computer equipment rather than purchasing outright.

Look for a place that is convenient to get to from your home, and that gives you quick access to any services you may need, such as your bank or even a good restaurant or coffee shop. Pick an area that suits your needs and fits your budget. For more advice on what to consider before renting space visit **www.nolo.com**. Click on the "Business & Human

Resources" tab, then on "Starting A Business," then on "Finding and Renting Space For Your Business."

Serviced Offices

Another option for renting office space is to find a professional, serviced office where several professionals share a common receptionist and other office facilities such as conference rooms, printers, copiers, and so on. Many of these types of office rentals also offer additional administrative services like typing, correspondence, filing, etc. This can be an economical option for setting up a professional space for your business. Prices vary but can start as low as $500 per month depending on your location and any extra services offered.

There are many websites where you can find these services. One example is Instant Offices (**www.instant-offices.com**), which is a searchable directory of serviced office space available all across North America and the world. You can also type "serviced offices" and the name of your city into your favorite search engine or look in the Yellow Pages under "Office Rentals" to find more.

5.4.2   Start-Up Costs

The initial start-up budget is one component of your business plan that you will want to create first. After you calculate this amount, you'll know if there's any need for investors or loans. A major benefit to working in this field is the low amount needed to get started as a business owner. In general, service businesses are cheaper to launch than businesses that sell products, because there is no inventory to buy and no retail location to open.

As discussed in Chapter 4, a training program or workshop can have its rewards, but it will also have an enrollment fee. If you decide this is the right path for you, be sure to include tuition and other training related costs in your start-up budget. Be sure to add association membership fees as well.

Start-Up Financing

Depending on how you set up your business, the cost of starting your practice might range from almost nothing to thousands of dollars. Obviously, your start-up expenses will be much higher if you decide to rent space and buy office equipment. You will also need to consider your "working capital" requirements. This is the money you will need for day-to-day operations. But there are other expenses that will come out of your pocket before you get your first client—such as business cards, telephone, etc.

Many entrepreneurs are optimistic about how much money they will earn from their business, and how quickly they will earn it. While you may be tremendously successful right from the start and exceed your own expectations, it is wise to be prepared for the possibility it may take longer than expected until your business is earning enough to support you.

One rule of thumb that's often cited is to have six months' living expenses set aside beyond your start-up costs. You might also consider remaining at your current job and working part-time as a life coach until it is established.

Depending on the start-up costs you calculate in your business plan, you may find you have all the money you need to get started in your savings account (or available to spend on your credit cards). If your own resources won't cover all the things you would like to do, you will need to look for financing.

Financing Options

Personal Savings

Evaluate your bank accounts, retirement plans, and investments for available funds to finance your new venture. Who better to borrow from than yourself? You might pay penalties for withdrawing funds early from certain plans and investments, but it keeps you from accumulating excessive debt.

Family

One place to look for financing is from family members. They may be willing to invest in your company or give you a loan to help you get started. To avoid any misunderstandings, it's wise to get any agreements in writing even with family members.

Moonlighting

You could always keep your day job and coach in the evening and on weekends, or you can downgrade to a part-time position and run your business with the extra time. This allows you to safely test being your own boss, while still having the shelter of a steady paycheck and benefits. Continuing to earn a salary of some kind to help cover your living expenses will keep your start-up costs way down.

Credit Cards

Using plastic to finance a business should generally be avoided because of the potential for extremely high interest rates. However, if you've exhausted all of the other options, then this is something to think about using carefully. There are also lines of credit that can be obtained from various other lenders which give you access to a pre-approved loan amount as you need it.

Banks and Credit Unions

Another place to secure a small business loan is through a conventional bank, credit union, or other lender. If you decide to give this a try, you'll need a comprehensive and professional business plan in order to impress the loan officer.

If you decide to approach a bank for a business loan, be prepared. Write a loan proposal that includes detailed information about your business, how much money you want to borrow, what you plan to do with the money, and so on. Some good advice about financing can be found at the websites listed below. Look into the Small Business Administration business assistance programs. The SBA has a Loan Guarantee Program that provides loans to small businesses. A similar program is available in Canada.

- *SBA: Financing*
  www.sba.gov/services/financialassistance/sbaloantopics/ index.html

- *Canada Business – Financing a Business*
  www.ic.gc.ca/eic/site/csbfp-pfpec.nsf/eng/Home

- *Nolo.com Resource Center*
  (Click on the "Business & Human Resources" tab, then on "Starting A Business," then on "Financing Your Business.")
  www.nolo.com

Start-Up Expenses

Expenses to Expect

Let's take a look at the foreseeable costs involved in launching your business, so that you can quickly and easily calculate your start-up budget. You should keep your initial expenses as lean as possible. After you have some cash flow from a few coaching sessions, you can buy the extras that were not in the original budget.

A start-up worksheet has been included at the end of this section to help simplify the process. Once you've researched how much each item will cost, fill in those amounts and total up your starting budget. The overall amount will largely depend on what items you already own. Here are the basic needs and expenses to anticipate:

- **Office equipment and supplies:** See section 5.4.3 for a list of supplies you likely will need

- **Marketing and advertising:** This includes building and hosting your website, networking costs to attend luncheons or meetings, and any paid advertising activity such as printed advertisements, radio and TV spots, etc. (see Chapter 6 for more about marketing)

- **Business licenses:** While the fees shouldn't be too large, they should be added to the start-up budget.

- **Legal or accounting fees:** If you will need the counsel of an attorney, accountant, or bookkeeper, this expenditure should be estimated and taken into account.

- **Insurance:** While not usually mandatory in this industry, starting with the minimum of at least general liability insurance for your business can provide peace of mind. Find out if this is legally required in your area for your type of business. As mentioned in section 5.3.3, you may also need to add in costs for health, disability or other insurance, if you need these policies.

- **Living expenses:** Since you won't have a steady paycheck as an entrepreneur, it is crucial that you save up about three to six months worth of living expenses, especially if you have no other sources of income to drawn on while you build your business.

- **Business capital:** Just like living expenses, you should start with enough money to fund your business for at least three to six months. This basically covers your costs to run the operation until you can use business revenue to pay the bills.

- **Training:** Any programs or workshops in which you enroll should be added into the budget. In many cases, training may end up being one of the top expenses. There are also small business classes or continuing education classes that you may decide to take.

Sample Start-Up Expense Worksheet

Item	Amount
Advertising/Marketing	$
Association fees	$
Bookkeeping fees	$
Business cards and printing	$
Computer/Printer/Fax/Copier	$
Equipment and supplies	$
Insurance	$
Legal fees	$
Licenses and permits	$
Living expenses (3-6 months)	$
Misc.	$
Office furniture costs (desk, file cabinet)	$
Office supplies	$
Telephone costs and utilities	$
Training and education	$
Working capital (3-6 months)	$
Total Expenses	$
Minus available startup capital	$
Total Amount Needed	$

5.4.3   Office Equipment and Supplies

You will need a variety of office equipment and supplies for your coaching business. If you don't already have everything you need, you will have initial expenses for these items. However, once your office is stocked, your ongoing expenses should be minimal. See section 5.4.2 for more about calculating and preparing for start-up expenses.

Of course you will need the basic supplies any business needs, including pens and pencils, paper, stapler, clips, Post-Its, scissors, tape, Liquid Paper, etc. Check with your local office supply stores, such as Staples and Office Depot, to find out about sales on supplies and the larger items listed below. The sales reps who work there can also be of assistance when it comes to getting help putting together everything you need for your office.

Office Supply List

By looking around your home, you can probably gather together most of the basic office goods needed to set up your new company headquarters. However, if you are starting a home office from scratch, you'll need to visit your local discount office supply store.

The major furniture requirements will be a desk or large table, a desk chair, a filing cabinet or file box, and shelves for the storage of reference materials. Useful office supplies to have close at hand include these practical items:

- Business card file

- Calculator

- Correction fluid or tape

- CD ROMs/flash drive for backing up computer files

- Day planner or PDA

- Envelopes, #10 size and 9" x 12" (business size)

- File folders, file labels, file jackets, and expanding file pockets

- Glue stick

- Laser pointer and other supplies for making presentations

- Paper clips and binder clips

- Pens, pencils, colored pencils, and markers

- Printer paper and stationery

- Stamps and return address labels

- Stapler and box of staples

- Tape with dispenser

- Writing pads and self-stick note pads

Any of the stores listed below can help you stock your home office with supplies. Most items can be ordered online, too.

- *OfficeMax*
  www.officemax.com

- *Office Depot*
  www.officedepot.com

- *Staples*
  www.staples.com

Computer and Software

Most people these days have access to a computer. However, if you don't have your own computer, you should consider buying or leasing one for your business as soon as you can afford it. In addition to the computer, it's a good idea to get a printer and something to back up your files (such as a flash drive or CD-RW).

Many computers already have the basic software needed to run a business. Some versions of Microsoft Office come with a whole suite of small business tools. You may also want to get a bookkeeping program such as Quicken or Quickbooks as well as a database program to keep track of your clients. The MS Office Small Business Suite has one, or you can buy a database program such as ACT! or Filemaker Pro.

For basic computer equipment and software, the staff at a computer store or your office supplies store can give you more information and help you decide which products are best for you.

Coaching Software

There are a number of websites with integrated tools for tracking and managing client information online. CoachTrack, designed by two Canadian life coaches, allows you to quickly and efficiently search client records, keep track of session notes, automatically send invoices and other forms, and check payment history and personal information. CoachTrack can automatically send you reminders about important dates or events, such as clients' birthdays, scheduled sessions, etc. Online help is also available.

Initial access costs $229 U.S., with annual upgrade fees of $79 at the time this book was published. However, you can simply choose to continue using the original version you downloaded without renewing. They also offer a 30-day free trial, with no obligation. Check out **www. coach-track.com** for more information.

Another software program designed specifically for life coaches is Client Compass™, available from John Wiley & Sons, Inc. Client Compass™ helps you to manage client intake, and has sophisticated recordkeeping and billing tools such as automated invoicing. It also allows you to track the number of hours you spend with each client. You can learn more about Client Compass™ at **http://ca.wiley.com/WileyCDA/WileyTitle/ productCd-0470008563.html**.

Fax Machine and Photocopier

These used to be considered optional equipment for small businesses. But today, when you can get a unit that is a combination photocopier, fax machine, scanner, and printer for a few hundred dollars, you should consider getting one.

You are unlikely to need dozens of photocopies; you might need to make a copy or two of an agreement from time to time, and if you have the equipment right there, you won't have to go all the way to Kinko's to do it. And remember, time is money, especially when you have a lot to do and a lot on your mind.

File Cabinet

You'll need to keep files for each client. Your desk may have drawers that can hold files, but you will probably eventually need a file cabinet. Your options include two-door or four-door filing cabinets, or you may find a lateral file cabinet with a wood finish that fits beautifully with the rest of your office furniture.

Telephone and Fax

The number of different telephone plans can be bewildering, but there are steps that you can take to keep everything fairly simple. If you choose to work out of your home, you probably do not even need to make any changes to your current telephone service. You will generally know when clients are calling, as you have already pre-arranged the times with them. You can install a separate business line, subscribe to Caller ID, or even get a different ring for when a client calls.

However, to ensure professionalism consider making your main office phone number a business line. You don't want your six-year-old picking up on a client calling in for a session, after all. That just doesn't come across as very professional.

A business line will cost a little more than a residential line, but you will be listed under your business name in the white pages and with directory assistance, which makes it easier for clients to find you. You can also get a listing in the Yellow Pages under "Coaching Services" (or whatever category coaches are listed under in your local Yellow Pages).

Make this phone off-limits to the rest of the family. Always be sure it is answered professionally with a greeting such as stating your business name followed by "How can we help you?"

These days, even large corporations have their phones answered by voice mail systems, so you might also want to install an answering machine or subscribe to the voicemail services offered by telephone companies.

Once you have developed a client base, you might want a toll-free number for coaching calls. Give this only to your clients, though. People calling for the initial consultation can call your regular number.

Although email has replaced fax machines in most cases, you might still want to be able to send and receive faxes, particularly if you market yourself to executives or businesses. Rather than buy a fax machine, you might also consider an online service. eFax.com allows you to send and receive faxes through your email account for less than $20 per month. You can try it free for 30 days before subscribing.

5.5 Financial Matters

Keeping Track of Your Finances

Being self-employed offers you the freedom to set your own schedule, work from home and choose your clients. However, you will be responsible for keeping track of your earnings and any applicable deductions. The only way to really know where your business stands is by having adequate financial records at your fingertips.

Keep accurate track of all invoices, receipts, telephone bills (related to coaching), and other business paperwork. If you're not used to keeping receipts for everything you buy, you should quickly develop this habit. Any supplies you buy for your office, right down to pens and paperclips, are legitimate business expenses and deductible at tax time. You don't have to print hard copies of everything, but be certain that the information is easily accessible if you need to look up or produce something.

Knowing exactly where your money is going will help you plan better and cut back on any unnecessary expenses. So, again, make it a habit to ask for a receipt for every expense related to business. At a glance, you should be able to see how much money has been brought in, how much money has been paid out, what amounts are waiting to be collected, and what debt amounts are still owed.

Bookkeeping System

Your bookkeeping system is a record of your expenses and income. Monitoring your expenses and income with a consistent bookkeeping system will help you build a more profitable company. By making this part of your daily activities, your financial position will be much clearer, and you will have the records needed at tax time.

The first step is to choose an accounting method for your business. The two basic types are the accrual accounting method and the single-entry cash accounting method. The accrual method is not generally used in service businesses because it categorizes money that is still owed as collected money, even if you haven't received payment yet.

The single-entry cash method is much simpler, since all incoming money is posted as a credit and any money spent is posted as a debit. Your credits minus your debits will equal your ledger balance.

A good way to learn more about using a bookkeeping system is to take a small business accounting course. These usually are fairly inexpensive, last a few weeks or a few months, and many are offered online. Check with your local college educational extension or continuing education departments to find out more, or check online at **www.petersons.com** or **www.schoolfinder.com**.

Financial Reports

There are several key financial reports that you will want to regularly update and maintain as a small business owner:

- Cash flow statement. This is a basic record of income and expenses, otherwise known as credits and debits. It is usually tracked on a daily or weekly basis and then tallied up for a given month. When you look at this data across several months, you can perform cash flow projections for upcoming months. Knowing your cash flow will tell you if there is enough money to pay the bills.

- Balance sheet. This helpful document compares your total assets to your total liabilities. Assets include current assets like cash, prepaid expenses, accounts receivable, and long term assets like property and equipment. Liabilities consist of any owed amounts such as loans, taxes, and accounts payable. By subtracting the liabilities from the assets, you will discover your owner's equity amount.

- Income statement. This report is also called a profit and loss statement, or P & L. It shows all generated income minus the business expenses, resulting in the gross profit before taxes.

Bookkeeping Software

When in doubt, get some help with your bookkeeping endeavors. One solution is to invest in accounting computer software such as Intuit's Quicken or QuickBooks (**www.intuit.com**) or Peachtree Accounting (**www.peachtree.com**). You can buy the basic edition from either company for less than $100. These powerful, bundled software packages can help you manage the following accounting functions:

- Accounts payable

- Accounts receivable and collections

- General ledger, balance sheet, and cash flow

- Invoicing and billing

- Payroll

- Report generation

- Stock and inventory

- Tax deductible expense tracking

Financial Experts

Just as people will hire you as an expert to coach them through their problems, you may want to hire experts to assist with your finances. An accountant or tax advisor can be expensive (e.g. you might pay $100 per hour compared to the $20 per hour you might pay a bookkeeper), but their advice could possibly save you hundreds or even thousands of dollars at tax time.

An accountant is someone who takes all your recorded transactions and creates financial reports in order to analyze your business. They can also provide valuable financial guidance and help with filing tax returns. To lower your expenses when hiring an accountant try to do some basic bookkeeping so the professional accountant doesn't have to sort through and organize your paperwork. Remember, they charge by the hour.

If you find yourself so busy with coaching work that you don't have time to do your own bookkeeping, consider hiring a part-time bookkeeper on a contract basis to do your bookkeeping for you. A bookkeeper can assist with your daily and weekly transactions in regards to accounts payable and accounts receivable. They will record all of your incoming money and process any money that you owe. Depending on how busy you are, it may take the bookkeeper a few hours per week to get your books up to date and balance them with your bank statements.

You can find a bookkeeper by checking your local newspaper classified ads or in the Yellow Pages under "Bookkeeping Service".

Financial Institution

Open a business account at a bank, trust company or credit union, even if you are using only your own name to do business. And use this only for paying the bills of the company and your own salary, which you then deposit in your personal account.

You can shop around to find a financial institution that is supportive of small business, or use the same one that you use for your personal banking. In addition to your checking account, a financial institution may provide you with a corporate credit card you can use to make purchases for your business, and a merchant credit card account if you want to accept credit card payments from your customers.

Get a style of business check that makes it impossible for you not to record checks you've written. Avoid using electronic payments unless you can print out a receipt for them. You want to create a paper trail for your business account so you are able to:

- Prove your deductible expenses at tax time

- Create a balance sheet that lenders may request from time to time

- See at a glance where your money has gone

5.6 Setting Your Fees

There is a great variety of ways for life coaches to charge for their services. In large part, these are based on the format of the coaching delivery (as explained in section 3.3), that is, whether you are coaching in person, by phone, doing e-coaching, presenting workshops or other group coaching, and whether you are coaching for individuals or corporate clients. In addition to these considerations there are other variables to consider when setting your fees.

Other factors affecting the fees you may charge include:

- Your income requirements (this includes how much you want to be paid, your business expenses, and how much profit you want your company to earn)

- Your reputation

- Your specialization

- Your client and their budget

- Your relationship with the client

- Your competitors' fees if you will be competing for projects

- Your geographic location (i.e. for coaching in person; coaches in larger urban areas will likely be able to charge more than those practicing in smaller cities or towns)

Many of these factors overlap and, as a result, there is no one way to set your fees. In this section we will explore the different types of fee structures normally employed by life coaches to help you understand how you can set your fees in your own coaching business.

5.6.1   Calculating an Hourly Rate

In the beginning phases of coaching, calculating an hourly rate is important because you can then use it as the standard by which to calculate many other time-based fees. As an example, laser coaches allocate from 5 to 15 minutes for laser sessions and can charge on a proportionate hourly basis for this time (for example, an hourly rate of $150 becomes $37.50 for a 15 minute session).

There are several different ways to calculate your hourly rate. You could simply pick a rate that you would like to charge, such as the $150 per hour used in the example above based on a bit of research about your competitors, but this is not recommended. One consequence of this method is that you might never really know if your prices are reasonable compared to your competitors given factors like your experience, the kinds of specialty services you offer, and so on. Also, you need to know that you will be able to cover your expenses and make a profit.

Another way to calculate your hourly rate is to start from the basis of the yearly earnings you expect and the number of hours you expect to work in a year. Let's say you want to earn a minimum of $50,000 in your first year, work 40 hours per week and have a two-week vacation. To calculate your hourly rate you would divide your total expected salary by your total hours worked per year.

40 hours per week x 50 weeks = 2000 hours per year

Your hourly rate would be $50,000 divided by 2000 hours, or $25 per hour.

$50,000 ÷ 2000 hours = $25 per hour.

However, this calculation by itself is a bit simplistic and leaves out a number of other factors, such as the number of paid (as opposed to unpaid) hours you will work, your operating expenses, and a reasonable level of profit for your business. You will want to include these elements in your hourly rate calculation as well. Once you have included these elements you will know that you are charging a reasonable rate based on the needs of your own business model.

Estimate Your Paid Hours

The next step is to estimate the percentage of your working time that will be spent on revenue-generating activities. This is a key consideration that is sometimes overlooked by entrepreneurs. However, the reality is that you will not be spending 100% of your working hours on revenue-generating activities. Instead, you will need to assume that some of your time will be spent on other activities.

Here are a few examples:

- Administrative work

- Attending networking events

- Preliminary consultations (many coaches provide the first meeting to prospective clients for free)

- Other marketing activities

- Submitting proposals that don't result in work

- Learning (reading, taking courses, etc.)

- Down time (sick days or time off)

Because your first year in business is likely to involve additional work to get the business off the ground, you should estimate a higher percentage of time spent on such tasks in your first year than you might estimate for subsequent years. For the purpose of our example, we will assume that 40% of your time will be spent on tasks that don't generate revenue, so 60% of your hours will be paid.

60% of 2,000 hours = 1,200 paid hours per year

Determine Your Overhead Costs

Overhead is all the non-labor expenses needed to run your business. Some examples include: rent, utilities, insurance, office equipment, and membership fees. Overhead costs can vary tremendously from one coaching business to another. For example, a home-based business is likely to have considerably lower expenses than a coaching practice with office space and an administrative assistant.

Use the total amount of expenses that you came up with in section 5.4.2 for your initial overhead costs for your first year in business. For example, if you estimated that your monthly operating costs will be $1,000:

$1,000 per month = $12,000 per year

Decide how much profit you want

Profit is generally expressed as a percentage of your total operating costs (your salary plus operating expenses). How much profit would you like your coaching business to earn? Unless you want to start a non-profit organization, the answer should certainly be more than 0%. Exactly how much more is entirely up to you.

There's no standard for how much profit you should be earning. We found that most recommendations ranged from 10% to 25% annual profit. Because you may have higher costs in your first year, you may want to aim lower than you might in subsequent years. So for the purpose of our example, we'll assume you want to earn a profit of 10% in your first year. Here's how you would calculate that based on our previous figures:

$50,000 salary + $12,000 expenses = $62,000 total costs

$62,000 x .10 = $6,200 profit

Calculate your hourly rate

Once you have figured out the other numbers, you can easily come up with a more reasonable estimated hourly rate, which you would then round up or down to come up with a fee that appears professional.

Here's the hourly rate calculated from the numbers used throughout this example:

$50,000 salary + $12,000 expenses + $6,200 profit = $68,200

$$\$68,200 \div 1,200 \text{ paid hours} = \$56.83 \text{ per hour}$$
(which you might round to $60 per hour)

To see what you would need to charge in order to earn a larger salary, work fewer hours, spend more on overhead, or make a larger profit, you can plug other numbers into the formula.

For example, if you want to work the same number of hours, but earn $100,000 per year instead of $50,000, spend $5,000 per month on overhead instead of $1,000, and earn a profit of 15% instead of 10%, here's how you would calculate your hourly rate:

$$\$100,000 \text{ salary} + \$60,000 \text{ expenses} + \$24,000 \text{ profit} = \$184,000$$

$$\$184,000 \div 1,200 \text{ hours} = \$153.33 \text{ per hour}$$
(which you might round to $150 per hour)

Likewise, if the figure you come up with doesn't seem reasonable for your market (e.g. you want to coach individuals who will be paying for your services out of their own pocket, rather than coach executives whose companies will be paying your fee), and you are willing to work more hours, earn a lower annual income, spend less on overhead, or make a smaller profit, you can plug in figures that will reduce your hourly rate.

To ensure that your costs are covered and that your business can prosper, you should do some number-crunching using the formulas above. Try it with different figures (such as different annual incomes) to help you settle on an appropriate hourly fee to charge.

Now that you've determined what your ideal hourly rate should be you can begin to apply that to a number of different coaching fee scenarios. Below, we will examine a number of different fee structures for a variety of coaching services.

5.6.2 Fees for Individuals

Initial Consultation Fees

Many coaches offer a free initial coaching consultation. Typically, this is a free half-hour coaching session used to introduce the client to the coach and the coaching methods that will be used. You may wish to provide a free consultation like this and then charge for the intake session. For our purposes, we will assume that the initial consultation and the intake session (see section 3.1.1) are the same (the first "real" coaching session).

The initial consultation will usually use up a full hour so you should charge according to your hourly rate that you have decided upon. For instance, from our example above, you would charge a fee of $60 for the initial consultation, although most coaches charge a much higher one-hour rate than this. You can also choose to include the intake session as part of your monthly coaching package fee (see below) or make the initial consultation refundable if the client signs on for a monthly package.

If you're a carbon coach who decides to offer in-home consultations, consider charging a flat rate higher than your usual hourly rate for a minimum of one hour for the initial consultation. You can then charge your regular fee for each half-hour session beyond the initial consultation. This way, if your client chooses not to continue with carbon coaching, you aren't giving your services away for free in the hopes that you will land a new client.

Often, carbon coaching engagements with individual clients can be of limited duration compared to other forms of life coaching so you should probably charge in the expectation that most clients will only be receiving a month or less of coaching. Remember that you are charging for a premium service that will likely save clients a lot of money in the future.

Coaching Packages

Most coaches who coach for individuals offer monthly coaching packages. Monthly fees for coaching tend to run from about $200 to about $600, although they can be higher or lower depending on the client, the coach, and a number of other variables such as the coaching delivery method (section 3.3), session length, services included, etc. While this is a very broad range of fees, there's a good reason for the range, because coaches offer a variety of packages based on different time increments.

Another way to look at coaching fees when you're coming up with a coaching package is to see them on a per minute basis. For example, if you've decided you are going to charge $150 per hour you would divide this by 60 to get your per minute charge, in this case, $2.50 per minute (many established coaches charge more than $3.00 per minute). This gives you great flexibility to offer clients a variety of coaching packages based on time increments of your (or your client's) choosing, such as 30, 45 or 50 minutes.

You might consider offering clients a choice between 3 one-hour sessions per month, three 50-minute sessions per month or three 45-minute sessions per month. The cost for the client on a per minute basis would be the same, but the total cost would be different for each package. As an example, a package of three 30-minute sessions per month would be, using our example of $2.50 per minute:

$2.50 x 30 minutes = $75 per half-hour session

Three 30-minute sessions per month = $75 x 3 = $225

For a package of three 45-minute sessions you would charge:

$2.50 x 45 minutes = $112.50 per session
(which you might round up to $115)

$112.50 x 3 sessions = $337.50
(which you might round up to $345)

In addition to the regular monthly coaching sessions included in the package, many coaches also include additional "free" services such as unlimited email check-ins, a set number of laser coaching sessions, and so on. Try offering some of these types of services until you settle on a total package that works best for you. Just be sure that you're not investing too much time on responding to extras like email check-ins, because that will result in an excess of unpaid hours.

Laser Coaching Fees

Coaches offering laser coaching as a separate service usually charge a monthly fee for a set number of laser coaching sessions. If you choose to offer laser coaching in addition to regular monthly coaching packages, consider charging a bit more for this service.

Just as with offering regular monthly packages, you can set your fees for laser coaching packages based on a per minute fee for a single session. In this case, though, you will probably charge at a higher per minute rate, perhaps 25-30% higher, because of the extremely focused, intense nature of the coaching and because it can put you "on call" in a sense.

You can also work out a rate based on your regular half-hourly or hourly rate (for example, your one-hour rate divided by four, for a fifteen minute session). So, if your hourly rate is $150, you might offer a package price of $300 for 8 fifteen-minute sessions per month.

Sometimes you will encounter a client who constantly goes beyond the 15-minutes (or whatever the time increment you offer) their contract specifies. In this case, you will need to remind them of the terms of their contract and let them know that you will need to charge for any overruns. If sessions with a particular client continually run over the 15-minute mark, you can then use your per minute fee to invoice the client for the additional time.

In-Person Coaching Fees

Most coaches we talked to told us that they charge a bit more for coaching in person. One coach offers 45 minutes of telephone coaching for $100, while a 60-minute in-person session costs $200, meaning the in-person coaching is charged at 33% more than telephone coaching. Mainly, price differences like these have to do with the higher costs associated with offering this service. Some of the additional costs include travel time for coaching at the client's preferred location, office or other meeting space rental, and the longer meeting times associated with in-person coaching. When setting your fees for in-person coaching, be sure to include the extra costs in your rate.

For example, if you live in a large urban area, travel across the city to the client's home might take you 20-30 minutes. This travel time is time wasted if you are not charging for it. You could charge an additional fee based on your per minute rate (such as 20 minutes x $2.50 per minute = $50) or just a flat rate that you think is reasonable for compensating your otherwise unproductive travel time. Include this in your coaching session fees.

Alternatively, if you plan to offer the majority of your coaching services in an office setting to clients who come to you for coaching appointments, you will need to take into account your increased operating costs related to office rental, administrative costs, etc. Be sure to look at all the daily costs of running your business from your rented office space (rent, utilities, insurance, repairs, etc.), and include those in your fees as mentioned earlier.

Other Fees for Individuals

Many coaches offer online assessments or tests in one form or another as a separate service from coaching. These could include career assessments, educational goals assessments, various health and wellness or spiritual assessments, etc. Generally, these are an outgrowth of the coach's specialty area and are often based on coaching instruments like those discussed in section 3.4 and the coach's experience in past intake sessions.

Online assessments usually involve an individual downloading the test, completing it and returning it to the coach for evaluation; all of this for a set fee. Prices vary, but the most important thing to consider is how much time you expect to spend on evaluating the test and following up with the client. The best bet for offering this type of service is to treat it as you would a one-time hourly client session and charge your hourly rate.

Career coaches offer a variety of job-hunting packages, including resumes, cover letters, thank you notes, approach letters, CVs, and so on. To write a resume for a recent college graduate, for example, you might charge $100. This might include 25 resumes on good quality paper, plus a CD containing the resume file. For an additional $25, you would also compose a cover letter. Don't focus on how much you can charge clients for every little extra, though. These are just considerations in determining a price.

Career coaches typically charge different prices for resume and cover letter preparation, depending on the job level that the client is seeking. Prices range from $75 to $150 for an entry-level resume to between $200 and $400 for a mid-level position to $500 to $700 for a senior level position. Executive and "C-level" (i.e. CEO, COO, CFO) resume prices may exceed $1,000.

Some coaches offer e-coaching or cyber coaching as a separate service (see section 3.3.3 for more about e/cyber coaching). Usually this type of service is offered in a package form of a set number of emails for a set price or a package price for messaging or chat room sessions of a designated length. For email coaching, the package price should reflect the amount of time you will invest in responses to client emails. Again, use the hourly or per minute rate as your guide when offering cyber coaching services.

5.6.3   Group Coaching Fees

Group coaching enables you to lower your fees for individuals taking group sessions. There a number of different ways to offer group coaching, including teleclasses, workshops, and retreats (as explored in section 3.3). In this section we'll offer tips for setting your fees for these group coaching methods.

Teleclass Fees

Teleclasses are a frequent feature of coaching practices. Many coaches offer teleclasses as an introduction to their coaching services for no charge. Classes usually range from 30 to 60 minutes in length. Teleclasses can be a great way to bring in new clients who might not otherwise pursue coaching. So think of them as a good marketing technique and price accordingly.

Probably the safest way to ensure that teleclasses are profitable, is to mandate a minimum number of participants and charge each participant enough to cover the cost of your session with the minimum number of participants, whatever its length. For example, if your normal hourly fee is $100 you could specify a minimum of three participants and charge each one $35, for a total of $105. This covers your usual one-hour rate and any participants you have above the minimum number is extra profit. And $35 is a very reasonable rate for a teleclass. Also, don't forget to calculate the cost of long-distance or other telephone charges into your fee.

For this guide, we surveyed a number of coaches offering teleclasses and found a very wide range of fees for this service. Fees started at about $20 and went up to about $150 for a one-hour session, with a median price of around $35. Most of the coaches also offered one individual coaching session for each teleclass participant and some offered additional email coaching. If you decide to offer these extra services, be sure to factor the cost of your time into the final fee for the teleclass.

Workshop Fees

Like teleclass fees, workshop fees vary widely. Much of this fee depends on the type of coaching you offer, the clients you cater to and any costs associated with delivering the workshop. Online workshops are common and are reasonably inexpensive to run. The advice for setting teleclass fees generally holds true for setting online workshop fees.

You will need to charge more for in-person workshops than you would for one presented online. This is because of the additional costs of renting facilities and equipment, any materials you will need, additional marketing, and so on. Many workshops also include a lunch in the price if the workshop is all day.

For example, let's consider an all day (7 hours including a one-hour break for lunch) workshop you decide to hold in a conference room at a nearby hotel. To work out a fee, you should first calculate all the costs to you in presenting the workshop. Using the costs as a starting point, you can then work out a profitable final fee.

In this example, let's assume the hotel offers you a package price of $1,000, which includes a meeting room, buffet lunch, and audio-visual equipment. You've also spent $100 on additional advertising of the event and you've purchased miscellaneous materials to create workbooks and a CD for each participant totaling about $50. All told, your time invested is about 10 hours even before the event has taken place. Let's assume your usual hourly coaching fee is $100.

Your total costs are:

Facilities	$1,000
Promotion	$100
Materials	$50
10 hours time invested	$1,000
Total	**$2,150**

This is the minimum amount you will need to charge to break even with everything you've invested in getting the workshop off the ground. You hope to attract about 30 participants. So your breakeven fee (the minimum you should charge to meet your costs) is:

$$\$2,150 \div 30 = \$72$$

Remember that you will also spend a minimum of 7 hours of your time on the day of the event. Since your normal hourly rate is $100, your time is worth $700, which we'll add to the original total for a new total of $2,150 + $700 = $2,850. Therefore the new breakeven fee is $2,850 ÷ 30 participants = $95, which you might round up to $99 or $100 per participant. This is a very reasonable rate for an all-day event that includes lunch.

You can also factor in any profit you would like to make such as 5%, 10%, and so on. Add the profit percent to the final total and divide by the number of participants ($2,850 + 10% or $285 = $3,135 ÷ 30 participants = $104.50 per person).

To be safe, for your first workshop you should research your costs thoroughly and start promoting the event well before you commit to renting a venue and facilities. That way, you'll be better able to gauge public interest in the workshop as people begin to inquire about it. If you don't have a minimum number of participants sign up you will still have time to cancel the event and refund those who did.

Also, a good strategy is to plan for a minimum number of participants to arrive at a higher breakeven cost than to expect a higher number and not charge enough to cover your costs because you thought there would be more participants. In the above example, if you count on only 10 participants your breakeven fee would be $285. If you charge something like $150 (still reasonable), you are in a better position to cover your expenses even if you don't make any profit or a wage for your time invested.

Fees for Retreats

Setting your fees for retreats is similar in most ways to setting workshop fees. In the same way, you will need to figure out your costs for the event, including the venue, any materials you will need, a guest speaker if you decide to have one (or more than one), as well as accommodations for you, your guest speaker(s), and the participants. If travel is required, participants normally would cover their own travel expenses, but you would need to cover your own travel expenses and those of your guest speaker(s).

There are a couple of ways to structure fees for retreats. One way is to offer an all-inclusive price that includes accommodations and your retreat program. If you receive a special rate from the venue where you're hosting the retreat, you can also charge a markup, if you choose to do so, on the room rate that clients pay. But keep in mind that this can make your price look expensive if you're planning a retreat more than 2-3 days in length.

The second way to structure your fee is to separate the price of accommodations from your actual retreat program price. In fact, this is the way that many coaches present their fee schedule for a retreat. This also creates a bit more transparency with respect to accommodations pricing, since clients can easily compare the room rate to what the hotel, resort or other venue normally charges.

Reducing Costs

One way to lower your costs is to have individual clients double up in one room, but only if they are willing to do that. This is a particularly good idea if your chosen venue is small with limited room capacity.

Another way to lower your costs and increase your profit is through networking (see section 6.3.1 for more about ways to network). If you are a member of an association, check with other coaches who host retreats similar to what you are interested in hosting and consider partnering with others if they are willing. This is also a good way to get some experience and avoid making costly mistakes, since you will be working with someone who already has practical knowledge of hosting a retreat.

Consider trying to find discounted accommodations and facilities if you can. If you are able to find a nearby retreat facility, or if you often visit a certain resort or other getaway spot and they know you already, speak to the owner or management and try to negotiate a special rate. If you hold your retreats in the same spot year after year or several times in one year, most will consider giving you a better rate for the business you can guarantee them.

Alternatively, if you find a resort or other retreat facility that is willing to host your event, you could partner with them to offer similar events to a general clientele (i.e. not just your regular clients). You would then leave all the facility, food and accommodations arrangements up to them and you would only have to worry about your own promotion and program development/delivery. This can be a very cost-effective arrangement for you.

5.6.4   Fees for Corporate Clients

Corporate coaches tend to charge much higher fees, particularly those whose clients are multi-million dollar companies that deduct the coaching as a business expense. According to Terri Levine, founder of the coach training school ComprehensiveCoachingU.com, monthly fees for corporate coaching range from $1,000 to $3,500. Coaches who work with executives in weekly telephone sessions may charge $300 to $400 per hour.

Fees for training programs are typically charged by the day. Fees vary, but it is not unusual to charge several thousand dollars a day for a training program. One trainer interviewed for this guide charges $1,500 for a half day and $2,500 for a full day, plus $1,500 for program development (if it is not a program she usually presents). Other trainers charge from $500 to $7,000 or more per day.

There are a number of ways to set your fees based on different services when you're working for corporate clients. The following discussion examines the most common of these and is adapted from the *FabJob Guide to Become a Business Consultant*.

Daily Rate for Individual Coaching

Many coaches who offer services for corporate clients use a daily fee rate (also known as a per diem) instead of, or in addition to, their hourly rate. This is a usual fee structure for day-long training programs, such as a team-building training program.

There are two systems most used by coaches to come up with a daily rate. The first, and most commonly used, is to simply multiply your hourly rate by eight (see section 5.6.1 for information about how to calculate your hourly rate). The daily rate is based on the assumption that you work eight hours per day on average. So if your hourly rate is $150, you can quickly calculate your daily rate as follows:

$150 per hour x 8 hours = $1,200 daily rate

Although you will bill your clients your daily rate for each eight hours you work, you can still have flexibility in your schedule. For example, if your coaching program lasts for two days you might put in 12 hours one day and four hours the next, and still charge for two full 8-hour days.

The other system for calculating your daily rate is to give clients a discount from your hourly rate as this may encourage clients to hire you for a period of days rather than hours. We found such discounts ranging from 4% to 20%. Here's how you would calculate a 5% discount off the $150 per hour rate:

$150 per hour x 8 hours x .95 = $1,140 daily rate

5.7 Getting Paid

5.7.1 Individual Clients

Payment Methods

Note: The following section includes a discussion about a variety of merchant services available to small business owners. Their inclusion does not represent an endorsement by either FabJob or the authors of this guide, but are provided as examples of the kinds of services available. You will need to thoroughly research the available services and decide for yourself which, if any, is best for you and your business.

Online Payments

With individual clients, coaches generally request payment at the beginning of each month for a set number of sessions during the month.

As we've mentioned previously in this guide, many coaches deliver the bulk of the services by telephone or other electronic means and, since they often never meet their clients face to face, most have some means of allowing clients to pay online.

There are a couple of different ways you can get set up for allowing clients to pay online. There are online services offering the ability to make secure payment such as PayPal to allow your clients to pay for their coaching package or other coaching services that you offer. Alternatively, you could also set up your own online "store" using a service provider like Total Merchant Services.

PayPal

If you're not familiar with PayPal, it is an online service that allows individuals and merchants to send and receive money. It allows you to accept both credit card and cash payments and is a simple, secure method of transferring funds. All that you need to use PayPal is an email address and a bank account. PayPal is available in both the U.S. and Canada.

There are no monthly service or other account-related fees, but you will surrender a small percentage of each transaction. If you would like to accept credit card payments through PayPal, there is an additional small charge per transaction (1.9%-2.9%) plus an additional 30 cents per transaction. There is a small cross-border fee of up to one percent applied to foreign payments, but this is waived for funds coming from the U.S. to Canada. To find out more about PayPal's services visit their website at **www.paypal.com** and click on "Business," then on "Merchant Services."

Setting Up an Online Store

One beneficial aspect of setting up an online store is that you can take advantage of the many "one-stop" type services available that allow you to set up your ecommerce website and domain at the same time such as eBay's Merchant eCommerce Solutions (**http://pages.ebay.com/merchantsolutions/**), Yahoo's Merchant Solutions (**http://smallbusiness.yahoo.com/ecommerce/**), and many, many more. There are also companies that can help you to add a store onto your existing website (see section 6.2.3 for more about setting up a website for your business).

As an example, Total Merchant Services lets you choose between different set-up options for your online store. They offer options such as their Total Merchandiser which you use to build your website, register your domain, and set-up a shopping cart allowing you to accept PayPal and credit card payments. The service costs $29.98 monthly or $299.40 per year if paid annually. You can also choose from their other options for businesses that already have their own websites and want to add on an online store. For more information about these services visit **www.merchant-account-4u.com**.

Another popular service is **1shoppingcart.com**. They offer a professional online marketing system that includes a shopping cart, ebook delivery, autoresponders (an email managing system that can automatically respond to people who email you from your website), and other Internet marketing tools. There is no software to download or install; it's all online. Service packages start at $29 per month, although there are additional, low-cost access and transaction fees involved.

To find other companies offering services like these type "merchant solutions for ecommerce" into Google or your favorite search engine. If you would like to learn more about ecommerce, you can download a free copy of "Beginner's Guide to Ecommerce" from Nightcats Multimedia at **www.nightcats.com/ebooks/ecom2.pdf**. This guide offers a general introduction to the subject and includes information about how the technology works, how to avoid fraud, online security, and more. Buyerzone.com also has many helpful articles about ecommerce on their website (**www.buyerzone.com/internet/ecommerce/index.html**).

One thing to be aware of is that some companies offering ecommerce website hosting also charge fairly high set-up fees (anywhere from $500 and up), so be sure to look for those before you sign up. If you're good with computers and the Internet you might want to think about doing your own online store setup. There are companies that offer software that you can use to set up your own store on your own domain. To start, you can check out ZDNet's list of available software by going to **http://updates.zdnet.com** (click on "O" and look for "online store") or type the following direct link into your browser: **http://updates.zdnet. com/tags/online+store.html?t=14&s=0&o=0**.

Pay-at-the-Table

If you plan to do most of your coaching in person in your home or other office, you will need to accept a variety of payment methods. These "pay-at-the-table" payments include check, cash, credit cards and debit cards. If you accept cash and check payments you should purchase a secure cashbox to keep these payments in until you can deposit them at your bank.

Since you probably will already have a business account at a local bank or other financial institution, one of the easiest ways to get set up for credit and debit card processing is through that institution. Check with their business services representative for more information.

Whoever provides your card processing services likely will provide you with the Point of Sale (POS) equipment. This includes a computer, a PIN pad (for swiping client cards and for clients to type in their account information and PIN), an Internet connection, and a printer for print-ing receipts. Many companies offer integrated systems that include the peripherals you will need to add to your computer.

For example, Moneris offers a system for professionals called eSELECT-plus that integrates your computer with their POS system and allows you to accept all major credit cards and Interac debit cards. You can check it out at their website **www.moneris.com**. (Click on "Industry Solutions" then on "Professionals" and near the bottom of the next page choose the link for "eSELECTplus Card Present.") At the time of publication the direct link was **www.moneris.com/index.php?context=/products/possolutions/ecom_eselectplus**.

The major banks and credit card companies all offer POS solutions for small businesses as well, but remember that there are setup charges, monthly maintenance fees and other costs involved. For information about different credit/debit card processing options, check out the links listed below.

- *Visa Merchant Payment Technologies*
  (Click on "Merchants" then "Payment Technologies")
  www.usa.visa.com

- *MasterCard PayPass System*
  www.mastercard.com/us/merchant/solutions_resources/paypass/

5.7.2   Corporate Clients

To keep your business financially healthy when working with corporate clients, you will need to ensure that you are paid in a timely manner. The first step is to ensure you have a contract that states when you will be paid. See section 5.7.3 for a sample contract. This section provides a detailed overview of when and how to invoice your corporate clients.

Corporate clients are usually invoiced at the end of a training program, or they can be invoiced monthly if coaching is ongoing. A challenge with invoicing corporations on a monthly basis is that your bill usually has to pass through their accounts payable department and you can wait awhile before receiving payment.

To make the process go smoothly and prevent any delays in payment, your invoice should be on your letterhead and include the following (see the Sample Invoice included later in this section):

- The client name and contact information

- The date of the invoice

- A purchase order number (if the client gave you one)

- Services you provided

- Any expenses and taxes payable

- The total amount due

- Terms of payment (e.g. "Payable upon receipt" or "Payable within 30 days")

In addition to these considerations there are a number of other things to think about when dealing with corporate clients. How and when to ask for payment are also important. You will find tips for dealing with these invoicing issues in this section.

When to Ask for Payment

Many organizations have a policy of paying invoices after 30 days, although some stretch that to 45 days, 60 days, 90 days or even longer. As a small business owner, you may not be in the position where you can wait a month or longer to be paid after a project ends. You can therefore ask for a deposit and interim payments.

Deposits

It's acceptable to ask the client for a deposit (advance payment) to be paid before you begin working. The deposit helps you cover your overhead costs until subsequent payments come in. For a short-term project you might require a deposit of 50% and payment upon completion of the assignment.

For long-term projects, for example if you have a year long contract where the fee is on a monthly retainer basis, you could ask to be paid up front for either the first month alone, or both the first and last month. For example, if the monthly retainer is $2,500, you could ask for a deposit of either $2,500 or $5,000 before beginning work.

Interim Payments

Even if you collect a deposit, you don't have to wait until the end of the project to collect the rest of your fee. The general rule for invoicing frequency is to do it often. Clients prefer to pay out small amounts at several intervals rather than one large, lump sum; it's easier on their accounting books and will provide you with a steady cash flow throughout the engagement.

You could invoice the client at the end of each phase of a consulting project, upon completion of specific project milestones, or based on elapsed time. For example, if you're actively engaged in a year-long project, invoicing on a bi-weekly or monthly basis is an appropriate frequency for both parties.

On the other hand, if the engagement is only for a few weeks or a month, it's appropriate to submit the invoice for the balance of your fee promptly upon completion of the project. If you're ever in doubt about the frequency of invoicing, simply address the issue with the client; they will appreciate knowing what to expect, and you will be fully aware of how to approach the process and can adjust your accounting accordingly, based on cash owed.

How to Invoice

There are two basic types of invoices used by corporate coaches, itemized and non-itemized. An itemized invoice contains a breakdown of what is being charged for, and a non-itemized invoice simply presents a bill for the agreed services that have been performed. In most cases it is better to present an itemized invoice, but in cases when there is an agreed single fee for a short-term engagement, including expenses, a non-itemized invoice is acceptable. The items that should be included in an invoice are listed below, followed by a sample invoice. Remember to keep both a hard copy and an electronic copy of each invoice for your records.

Your Business Name

Make sure the client has no doubt about whom the invoice is from. For a professional appearance, print the invoice on letterhead.

Invoice Number

Invoice numbers are like check numbers, they allow you to keep track of what invoices have been issued and what is still outstanding (see the Sample Invoice Tracking document included later in this section).

There are several different numbering systems that can be used. You can use several-digit numbers or incorporate letters to distinguish the type of project or the city, state or province in which the project took place. Many coaches prefer to use a numbering system that incorporates several digits in anticipation of growth of the business, and your client gets the impression that you have many clients and more business with an invoice number that reads 100-000-001, rather than just 001. Your tracking number can appear anywhere you like on the invoice.

Client Name and Contact Information

Be sure that your invoice identifies the company (full legal business name) you did the consulting work for and includes the name of your contact at the company. For your reference, include the company address and other contact information.

Invoice Date

This date will be the date that the invoice is submitted. The project dates will appear in the body of the invoice.

Purchase Order Number

Some organizations use purchase order (PO) numbers to manage expenses. If a client uses purchase orders, they will either give you a paper copy or your contact person at the company will tell you the purchase order number. Be sure to make reference to the PO number on your invoice.

Reason for Invoice

This is a brief summary of the services provided to the client. It usually has the prefix "Re:" and allows busy people to glance at the invoice and know what the invoice is for. For example: "Re: Coaching services for training sales division." Including only "Re: Coaching Services" may suffice, but a large company may be employing more than one coaching consultant at a time, so use your judgment.

Services Provided

Under this heading you will be more specific about what services you provided to the client. If the payment structure was per engagement plus expenses, then this section should reiterate, or point to, what was agreed upon as the scope of services to be provided, as laid out in the letter of engagement.

For example:

> Coaching services, as per
> letter of engagement $4,000.00

If, however, you are charging by the hour, the services section of the invoice will have to be more specific.

For example:

> Initial meeting – 2 hours @ $100/hr....................... $200.00
>
> Team meeting – 3 hours @ $100/hr........................ $300.00
>
> Preparation of employee questionnaire –
> 5.5 hours @ $100/hr $550.00

Expenses

If expenses have not been built into your fee and will be paid individually, they should be itemized much like Services as shown below. Whenever possible, attach receipts for expenses to your invoice.

> Meeting with Client,
> round trip 100 miles @ $0.30/mile $30.00
>
> Airport Parking $15.00
>
> Hotel and meals for conference $380.00

Total Amount Payable

Despite the fact that any good business person will double-check the numbers, do not make the client do the calculation, but provide a visible and accurate grand total. Be sure to denote if payment is to be made in U.S. or Canadian dollars.

Terms of Payment

An invoice should state when payment is due, for example: "Payment due upon receipt" or "Payable within 30 days." Closely related to the above is the inclusion of a single line, either included with payment date or by itself, that stipulates additional charges are applicable if payment is not received by a certain date.

For example: "2% interest per month on overdue accounts"

Where to Send Payment

Even if the invoice is printed on your letterhead, it's a good idea to place a "Payable to:" line on your invoice that includes your business name and address.

Business or Tax Information

An important item to remember to include on an invoice is any business or tax number. In the U.S., if you're a registered business you'll be provided a Federal ID number. In Canada, businesses are required to charge the Good and Services Tax (GST). So be sure to include this number, as you'll be required to charge your clients this tax. To get this number, contact your local government tax office. See section 5.3.3 for more about taxes.

Designing an Invoice

There are several ways to create an invoice. It can be done using a template in any of the numerous software packages designated for the home office, or it can be made from scratch using Microsoft Word or Excel. Use what you're comfortable with, but ensure it is as clear and concise as possible.

On the next few pages, you will find two sample invoices for coaching services to corporate clients. The first is an invoice for a training program without any additional expenses being charged, and the second one includes expenses being charged separately along with the coaching services.

Sample Invoice #1

(On Coach's Letterhead)

Invoice #: 100-000-001   **Date:** October 23, 2009

To: Jane Jones
    Human Resources Department
    ABC Company, Inc.
    123 Main Street
    Sunnyday, CA 90211

Re: ABC Company, Inc. Leadership Training Program

SERVICE PERFORMED	FEE
Design of Seminar	$1,500.00
October 21, 2008 Workshop Delivery	$3,000.00
October 22, 2008 Workshop Delivery	$3,000.00
Subtotal	*$7,500.00*
7% tax (include your own tax rate here) (Federal Tax #: 54321)	$525.00
TOTAL – PLEASE PAY THIS AMOUNT	$8,025.00

Terms:

Payable within 30 days. 1.5% per month charged on all over-due accounts.

Make check payable to:

I. M. de Coach
[Your company name]
[Full business address]
[phone number]

Thank you for your business.

Sample Invoice #2

(On Coach's Letterhead)

Invoice #: 100-000-002   **Date:** November 13, 2009

Client: XYZ Corp.   **Federal Tax #:** 54321
452 Long Rd.
Portland, OR
555-123-4567

Attention: Accounts Receivable Department

Re: Coaching Services as per the [date] letter of engagement. To deliver leadership training program.

SERVICES AND EXPENSES

SERVICE PERFORMED	PRICE
Coaching Fee (as per agreement)	$4,000.00
Meeting With Client (round trip 100 miles @ $0.30/mile)	$30.00
Airport Parking	$15.00
Hotel and Meals for Conference	$380.00
Less Deposit (paid October 31, 2008)	*($2,000.00)*
BALANCE DUE	$2,425.00

Terms:

Payment is due within 30 days. Interest of 2% per month is charged for overdue accounts.

Please make check payable to:

I. M. de Coach
XYZ Business Coaching Services
Somewhere, Somestate

Thank you for your business.

Be sure to keep accurate track of all invoices, receipts, telephone bills (related to coaching), and other business paperwork. You don't have to print hard copies of everything, but be certain that the information is easily accessible if you need to look up or produce something. This will save you a lot of hassles during tax season.

Submitting an Invoice and Following Up

There are a variety of ways to submit an invoice to a client. You can deliver it by email, fax, mail, or courier, or present it in person. The key is to determine what works best for you and your client.

It is also important to establish where to send the invoice itself. For example, a large company may require the billing or accounting department to receive all invoices, whereas the owner of a smaller company may take a hands-on approach and oversee all of the expenses. Check with your client contact to find out where to send it.

If a client doesn't pay within the time requested on the invoice, then send another invoice, noting that payment is expected within a shorter time, perhaps five or ten days. This gives your client a reminder to quickly make the overdue payment.

If a bill is not paid within 60 days, you will need to contact the client again. You can do this by phoning or writing. If you send a letter, you can make arrangements with the courier or post office to get confirmation that your client actually received it. If you're dealing with a corporate client that is slow to pay, you may have to make more than one phone call. If you work with that client again, you may want to consider requiring a larger deposit or interim payments before proceeding with work.

An invoice tracking document may help you to keep track of invoice. Use this to track clients who have/haven't been billed, who has paid, who has made partial payment, and so on. See the Sample Invoice Tracking form on the next page. And see section 5.4 to learn about computer software that can help you with your billing and invoicing.

> TIP: To ensure you are paid by corporate clients make sure you have a contract in place. See the following section for information about client contracts.

Sample Invoice Tracking Form

Invoice #	Client/Address/ Phone	Date Billed	Sent to…	Amount	Date Payment Received
100-000-001	ABC Inc. 123 Main St. Sunnyday, CA 555-555-5555	Oct. 22, 2009	Jane Jones	$8,025.00	Nov. 30, 2009
100-000-002	XYZ Corp. 452 Long Rd. Portland, OR 555-123-4567	Nov. 13, 2009	Accounts Receivable Dept.	$2,425.00	Not yet received
100-000-003	Acme Ltd. 1107 4th St. Santa Fe, NM 555-111-1212	Nov. 26, 2009	Sam Smith	$3,675.00	Dec. 11, 2009

5.7.3   Client Contracts

With any business relationship, you must establish what services are to be provided, what the charges will be, and set boundaries stating what is and is not covered. This is for your protection as well as the client's. With that in mind, avoid a contract that is too wordy or confusing. You can cover the major points clearly and concisely.

Different coaches set different time lengths for working with clients. Some arrangements are six months, others a year, others ongoing. An initial time frame of three months is a good starting point for coaching an individual, and the contract can always be renewed if the coaching is going well.

David M. Noer, president of Noer Consulting, who is an executive coach, author, and professor of business administration at Elon University, advocates setting a time frame for the coaching relationship. The idea, he says, is basically for the coach to withdraw and the client to become self-reliant.

The contract should state the fees for services rendered, as well as when payment is expected. Since coaching is usually on a pay-as-you-go basis, fees are paid at the beginning of the month. Occasionally a client will have to cancel or postpone a session. Protocol generally requires 24 hours notice, but understand that emergencies occur and that this is not always possible.

Privacy is a major issue. State that all conversations will be held in the strictest confidence. The only exception to this rule is if the client indicates that he or she has committed or intends to commit a crime. This may seem unnecessary to include, but some life coaches report that clients have admitted illegal activity to them.

Consider guaranteeing your clients a refund if they are not satisfied or wish to cancel for any reason before the contract expires. This is good business practice, and can save you a lot of future hassles.

On the next few pages you will find a Sample Contract between a life coach and an individual client. You may reproduce it in whole or part, amending it as you wish, but be sure to have an attorney review it before you use it in your own practice.

Sample Contract with an Individual

The following represents the Contract between [coach's name], hereinafter "the Life Coach" and [client's name], hereinafter "the Client". The Services contracted shall be that of life coaching, as set out below (The Services).

Contract Period

The Contract shall be in force for a period of ___ months, beginning the ___ day of _____, 20__ , and ending the ___ day of _____, 20__ .

The Services

The Life Coach shall assist the Client in clarifying his/her personal or career goals, and in working out a plan of action, as determined by the Client, to help achieve such goals. The Coach will accomplish this by carefully listening to the Client's concerns, providing open, honest feedback, and asking questions intended to elicit responses from the Client that will lead him/her to decide what steps to take to achieve the desired results.

The Services will be delivered by telephone [or other method you and your client agree on], for a period of ___ minutes once each week, at a mutually-agreed time. The schedule may be modified, if necessary, and if both Parties agree to such modification. Either the Client or the Life Coach may terminate the Services at any time with 48 hours notice of termination, with no further obligation, and the Client shall receive a full refund of all fees paid for the Services not yet delivered. At the end of the Contract Period, the Contract may be renewed if both Parties are agreed.

Payment for Services

Payment for the Services shall be $_____, payable in monthly installments of $_____, each installment to be paid in full on the first day of each month. Payment may be made using cash, money order, check, or credit card (Visa/MasterCard). The Client shall be billed for any and all missed sessions if at least 24 hours notice is not given for cancellation of the session(s).

Confidentiality and Limit of Liability

Any information divulged to the Life Coach by the Client shall remain completely confidential, except in the event of the Life Coach's knowledge of any illegal activity by the Client, or admission by the Client of the intent to commit an illegal act. The Client acknowledges the obligation of the Life Coach to cooperate fully with law enforcement and other authorities as required by law.

The Client acknowledges that the Life Coach is not in the business of providing advice, medical, legal or otherwise, and the Client should retain the services of a qualified professional in any particular area where such qualified advice is required. Furthermore, the Life Coach does not provide therapy or mental health counseling. Clients with psychological or other medical problems should consult a qualified health care professional. Any action taken in regard to therapy, medical advice, or mental health counseling, or any other activity not directly related to the Services provided to the Client by the Life Coach will be at the sole discretion of and will remain the sole responsibility of the Client, and the Life Coach will not be held accountable and shall remain blameless for any consequences arising as a result of any professional therapy, counseling or any other activity not directly related to the Services provided by the Life Coach.

Entire Agreement

This Contract constitutes the entire agreement between the Client and the Life Coach and the Life Coach shall not be held liable and shall remain blameless for any adverse or other consequences, including but not limited to financial, personal, employment or other losses, arising out of decisions or actions the Client may make as a result of the Services provided by the Life Coach.

_____   _____
Life Coach   Date

_____   _____
Client   Date

Corporate Contracts

If you are doing individual coaching for a corporation, you can adapt the Sample Contract as appropriate. Make sure the contract is between your company and the client company and not the individual employee who is your company contact. Otherwise, if some dispute arises in future the company cannot be held liable for their part of the contract and you may not get paid.

If a company is hiring you for a training program, your contract will need to incorporate additional details about the program. Some organizations will have their legal department create a contract, and you can review it with your lawyer to ensure it covers what you want.

If the company does not provide you with a contract, you will have to provide the contract yourself with the help of your lawyer. While you may feel you can trust the company to pay you, prepare a contract anyway. Circumstances can change. The person who hired you may leave the company. Their replacement may decide to cancel your program, or want to pay a lower fee. A contract can help protect you in such circumstances. Without a contract, you may not get paid.

One of the most important elements of a training contract is a clause specifying when you will be paid. Another important element is a cancellation clause, or a statement that explains what will happen if a training program is cancelled.

For example, some trainers have a clause which says if the client cancels the program, for any reason, less than a certain number of days before the event (e.g. 30, 60, or 90 days), the client forfeits the deposit.

If the program could possibly be postponed, you can also include a postponement charge. However, if the change does not inconvenience you, it's good for client relations to be flexible.

On the next page is a Sample Training Contract for a fictional coach-trainer (Chris Coach), adapted from the *FabJob Guide to Become a Motivational Speaker*, to give you some ideas for your own contracts. Make sure you review your own contract with a lawyer before using it.

Sample Training Contract

(On Your Letterhead)

Client

Jane Jones
Human Resources Department
ABC Company, Inc.
123 Main Street
Sunnyday, CA

Purpose

To deliver a Team Leader Training program for XYZ Corporation.

Details

The training sessions will be presented at the XYZ Center in Sunnyday, CA. The training will consist of seven sessions consisting of three hours each, scheduled to take place from 4:30 p.m. to 7:30 p.m. The session topics and dates are as follows:

Team Leadership and Supervisory Basics	April 27, 2009
Fundamentals of Effective Communications	May 4, 2009
Advanced Interpersonal Communications Skills	May 11, 2009
Delegation and Empowerment	May 18, 2009
Teambuilding	May 25, 2009
Conflict Resolution	May 18, 2009
Motivation and Performance Management	May 25, 2009

The trainer will be Chris Coach. In the event the chosen trainer is unavailable for a particular session, CBA Coaching Services will send a suitable and equally qualified trainer.

Client Responsibilities

- facility arrangements

- A/V equipment

Trainer Responsibilities

- printed materials for each participant
- delivery of training

Fees

Per session fee (based on the client's stated number of a minimum of 12 participants): $1,200.00 plus tax, payable within ten days after each session.

Actual billing may vary should the number of attendees exceed those quoted above. The minimum amount of per session fees as stated above is binding, even in the event that fewer than 12 participants actually attend.

If, prior to the commencement of the program, dates are postponed or sessions cancelled, CBA Coaching Services shall be paid the appropriate postponement/cancellation charge as noted below. (This does not apply to rescheduling of the order of topics or session start/end times, which may be changed on request.)

Days Prior to Scheduled Session	Postponement	Cancellation
0–90	10%	25%
11–29	25%	50%
10 or fewer	50%	75%

Signature and Date

Signed by:

_____   Date: _____

Jane Jones,
Vice President of Human Resources
ABC Company, Inc.

Signed by:

_____   Date: _____

Chris Coach,
President
CBA Coaching Services Ltd.

Letter of Engagement

A letter of engagement can be used as a contract for small coaching engagements or as a means of outlining the services to be provided to clients and used along with a regular signed contract (the contract would then refer to the letter of engagement for services to be provided). Like a regular contract, the letter of engagement should include all the client information (company name, contact name, address, phone number) as well as your own.

Use the letter of engagement to fully itemize all the services to be performed by you and agreed to by the client. Be sure to get both your signature and the client's or client representative's signatures to validate the agreement. When invoicing your client after services have been performed, instead of itemizing everything on the contract, you can simply refer to this letter of engagement.

5.8   Employing Others

Working with Other Coaches

As in many professions, there is a standard of professional courtesy within coaching. This means that in the coaching industry, coaches refer clients to other coaches with different specialties or in the same specialty when they are too busy to take on new clients, just as other professionals do in their industries.

For example, you may meet someone who wants to work with a coach on relationship issues, but you typically coach people in starting new businesses. Because of your diligent networking, you know two or three other coaches you think might be good matches. So you contact the first coach on your list, and she gladly agrees to talk with the client. Assuming that the two of them hit it off, there is generally no payment to you from the other coach; you merely expect that if she meets someone who needs a business coach, she will in turn contact you.

Another example of this professional courtesy is when coaches have more clients than they can effectively handle at one time and contract with other coaches. Suppose that you coach entrepreneurs, and you have developed certain proprietary procedures and coaching methods which you have found to be very effective with new business owners.

Sample Engagement Letter

(On Your Letterhead)

[Insert name of Client]

[Insert address of Client]

[Insert date]

Attention: *[Insert name of client]*

As promised, I have set out below a description of the services that [insert your company name] will provide to you.

I will provide the following services:

[Insert full and accurate description of the services, such as consultations with the client, reviewing documents, etc.]

My fee for the services performed will be as follows:

[Insert rates, when payment is due, etc.]

If you agree that the foregoing fairly sets out your understanding of our agreement, please sign a copy of this letter in the space indicated below, and return it to me at *[insert your address, fax number or e-mail address]*.

Yours sincerely,
[Insert your name]

Agreed and Accepted:

_____

[Insert name of client]

_____

Date

Because your current load of 17 clients leaves you little time to take on additional business, you have contracted with a couple of "junior" coaches who in turn use your coaching model. These coaches handle any "overflow" clients. The client pays you whatever fee you normally charge–say $500 per month–and you give each contractor coach 75 percent, which works out to $375.

Administrative Assistance

Coaches who have large practices or who maintain separate offices sometimes hire permanent employees to assist with clerical or administrative functions. You should be aware that there are many legal and tax issues involved with hiring employees, and you may be creating a lot more work for yourself if you put people on your payroll.

Also, when you are starting any new business you may find yourself obsessed with little details. If you are spending an excessive amount of time with non-coaching aspects of your business, contracting these mundane duties will make your life a lot simpler. You need to strike a balance between doing certain things yourself and hiring others to perform the less coaching-oriented tasks. There are many good temp agencies who can supply you with qualified workers to assist you with everything from accounting to cleaning to word processing.

Coaches are increasingly turning to virtual assistants (VA's) as another alternative to putting employees on their payroll. VA's are independent contractors who offer their administrative or technical services to busy professionals who do not want the hassle of dealing with full time employees. VA's may be secretaries, accountants, graphic artists, website designers, photographers or freelance writers, among a host of other specializations. The International Virtual Assistants Association (**www. ivaa.org**) has a database of hundreds of qualified VA's that you can search by keyword, location or area of expertise.

You will need to understand payroll taxes if you plan to hire employees, and each new employee needs to fill out paperwork when they are hired. In the U.S. this will be the W-4 and I-9 forms. In Canada, employees complete both a T-4 and a Canada Pension form.

Check with your state or provincial labor office to make sure you are clear about all the forms employees must fill out to work for you. The sites below have additional information on the legalities of payroll taxes and include information on where to get blank copies of the forms your employees will need to fill out.

IRS Publication 15, Circular E, Employer's Tax Guide, provides a thorough overview of employers' tax and fiscal responsibilities. You can download Publication 15 at **www.irs.gov/pub/irs-pdf/p15.pdf**.

Before you hire anyone, check with your local department of labor to find out all the rules and regulations required as an employer. Other state and federal rules and regulations may apply to you, including: health and safety regulations, Workers' Compensation, minimum wage and unemployment insurance. You can find excellent advice about hiring employees at the Small Business Administration website at **www.sba.gov/smallbusinessplanner/manage/manageemployees/**.

Canadian employers must also register with the government and comply with federal and provincial laws. For information on becoming an employer in Canada, visit the Canada Business website at **www.canadabusiness.ca/osbw** (under "Session 5" choose "Becoming an Employer").

Employees and Contractors

Whenever you hire someone, you will either sign them on as employees or as contractors. What's the difference?

- Employees may be trained by you. Contractors received training elsewhere.

- Employees work only for you. Contractors may have their own customers and may work for other coaches.

- Employees are paid on a regular basis. Contractors are paid per project.

- Employees work for a certain amount of hours. Contracted workers set their own hours, as long as they get the job done.

- Employees can be fired or quit. Contractors can't be fired in the usual way while they are working under contract. You may decide to have them stop working on a project, but you will be obliged to pay them according to your contractual agreement unless you are able to renegotiate the contract or successfully sue them if you are unhappy with their work. Of course that would only be in extreme cases; it is best to avoid lawsuits altogether.

Tips for Working with Contractors

You are ultimately responsible for how well strategic partners and other contractors do their jobs, so you will need to find people you can depend on to do the job right, by the agreed upon deadline, for the agreed price.

To help you choose contractors, make appointments to meet either by phone or in person. Ask what services they provide, their rates, and their availability. You need to know that you can depend on the contractor, and that they will be willing to work overtime if necessary to keep their agreements with you. (Unfortunately, some busy contractors consider deadlines to be "suggestions" rather than requirements.)

As the coach hired by the client it will be your job to supervise them and ensure they get the job done. Remember your name (not the contractor's) is on the line if you bring in a contractor and they don't come through in a timely or professional manner or within cost. So look for someone reliable, and have at least one back-up for each job.

Wherever possible, get agreements (e.g. for costs, delivery dates, services to be provided) in writing. Also check if the contractor holds liability insurance, which covers both them and you if the client's property is damaged while you're working with a corporate client, or the work is not satisfactory.

Before working with a contractor, check their references. It is also advisable to contact the Better Business Bureau to find out if any complaints have been lodged against them or their company. To locate them anywhere in the U.S. or Canada visit **http://lookup.bbb.org**.

6. Getting Clients

There are rare cases in which people jump into coaching full time, but the majority gradually incorporate coaching into their present occupations, or reduce the hours at their "regular" jobs while increasing the hours that they coach per week. Usually their current job exposes them to a lot of potential clients, and they use this as a springboard for starting and growing their coaching practice. Thomas Leonard began by coaching clients he had obtained working as a financial planner.

Those whose jobs do not afford them the liberty to set their own hours generally continue to work full time while coaching one or two clients during the evenings or on weekends until they have established enough contacts to transition to full time coaching.

> **TIP:** Between three to five clients a month is generally considered part time, whereas a full client load is between 15 and 20.

6.1 Choose Your Target Market

Before you start trying to sell your services to prospective clients, you should decide which types of clients you want to coach. This is your target market.

It's not unusual for a new coach to say something like "I want to work for anyone who'll pay me!" Avoid this kind of thinking. It is costly and time-consuming to try to market your business to "everyone" and the truth is that some people will be more interested than others in the services you have to offer. In fact, people are more likely to hire you if they see you as an "expert" who specializes in what they need.

When you are just starting out, of course you might take whatever business comes your way. However, you can still focus your marketing efforts on the target markets you most want to work with. Once you start getting more business, you may be able to give up work you find less rewarding and spend your time on work you find more rewarding.

The Coach Training Alliance website (**www.coachtrainingalliance.com**) states that "The most successful life coaches choose not only a narrow coaching focus, but also a narrow target market. The niche and the market will organically develop from the coach's skills, interests and life experiences."

Once you have decided on a specialty, you should start thinking about the kinds of services you will offer to clients based on your specific area of expertise. You will need to decide if you will offer only individual sessions (which is what most coaches initially do), or if you will also offer workshops, laser coaching and other services. This will be based mainly on your experience and the skills you are bringing into your coaching practice. Knowing in advance what you will offer and how you will offer it will help you to focus as you start marketing your services.

There are a number of considerations when thinking about targeting individual clients. Maybe you are a man who relates better to other men, or a woman who relates better to other women. If you are retired, you may feel an affinity towards people approaching that milestone in their lives. Start with your specializations (see section 2.1) to determine what kinds of people would need those particular coaching services.

Here are some additional questions to consider as you begin to focus on your target market:

- Is there a need for the services you provide or is the market already well served by others offering similar services?

- Is your target market easily identifiable?

- Can your target market afford the services you're offering them? In other words, if you want to earn a lot of money, you need to coach clients who can afford to pay you a lot of money. For example, if you want to do corporate coaching, you will likely find large and mid-sized corporations are more likely than small businesses to hire you, at the fees you want to earn.

- Are your competitors successful? In other words, if there are already a number of companies offering the same services you're planning to offer, and if they've been in business for some time, chances are the market for those services is strong.

- Does your expertise match the kind of clients you're targeting? It's fine to target executives as a career coach, for example, but if you've never worked in a corporate setting or have little understanding of the corporate environment, you may be at a disadvantage before you even start.

- Do your services benefit your target market? In other words, put yourself in the client's place and ask "what's in it for me?

Do Your Research

To answer these questions, you'll need to do some research. If you're a work/life balance coach or a weight loss coach targeting women, for example, join a few women's groups. At the meetings, talk to the women there and ask them how their needs could be met by your services. As a carbon coach, you could join some environmental groups and do similar research.

Another way to do some free research is to check polls online from companies like Gallup or Ipsos Reid. Both of these companies have literally thousands of polls that you can read. For example, one recent poll (July, 2007), found that 61% of the people polled were very concerned about global warming and more than 40% were willing to pay more for environmentally friendly products. Another poll found that 71% of adults wished they had gotten more professional career planning advice, suggesting plenty of opportunity for career coaches. And yet another poll conducted recently was featured on all the major news media indicating that fewer women in the U.S. are happy working outside the home. With this kind of information you can easily see that a number of opportunities present themselves for offering services as a life coach.

You can read more polls at **www.ipsos-na.com**. The site also has a search function that you can type keywords into. The Gallup website is at **www.gallup.com/poll/Topics.aspx**. The online encyclopedia Wikipedia has a list of polling companies and links to their websites at **http://en.wikipedia.org/wiki/Opinion_poll**.

Targeting Corporations

Many coaches start out coaching individuals and then make the switch to coaching for corporations. Some of the coaches we interviewed said that they had started out coaching for individuals but found that they couldn't pay the bills this way. Others found that their services were so much in demand they needed to expand their coaching practices beyond individual coaching. Here is what two of them told us:

"I started coaching individuals but due to demand I expanded my practice to include corporations and groups. I love working with women, especially those juggling full-time careers and families, since I have lived it myself. I am an advocate of busy, caring women juggling too much on their plate who always put themselves last. Many of my individual clients, women's groups, and audiences are these women. I do enjoy working with small business owners and entrepreneurs as well, since it is challenging and very rewarding to see their businesses grow and my clients achieve success. Many coaches find that there is more revenue in working with corporations and have to work in that arena due to financial reasons."

— KC Christensen-Lang, Happiness Is...

"I initially focused on private clients – individuals who hired me directly. However, after 2 years in business for myself I switched my strategy and began primarily working with managers in corporations. This was primarily based on the unpredictable nature of private clients – it was difficult to maintain a revenue stream in terms of both volume of work and rate per hour.

I found that developing a few relationships with different companies provided a steady stream of clients as my reputation was established internal to the organization. Also, I was able to work with more senior managers which allowed me to increase my rates."

— Kevin Nourse, Executive Coach, Leap Advocates

Large companies often hire coaches after first posting Requests for Proposals (explored in detail in section 6.4.1) in newspapers or online ads, as well as on their own websites. This doesn't mean, however, that you can't offer an unsolicited proposal to a large corporation. Study their core business and use this information to generate ideas for offering your services outside the company's core operations.

You can find contact information for corporations through services such as Hoovers (**www.hoovers.com**), D&B (**www.zapdata.com**), and Lead411 (**www.lead411.com**). If you decide to subscribe to Lead411, join Women in Consulting (**www.womeninconsulting.org**) first, so you get a subscription for $200, a savings of 90% off the regular price.

If you prefer to create your own contact lists, you can find a list of large corporations in directories at your local public library or online at the Fortune website at **http://money.cnn.com/magazines/fortune/fortune500** or Report on Business's Top 1,000 list of Canadian companies at **http://v1.theglobeandmail.com/top1000**.

6.2   Promotional Tools

The promotional tools that can help market your business to your target market begin with your business card, but should also include a brochure, information package, and website.

6.2.1   Printed Materials

Business Cards

Do not underestimate the importance of a good business card. Simply listing your name, telephone number and "life coach" is not enough. Your card should say enough about you to give people an idea of what you can do for them. Include your specializations, your website so they can get more information, and consider a call to action, such as: "Call today for a free half hour consultation."

To get ideas for what to include on your own card, take a look at the business cards you have collected from other people. If you don't have business cards from other life coaches, take at look at Yellow Pages ads for coaches to see what kind of information they put into a small space.

Consider using heavy textured papers, raised printing, and a professional design. Check around for prices at print shops or office supply stores. If your start-up finances are limited, you might want to consider getting free business cards from VistaPrint.com. All you pay for is shipping.

They offer color business cards on heavy paper stock in a matte finish, available with a number of different designs. In return for the free cards they print their logo and "Business Cards are free at VistaPrint.com" on the back of the card near the bottom so you still have room to write something on the back if you want to. If you don't want anything printed on the back, you can get 250 cards for only $19.99 plus shipping.

Pass your business cards out whenever you can; you never know who will read it. Give them to your friends, your relatives, people you meet at social functions, your mechanic, your dentist, your mail carrier. They may pass it on to someone else if they don't need your services themselves. Mention that you are a life coach when handing out your card, so that people will look at it later and make the connection. When you mail bills or correspondence, stick a business card in the envelope.

Make sure that you carry plenty of business cards in your wallet or purse at all times. It can be embarrassing to spend time telling someone about your business, then when he or she asks for a card, you don't have one. Also, you should keep your cards in a business card holder that protects them from becoming damaged. Passing out crumpled or dog-eared business cards just doesn't look professional.

Brochures

Once you start marketing your services, you will probably find opportunities to give out a brochure — for example, when you give a presentation at a networking meeting (see section 6.3.1), participate in a trade show, or when people seem particularly interested in your services.

Your brochure will contain your company name and contact information, including your web address. It can also include information such as:

- Your photograph

- Your specialization(s)

- A list of the benefits of hiring a life coach.

- A list of the services you perform, such as individual coaching or corporate training programs

- Some comments from satisfied clients or, if those are not available yet, some comments from respected people on your integrity, abilities and so on.

- Your qualifications

Your brochure can be a bi-fold or tri-fold, in black and white or color. If you can afford it, have a commercial printer print them. They often offer design services, too, either for free or for a modest cost. Or you can design your brochure yourself on your computer using brochure paper from a stationery store such as Staples, OfficeMax or Office Depot and a computer program like Microsoft's Publisher. You can simply print and fold a few at a time, at first. They will not look as polished as commercially printed brochures, but they can serve to get your business off the ground.

When you decide you do need professionally printed brochures, check the Yellow Pages under "Printers" or use quick-printer services such as Office or Minuteman Press or even the printing services of your local office supply store. Your printed materials can also be easily designed, paid for and delivered without leaving the house. Here are links to some companies that provide online printing services for small businesses:

- *FedEx Office*
  www.fedex.com/us/office/

- *Acecomp Plus – Printing Solutions*
  www.acecomp.com/printing.asp

- *The Paper Mill Store*
  www.thepapermillstore.com

- *VistaPrint*
  www.vistaprint.com

Information Packages

Leadership coach and psychologist K. Denise Bane suggests preparing informational packages when approaching organizations. This works whether you are planning a corporate seminar or an inspirational speech in front of a community group.

Make up folders containing:

- Your business card

- Your resume

- Cover letter

- Your bio

- Articles that you have written (published or not)

- References and testimonial letters

- A reading list or reading materials explaining the basics of coaching (make sure you have permission to copy any materials you did not write yourself)

Keep a dozen or so of these folders by your desk. This will help you to be ready at a moment's notice if the phone rings and one of your contacts asks you if you can come for an interview the following morning, or asks you to mail out an information package for them to look at and learn more about you.

As well as including this core material, you can tailor your package according to the needs of the particular organization. If you can, find out from your contact person any relevant details about the interview—who is going to be there, what he or she is expecting, what the organization's needs are, etc.

Many successful professionals, especially those who do speaking engagements, have folders printed in color with their name and photograph. If you are interested in doing the same, you can contact local printers for information and price quotes. If you shop around you may be able to get personalized folders for as little as one dollar each for several hundred folders (although the price will depend on how many you order, how many colors you want, etc.). One company that specializes in printing folders is Presentation Folder Inc. (**www.presentation folder.com**).

If you are working with a limited budget, an inexpensive alternative is to buy some glossy two-color folders from a local stationer. For example, Staples offers a package of "twin-pocket laminated portfolios" for under $10. You could then personalize it by gluing your business card on the cover.

6.2.2 Resume and Cover Letter

Your Resume

Having a resume is standard practice in just about any business. For working exclusively with individual clients you may not see as much need for one, but if you are going to market yourself to corporations or other organizations, you should have one and update it at least twice a year. Some life coaches may argue, "A resume is for people who are looking for a job. I have a job: I'm a life coach, therefore I don't need a resume."

But a good resume should be used as a follow-up to a business card: one gets your foot in the door, the other gets you across the threshold. Your resume serves as a summary of your relevant life and work experience. You do not need to list every job that you held since high school (cashier, gas station attendant, etc.), only those that apply to life coaching. You can see what other life coaches think is relevant by reading the biographies they publish at their websites.

List short, bulleted points, such as those shown in the Sample Resumes that follow. When you are asked to elaborate on the above, you can supply that information. It should go without saying that keeping track of names, dates and places is important.

Put your name and address in the upper right corner of your resume. The theory behind this is that prospects will notice your resume first when they are thumbing through a pile of papers on their desk, whereas they might not if you center this information. Use bold text for your name, but keep the same-sized font (such as 11-point Arial or 12-point Times New Roman).

Summarize your objective a couple of lines underneath your name and address. Listing "Life Coaching" is too vague. Include a sentence or two about your specialty, if you have one, or a brief description of how you intend to help clients achieve more success in their business, personal or romantic relationships, for example.

List your skills and abilities, emphasizing those that relate to life coaching. Maybe you enjoy working with people, or relate particularly well to children. Perhaps you have exceptional sales abilities, are a speed reader, or understand sign language. Maybe you hold a stock broker's license, or some other kind of professional certification.

When evaluating potential clients, one of the first steps that many coaches take is to have the clients list those achievements that make them proudest. Do the same with yourself when writing your resume. Following your objective, include the heading "Accomplishments" or "Significant Achievements." List a half a dozen or so.

Summarize your relevant experience. You need not limit this to work-related experience. If you were the head of your company's human resources department for three years, by all means include that, but also mention that you coached Little League or organized charity fundraisers, or served as volunteer good will ambassador for your township. This should be a chronological list, starting with the most recent. Again, try to pick out those jobs and activities that have some relevance to life coaching.

Following, you will find two sample resumes for coaches with different specializations and levels of experience. The samples also show different resume formats.

Sample Resume #1

ASHLEY ANNE CARVER
123 Inspiration Drive
Jefferson City, MO 63000
573-123-4567
AAC@anyisp.com
www.ashleyannelifecoach.com

OBJECTIVE:

By offering support, assistance and encouragement, to help clients achieve success in whatever area/s they indicate, personal or professional. I accomplish this by listening, asking questions, and making observations designed to stimulate clients' thought processes and problem-solving capabilities.

SKILLS:

- Fluent in Spanish

- Excellent verbal communications skills

- Certified aerobics instructor

- Community volunteer work

SELECTED ACCOMPLISHMENTS:

- Received Employee of the Year Award at Helping Hands, Inc. (October 2005; Jefferson City, MO)

- Published 100-page book, "Your Perfect Life," Very Big Publishers, Inc. (December 2004; Littleton, CO)

- Organized youth visitation program — Green Gardens Retirement Home. (January 2004; Jefferson City, MO)

- Top fund-raiser during local Little League's annual telemarketing drive. (October 2003; Jefferson City, MO)

- Treasurer for Sarah Lawrence Chapter of Zeta Pi Phi Sorority. (September 1997–May 1998; Jefferson City, MO)

PROFESSIONAL EXPERIENCE:

LIFE COACHING
January 2006 to present   *Jefferson City, MO*

As a life coach, I use my interpersonal and communication skills to help people achieve personal and professional success.

HELPING HANDS, INC.
March 2004 — December 2005   *Jefferson City, MO*

As a caseworker, I assisted handicapped and developmentally-disabled individuals to find employment. This entailed helping them write resumes, fill out applications and practice interviewing techniques.

PRODIGIOUS PUBLISHING COMPANY
October 1999 — January 2004   *Jefferson City, MO*

While editorial assistant on PPC's Spanish language newspaper, La Gaceta, I proofread articles, contacted freelancers regarding assignments and occasionally contributed editorial columns.

MOM AND POP SOFTWARE, INC.
September 1998 — September 1999   *Jefferson City, MO*

As customer service associate, I assisted clients with questions, complaints and merchandise return, and also served on a volunteer employee incentive committee.

EDUCATION:

B.A. – Spanish
Sarah Lawrence College
Bronxville, NY
May 1998

Sample Resume #2

CHRIS COACH
4321 Solution Street
Sunnyday, CA 91111
Phone: (123) 555-1212
chris@chrisconsultant.com

SUMMARY

A problem-solving leader who consistently delivers team-building and performance-generating solutions for organizations.

COACHING EXPERIENCE

Successfully led team-building and leadership development projects for a variety of organizations including small businesses, non-profit associations, and the XYZ Corporation. For each project:

- Met with clients to conduct needs analyses and determine each project's scope, deadline, team, and budget.

- Carried out qualitative and quantitative information-gathering techniques including document review, case study analysis, interviews, and conducting surveys.

- Used appropriate problem-solving techniques such as 360° Analysis and SWOT Analysis to identify possible solutions.

- Presented recommendations and carried out training programs to assist organizations in implementing recommended solutions.

Sample projects include preparing an executive stress-management program to help executives cope better with the pressures of their corporate environment and developing a marketing team-building program for a corporation to address concerns about faltering sales. (The team's sales have increased 67% since implementation.)

Details of these and other project successes available on request.

SKILLS

- Skills include project management, analytical problem-solving, team leadership, sales, business writing, making presentations

- Proficient in a variety of computer programs including Microsoft Office, MS Project 2007, and PowerPoint

- Conversant in Spanish

"I have worked closely with Chris on a number of major projects and found her to be knowledgeable, professional, and extremely resourceful. She readily accepts a challenge and uses her intelligence and abilities to solve problems creatively."

> — Jane Jones, Vice-President of Communications, XYZ Co.

"Chris was our company's top team leader. Her teams consistently achieved their goals ahead of schedule and under budget."

> — Ed Employer, President, ABC Company

EMPLOYMENT AND VOLUNTEER HISTORY

- Owner-Coach, CC Corporate Coaching, 2007 to present

- Communications Manager, XYZ Corporation, 2001-2006

- Operations Coordinator, ABC Company, 1997-2000

- Humane Society, Communications Committee, 2005-2007 (Chaired the committee in 2006)

EDUCATION

- Enrolled in courses on project management and leadership at University of Sunnyday Business Studies Department

- Completed seminar on strategic planning offered by American Management Association, 2006

- BA in Communications, Wise University, 1996

MEMBERSHIPS

- Member, International Coach Federation

- Member of City of Sunnyday Chamber of Commerce, Executive Women International, and Toastmasters

Your Cover Letter

A solid cover letter complements a resume, and serves as an introduction or as a follow-up to a prior conversation. Some companies request that applicants only send a resume initially, with the understanding that they will screen the ones that they receive and contact those candidates whose qualifications match their needs.

But yours is not a traditional job search, and even if your resume somehow ends up in a pile with others, the fact that you also sent an effective cover letter will improve your odds of being contacted. People who run companies, professional organizations and civic groups are typically very busy, and your cover letter reminds them who you are and what you discussed with them.

Be considerate of the reader's time. Three to five paragraphs work best. This should allow you to make your point effectively. Break up long passages of text to avoid lengthy paragraphs. In all correspondence, including email, list your contact information–phone, fax, email, website––as well as specific credentials that you want to emphasize. Include a slogan if you have one.

On the next page is a Sample Cover Letter that might accompany the above resume. You will need to tailor yours according to your unique situation.

6.2.3   Website and Online Promotion

Your Website

Your website functions as an electronic business card, sales brochure and ongoing advertisement. Clients will expect you to have one. In addition to giving you an added degree of professionalism, your website will establish you as a presence in cyber-space, and provide 24/7 exposure to potential millions. Remember that life coaching is not limited by geographical boundaries, and the Internet provides a forum for international exposure.

Your website can complement your other marketing efforts. When someone looking for a life coach sees your web address on your business card, in a Yellow Pages ad, or elsewhere, they can visit your website 24 hours a day to learn more about your services.

Sample Cover Letter

October 27, 2009

Eligible Singles Network
Attn: James T. Busmani
P.O. Box 123
Herculaneum, MO 63011

Dear Mr. Busmani,

I enjoyed the opportunity to speak with you about life coaching during the Eligible Singles Network's monthly cocktail hour last Friday. The hors d'oeuvres were great, and everyone I met was very friendly. The guest speaker gave a very compelling speech about effective time management.

As a life coach, I help clients prioritize goals, and set reasonable time limits on accomplishing them. One client went back to school to become a paralegal after 30 years in sales. He had always wanted to work in the legal field, and felt burned out in his present job. I helped him come up with a plan for implementing his goal, and today he is employed by a prestigious law firm in Jefferson City. Another client found the courage to write and submit her first romance novel, and her book has been accepted by a publisher. Both have given permission to be contacted.

I would be grateful for the opportunity to speak to your organization at some time in the near future. I feel that such an opportunity would be beneficial to both of us.

Yours truly,

Ashley Anne Carver
Life Coach and author of "Your Perfect Life"
Phone: 573-123-4567
Email: AAC@anyisp.com
Website: www.ashleyannelifecoach.com
Don't just survive; thrive!

Starting and maintaining a website does not have to be expensive and complicated. If you are already experienced at creating web pages, or learn quickly, you can design your website yourself using a program such as Microsoft's FrontPage.

Many online companies provide free website hosting and development tools designed specifically for the non-technical computer user. They offer many tools and services, including site hosting; counters to track visitors; guest books where viewers can leave a personalized message; bulletin board set-up for posting online discussion forums; chat rooms; automatic bulk email capabilities and customizable newsletters.

A major drawback to the free website hosting services is that you must consent to banner ads and pop-ups. If you do not want advertisements on your website, or you want multiple email accounts or other enhanced features, most also offer premium accounts. Another major drawback is that you won't have your own domain but something like www.Janejoneslifecoach.freehost.com.

For a more professional look to your website, consider purchasing your own domain and have it hosted by a company specializing in such services. Your current Internet service provider most likely offers domain hosting for small businesses. You may pay a little more, but your website will also look far more professional when you have your own domain.

To find out whether your preferred domain name is available, visit **www.internic.net**. InterNIC is a service of the U.S. Department of Commerce that provides information about registered domains. In the Whois section you can type in your domain name and if it is already taken, you will know right away. They also provide a list of domain registrars you can contact when you're ready to register your domain.

If your preferred domain name is available, but you're not yet ready with your website, you can also "park" your domain. This means that you register the domain name in your business name so that someone else does not take it before you're up and running with your business website. To park a domain, contact one of the many registrar's listed on the InterNIC website.

If you plan to have an online store on your website (and most coaches who offer telephone and cyber coaching services do), your best bet is to use one of the many services that combine this functionality with domain registry and hosting services. See section 5.7 for more about these companies.

What to Include On Your Website

You are competing with a tremendous number of other websites online, so yours will have to quickly catch viewers' attention. At the same time, you don't want to overwhelm them with too much information on your home page (the main page). Put the most important stuff first. Make your website lively, interesting, and if possible, interactive.

Here are some suggestions of what you can include on your site:

- Include a recent photograph of yourself. Even though most coaching is done over the telephone, people like to have a face to associate with a voice.

- State on your home page that you offer a free 30-minute introductory consultation (if you plan to offer that).

- Many coaches have questionnaires and evaluations posted on their websites. This sparks potential clients' interest and enables them to establish initial contact with you. Some examples are: "Is coaching right for you?" "Defining your life goals" "Do you have a career or just a job?" "Are you ready for retirement?" "Do you know your Carbon Footprint?" Limit the questions to five or ten. Your website can also include the information from your brochure and information package.

- Include a disclaimer on your website that assures viewers' privacy. Let them know that you will not send them spam, nor will you sell or otherwise distribute their email or any other information.

- The Internet is becoming increasingly sensory, and to add more of a personal touch to their websites, some coaches have links where visitors can listen to them talk about their services, or even watch a short video clip. A professional web developer or your Internet hosting company will be able to help you add these features to your site.

- Many life coaches are adding audio messages to their websites as a personal touch. The message should ideally be between 15 and 30 minutes long. Suggested topics include your biography, an explanation of life coaching, answers to frequently asked questions, a recording of one of your classes or seminars, or a sample dialogue between you and a client (with permission from the client). To record an audio message you will need to purchase a microphone and voice recording software, which you can find at most stores that carry computer accessories.

- The more easily people can contact you, the more responses you will get. Instead of just posting your email, include an automatic email form. (This will also help cut down on spam.)

- Ask for permission to post testimonials from satisfied clients on your website. Nothing emphasizes your credentials like quotes from actual people whom you have helped. If it's a corporate client, include the company name, particularly if it's a well known company.

- A lot of life coaches make considerable income by selling on their websites books and CDs that they have produced. If you have written a book, or developed a series of CDs from seminars or speeches that you gave, offer these for sale on your website. You can set up links for people to purchase them online. See section 6.3.5 for more information on producing your own products.

- Many coaches don't mention fees on their websites. They prefer to have people call them to get more information, and the kind of clients that they want to attract are already successful and can generally afford coaching services. However, other coaches prefer to post fees to avoid getting calls from clients who are not a good fit. For example, if you offer corporate training programs for $3,000 per day, you may not want to field calls from individuals who are looking for a coach charging $50 per hour.

Promoting Your Website

The Internet is a powerful tool for business and communication, and its potential is always growing. Maintaining a website is an important first step, but with the millions of other websites out there in cyberspace, simply having a website is not enough. You need to make people aware that you're out there.

Registering your website with the major search engines is a good start. There are premium services that advertise exposure to hundreds of search engines for a fee–which can cost a couple hundred dollars or more–but paying to be listed on every single obscure search engine is, quite frankly, a waste of time and money.

Most people regularly use only a handful, such Yahoo, Google, MSN, and AOL. You can submit your website address (URL) to any of these search engines for free. Check out Google's tips page that tells you how to submit your URL and maximize search engine hits on your website at **www.google.com/addurl/?continue=/addurl**. Google also offers a variety of packages for advertising your website in their AdWords program. Visit **http://adwords.google.com** to learn more.

Also resort to traditional methods of promoting your website. Tell people. Mention it in conversations, include your URL on your business card, and at the end of your emails and letters.

You might agree to have links to other coaches' websites, or have links on your website where viewers can purchase other coaches' products, if those other coaches in turn do the same for you. If you are worried about "competing coaches," and you really shouldn't be, then sponsor links for coaches who have a different specialty (i.e. if you are a career coach, sponsor a relationship coach or a Christian coach, etc.).

You can also register yourself on an association website like International Coach Federation, if you are a member. Usually there is no charge once you are a member of the organization. If you take training with a training institute you will be able to add your information to their directory once you're certified.

Comprehensive Coaching U (**www.comprehensivecoachingu.com**) has an affiliate program whereby coaches can earn a percentage of sales from items on CCU's website, providing that the sales resulted from clicking on their banner link from the sponsoring coach's website. Coachville.com has a program that pays affiliates when new members join as a result of their link. Neither program costs the affiliate anything, and there is no membership requirement.

Other Online Tools

Blogs

The latest rage in Internet communication is the weblog, commonly known as a "blog." Blogs consist of a series of posts, usually on a particular theme or topic, and generally in chronological order. They often take the form of diaries or journals. Groups with similar interests use blogs to keep members informed of current events and updates. Blogs are also useful for writing online columns or newsletters.

There are many blogging websites, featuring hundreds of posts divided into different categories—politics, religion, entertainment, relationships and even coaching. Readers are also able to post feedback. Most blogging websites offer free membership, and allow you to establish a user profile where you can post your website, email and contact information. Popular sites include: Blogger (**www.blogger.com**) and Blogit (**www.blogit.com**). With Blogit you have to pay a subscription fee, but you also get paid based on how many people view your posts.

Autoresponders

Autoresponders are programs that automatically respond to email. They can be an efficient method for marketing your business and keeping track of potential clients.

With an autoresponder you can send one message, or a series of messages. You might have a link on your website for people who are interested in learning more about your services, or a link for a seminar or teleclass you are giving so that people can register in advance or receive reminders as the date approaches.

Autoresponders keep lists of people who have contacted you, and these lists can be updated and modified as necessary. You can usually customize the emails to some extent, changing variables such as names. They are tremendously helpful for managing newsletters. Two popular autoresponder services that you can check out are **AWeber.com** and **GetResponse.com**.

You can also use autoresponders to send complimentary or fee-based e-coaching programs to clients. For example, a life coach specializing in assisting entrepreneurs could have an e-program titled "Ten super secrets to building your new business." A coach working with artists or creative individuals might have one called "Three steps to finding your muse." Generally, e-programs are spaced over a period of time. This gives recipients time to absorb the information and implement the ideas contained in them.

Chat Sessions

Some life coaches hold regular (e.g. weekly) online chat sessions. This is not the same as e-coaching, which was discussed in section 3.3.3. In a chat session, you invite interested people to "attend" and participate in a coaching-related discussion. These sessions might focus on different topics, or give you the opportunity to answer questions about life coaching. You do not charge for these chat room sessions; they are merely marketing and informational tools.

There are many resources available for setting up free online chat rooms. Freeware Java lists numerous links at **http://freewarejava.com/ applets/chat.shtml**.

6.3   Marketing Techniques

Effective marketing is the key to a successful business. After all, people will need to hear about you and your services before they can consider hiring you as a coach. In this section, you will read about ways to promote your business to potential clients.

6.3.1   Networking

Networking is probably one of the most important marketing techniques you should use. Networking is the key to referrals and word-of-mouth advertising, and will open up endless windows of opportunities for you. Executive Kevin Nourse stresses: "Build relationships! When I was an internal HR manager, I didn't realize how important it is as an entrepreneur to have a broad base of support and connections to start and sustain a business."

Personal Contact

A simple but effective way to begin networking is to make a list of everyone you know. If you sit down and think about it, you can probably come up with at least a couple of hundred people. They can be friends, family members, co-workers or acquaintances.

Don't be concerned with editing the list or crossing off names. Just start by brainstorming. After you have compiled your list, go over the names and check the ones that you will contact first. A phone call works best.

So what happens after you say hello and exchange amenities? Without being abrupt, try to get to your point fairly quickly. Say that you are embarking on a new profession, life coaching, and ask the person if he or she would be interested or knows anyone who might benefit from your services. Come up with a brief description of life coaching, as a lot of people still don't know what it is. Maybe something like the following:

> "Life coaches offer ongoing support for people trying to clarify and attain their goals or to find balance in their life and work. Through weekly, half-hour telephone calls, life coaches listen to their clients, ask thought-provoking questions and hold clients accountable for following through on the plans of action that they have developed with the coach."

Rehearse what you are going to say until you sound natural, and remember that you don't have to recite it verbatim for every single call. You don't want to sound like you are reading from an index card.

Referrals

Do some volunteer or pro bono (free) coaching to get both practice and exposure. (See section 4.2.3 for more about ways to get volunteering experience.) When talking to potential clients, you will be able to say that you have already coached a number of people. You don't need to tell them that it was for free. This is a good way to get referrals from satisfied clients.

Offering referral bonuses to current clients can lead to new business. Consider taking 10 percent off the next month's fees for every person they refer who calls for a consultation, or 25 percent off for every new client who comes from that referral. If you obtain four new clients as a result, it is worth it to give the client who referred them a free month of coaching.

Joining Organizations

Local organizations can offer wonderful opportunities to network and establish contacts.

Networking Clubs

A valuable form of networking is through a networking club. Some of these are general business groups, but many have a target group of clients and include one member from different industries (e.g. insurance, financial planning, law, professional photography, real estate, etc.) to reach those in the target group. Each member of the club is expected to bring a certain number of leads to the group each week or month.

Fees will vary but can be as low as the cost of breakfast once a week or breakfast plus a membership fee. You may also be required to serve on the executive board after a time. In addition to the marketing opportunities, benefits of joining networking groups may include discounts on services provided by other members of the group.

To become a member you are either recommended to the group by an existing member, or you might approach the group and ask to sit in as an observer for a meeting or two, and get accepted from there. Most groups will allow a trial period before demanding that you join or stop coming to meetings. You may be asked to give a short presentation about your own business, and on what business and personal skills you can bring to the group.

The types of participants will differ with every group, so don't settle for the first one you visit. Check around first before deciding which one to join. Make sure the members represent the kind of very busy people with reasonable incomes who might become clients for you, or who would know others who could benefit from your services.

One way to find a networking club is through word of mouth. You can also look for networking groups online. Business Network International (**www.bni.com**) has more than 2,300 chapters in cities around the world.

Membership Organizations

In addition to networking clubs, consider joining or attending events organized by groups that members of your target market belong to. For example, if you want to work with singles, get involved with singles organizations. If you want to work with women in business consider joining the National Association for Female Executives. Learn more about them at **www.nafe.com**.

Joining your local Chamber of Commerce is also a good idea. Your local Chamber will host various social and business-related meetings where you can meet a great variety of people, and get some great business advice besides. To find your local U.S. Chamber of Commerce visit **www.chamberofcommerce.com** or in Canada go to **www.chamber.ca/article.asp?id=286**.

Service Clubs

International service clubs like the Rotary Club (**www.rotary.org**), Kiwanis (**www.kiwanis.org**), or Lions Club (**www.lionsclub.org**) are also good starting points. If you're a carbon coach, for example, the Lions

Club has a well-developed environmental service program and its members might like to learn more about your services.

Joining service clubs is a great way to network and you'll meet people from all walks of life you can discuss your service offerings with. This can also help you gauge the demand for the services you plan to offer as well as help you to refine your target market.

Effective Networking

One of the first questions people ask when they meet is "What do you do?" This generally comes shortly after "What's your name?" When you respond, "I'm a life coach," most of them will ask you what that is. You have a perfect opening.

Ken Abrams, MCC, co-founder of the Philadelphia Area Coaches Alliance (PACA), likes to pique potential clients' interest. He tells them:

> "People who work with me work less, make more in less time, and have more fun. Doesn't that sound of interest to you? The first question that comes out of their mouth is 'How do you do that?' I tell them, 'The process of coaching is a strategic partnership. All your life, you've had strategic partners—your parents, your teachers, your mentors. Coaching is a strategic partnership. It's your choice whether or not you want to be supported in the next 90 days, 5 years, or whatever. My job is to focus on your goals and wants."

Also take an interest in the other members of any group you join. If you join a group with the intention of simply trying to cull as many business leads for yourself as possible, you probably won't be too popular. To make the most out of your membership in an organization, there are several things you can do to raise your profile, including:

- Serve on a committee
- Write articles for the association newsletter
- Offer to give presentations on topics of interest to the members
- Do volunteer work that will bring you into contact with other members
- Run for election to the Executive Committee

Although networking and meeting as many people as possible are paramount, don't spread yourself too thin by joining more groups than you can possibly handle. Between attending meetings regularly and paying membership dues, becoming involved with too many groups can become a burden on your time and money.

Following Up

If you meet someone who seems genuinely interested in your services and you exchange business cards, don't stand on ceremony waiting for the person to call you. If you don't hear anything in a week, call him or her. K. Denise Bane remembers how not following up cost her a client once:

> "I met a woman at a breakfast sponsored by the National Association for Female Executives. She said that she might be interested in coaching, took my card, and said that she'd give it some thought. Months went by, and I finally called her. It took her a second to remember who I was, then she said, 'Oh, Denise, I'm sorry! I lost your card, and I didn't know how to contact you.' She had just signed up with another coach the previous week!"

6.3.2   Speaking and Events

Give a Speech

Even if you don't join an organization, you may still be able to connect with their members and get new business by being a speaker at a breakfast meeting, luncheon, or workshop. If you give a good talk and offer useful advice, you will be seen as an expert. As long as there are people in the audience who need coaching services, this can be an excellent way to attract clients.

The topic can be anything related to coaching that their members would be interested in. Focus on what you really know and develop that theme into something workable. This is not to say that you should never come up with new ideas, but your credibility will be better if you draw on your core knowledge and experience. A lot of coaches give the same presentation to many different organizations, occasionally tailoring it to fit the needs of a specific group.

For example, perhaps you are particularly good at time management, which is a very important topic nowadays. Tell people how you do it, give them tips for effectively organizing their own lives or their own schedules.

While you probably will not be paid for your presentations, it can be an excellent opportunity to promote your business. Your company name may be published in the organization's newsletter, it will be mentioned by the person who introduces you, you can distribute business cards and brochures, and you will be able to mingle with attendees before and after your presentation. (You may get a free breakfast or lunch too!)

Approach community groups whose interests are similar to yours, or those you feel might benefit from a seminar or presentation that you would like to give. Check your local newspaper to find out when these groups meet, and attend some of their events. Offer to speak for free until you have established yourself and generated some publicity. Do not forget the resources that you already have. Are you a member of a civic, professional or even volunteer organization? Do you belong to a church or synagogue? How about your college or university alumni organization? You would be amazed at how many contacts you actually have.

Ask for referrals. If one group turns you down for a speaking engagement, ask them if they know of another group that might be interested. When you do have the opportunity to speak to an organization, you can also ask for referrals afterwards. Request that the head of the organization write you a letter of recommendation. Or, to make it easier, write one yourself and have the person sign it. As always, leave a business card.

Give a few free speeches to establish some credentials first. Later, you could offer to charge the public to attend, maybe $5 or $10 per person, and split the revenue with the sponsoring organization. If your presentation doesn't draw a large crowd, it hasn't cost the sponsoring organization anything, and still gives you one more credential.

Joining Toastmasters (**www.toastmasters.org**) can provide excellent practice for designing and delivering public presentations. An international organization with chapters in about 106 countries, including the United States and Canada, their goal is to help members become more effective public speakers. They offer a variety of programs and hold regular meetings where members offer each other critiques, evaluations and feedback. Membership dues are about $35 per year.

Brushing up on your speaking skills is useful even if you don't give that many public presentations. Your voice is your primary method of communicating with clients, so it behooves you to speak as effectively as possible. How you sound can be as important as what you say, and an organization like Toastmasters can provide you with some objective feedback that you might otherwise not have.

Moderate a Support Group

Moderating a support group in your area of specialization is a good opportunity for you to market yourself, as well as possibly obtain clients and get referrals. For example, if you are a career coach, you might host a job hunting support group. Limit group size to about 10 to 12 members, and meet in a public place for one hour per week.

Make the first coaching session somewhat informal and introductory. Give everyone time to assemble, and provide some refreshments. A few boxes of donuts and a couple of pots of coffee shouldn't break you financially, and will give the attendees time to relax and unwind.

Then introduce yourself. Tell them about your background, what led you to coaching, and how you plan to help them. Tell them that you are going to assist them, but don't use language like "I'm going to do this for you," "I can promise you this," or "I guarantee you." Tell them that they are here to support and encourage each other, and even to offer constructive criticism when necessary.

After your introduction, give the group members five or ten minutes to mingle. Tell each person to introduce him or herself to at least two other members. Tell them to shake hands, give their names, and one or two sentences about themselves.

At this first session, you might want to give them a brief questionnaire or evaluation. Also have them fill out a card with their name, address and contact information. They should include a brief statement about what brought them to the group, and what they hope to achieve.

Moderating a support group is similar to group coaching. For more information about group coaching, see section 3.2.

Teach a Class

Teaching a class can be a great way to earn extra money, establish your reputation, and meet prospective clients. You don't have to have a degree to teach adults—just lots of enthusiasm and knowledge of your subject. If you've already designed teleclasses or workshops, you can use material from those as a starting point.

The first step is to review the current catalog of continuing education courses offered by local colleges, universities and other organizations that provide adult education classes in your community. Call and ask for a print catalog if they do not have course information at their website. Once you have reviewed their current list of courses, come up with some ideas for new courses. (They already have instructors for any courses that are in their catalog.)

Once you have an idea for a new course in mind, call the college or organization and ask to speak with whoever hires continuing education instructors. They will tell you what you need to do to apply to teach a course.

Your Own Workshops or Seminars

While teaching continuing education courses can be rewarding, it normally takes months for a new course to be offered (and there's always the chance the continuing education program may decide not to offer it). If you'd like to start presenting courses right away, consider designing and giving your own workshops or seminars.

We looked at the logistics of hosting workshops in section 3.3.5. Workshops and seminars are also great opportunities for coaches to get their names and businesses known. If you can find a free or low-cost venue, consider conducting one or two seminars for free to get publicity for yourself. This is also a great time to put out a press release to get even more publicity (see section 6.3.4).

The following detailed advice on how to market a seminar comes from the *FabJob Guide to Become a Motivational Speaker*:

When preparing your marketing materials, remember to focus on communicating all the benefits of attending. As well as the information, benefits of attending a seminar may include: a fun night out, a chance to network, or personal advice from an expert. Among the other items you might include in a brochure:

- Who should attend

- When and where the seminar takes place

- The speaker's credentials

- Testimonials

- That enrollment is limited (mention if past seminars sold out)

- A call to action such as "Register now!"

- How to register, including your phone number and web address

Brochures with this information can also be used to market seminars to the public. The ideal brochure for a public seminar is one that can double as a poster (e.g. printed on one side of a colorful 8½" x 11" sheet). If permitted, try posting them at bulletin boards, especially bookstores and college campuses – two places you're likely to find people interested in seminars.

Trade Shows

If you specialize in coaching on issues such as body image, relationships, etc. you may be able to find prospective clients at public shows such as women's conferences. The cost to become an exhibitor (i.e. to get a booth at the show) will vary depending on the particular show, the location, the number of people expected to attend, and the amount of space you require. It may range from as little as $50 to $1,000 or more for public shows. To cut costs, you could partner with another non-competing exhibitor and share a booth space.

However, before investing in a trade show booth, attend the event if possible, or speak to some past exhibitors. While you may find a $100 booth at a women's show is a good investment to market relationship coaching, $1,000 spent on a trade show booth to promote executive coaching services could give disappointing results. (Trade shows are often used to raise awareness rather than generate immediate sales.)

You can find out about upcoming shows by contacting your local convention centers, exhibition halls, or chamber of commerce. Many shows now have their own websites and provide registration information as well as site maps and logistical information. When setting up your booth you should bring business cards, your company brochures, and your portfolio for display at your booth.

When you speak with prospective clients, mention a few of the ideas you have for coaching the client, employees or executives (but don't give away too much for free). To arrange consultations, bring an appointment book.

> **TIP:** If you don't have an assistant, find a partner or even a spouse or close friend to help out at the show. The days can be long and tiring, and you won't want to close down your booth to take breaks.

6.3.3 Advertising

Yellow Pages

Life coaches can be found in the Yellow Pages under categories such as business, consulting, training and, of course, coaching. However, many coaches do not rely heavily on this type of advertising, for several reasons. First, the relationship between a life coach and a client is more personal than a traditional business relationship. People who search the Yellow Pages for a plumber, an electrician or a pizza parlor that delivers are not looking for someone who is compatible with their personality.

Second, life coaching is still new enough that people might not think to look for a coach in the telephone book. They first need to understand what life coaching is, and then how it could benefit them. As a result, coaches are more likely to get business through networking, referrals, giving presentations, and the Internet.

Before you buy a Yellow Pages ad, you should carefully investigate the costs compared to the potential return. Many coaches find a Yellow Pages ad does not make the phone ring off the hook with clients. If someone does respond to your ad, they may be "shopping around," so you must be prepared to invest time as well as advertising dollars if you use this method of advertising.

To minimize your risk, you might want to consider starting with a small display ad, such as a 1/8 page ad. If you can get your hands on a previous year's edition of your local Yellow Pages, compare the ads for other coaches from year to year. If you notice others have increased or decreased the size of their ads, this can give you an indication of what might work for you. Also, if you meet other coaches at networking events, you can ask how well their Yellow Pages ads are working for them.

You can either design the ad yourself, have the Yellow Pages design it for you, or hire a designer. Take a look at the ads in the relevant category of your current Yellow Pages for ideas. If you are interested in advertising, contact your local Yellow Pages to speak with a sales rep. Check the print version of your phone book for contact information.

Some localities also have "pages" or "books" of other types. In many areas, community-based Yellow Pages are alternatives. These are limited to smaller geographic areas than, for example, a whole state or city. Advertising in these is usually a bit cheaper than in the regular Yellow Pages.

Magazine and Newspaper Advertising

Advertising can be expensive, and may not generate the results you want unless you do it repeatedly. Most people need to see an advertisement three to seven times before they buy. Therefore, if you choose to buy advertising, it will probably be most cost effective to place ads in local magazines or newspapers aimed specifically at your target market. For example, if you specialize in working with families, you might advertise in local parenting magazines.

Here are some tips for effective advertising:

- Make your ad about your customers. Explain how they can benefit from your services rather than just listing the services you provide.

- Make them an offer they can't refuse. Your ad should describe a service or special promotion that makes you stand out from your competition. It should also include a call to action (i.e. saying "Call today" or including a coupon that expires by a certain date).

- Make sure you're available for people who respond to your ad. If someone wants to talk to you but keeps getting your voicemail, they may give up.

- Make long-term plans for your advertising program. Chances are that running an ad only once won't give you as much business as you would hope. Develop a long-term advertising strategy and stick with it.

The publications you advertise in will usually design your ad for an additional cost and give you a copy of the ad to run in other publications. However, you will get much better results if you can manage to get free publicity in those publications, instead of paying for advertising. In the next section we'll at various ways for you to get free publicity for your business, which can be far more effective in getting your name out and for a lot less money.

6.3.4   Free Publicity

When a business gets publicity in a magazine article, newspaper story, radio or television talk show, it can result in a tremendous amount of new business. Here are some ways you can get publicity like this.

Press Releases

A press release is a brief document that you submit to the media in order to gain publicity for your business. Editors prefer to see a press release as a single page (under 500 words) and written as if it were a news story. But don't expect it to be run "as is." Most editors will rewrite your press release slightly to fit their standards.

Here are some tips for writing a good press release:

- Make sure the press release is newsworthy. For example, you could write about an upcoming event you'll be speaking at.

- Give your press release a strong lead paragraph that answers the six main questions: who, what, where, when, why, and how.

- Include factual information about yourself and your services. Remember, a press release should read like a news story, not an advertisement.

- Keep it short. Aim for a maximum of 500 words.

- Include your contact information at the end of the press release so that reporters and readers can get hold of you.

You can find many online resources to help you write press releases, including **www.publicityinsider.com/release.asp** and PR Newswire at **http://prntoolkit.prnewswire.com**. PR Newswire offers a PR Toolkit on its website, which includes advice on whether or not to use a press release, details about what to include in a press release, how to write an effective press release, and writing tips.

Most magazines and newspapers publish contact information for their editors. Newspapers may have dozens of editors, so make sure you send your submission to the appropriate one. For example, you would probably want to contact the Business Editor for your new business announcement, and the Lifestyle Editor if your specialty is relationship coaching. As an alternative to writing a press release, you could call the editor or send him or her a brief "pitch letter" to suggest an idea for a story.

Writing Articles

By writing articles for magazines and newspapers, you demonstrate that you are passionate about the business of coaching. Stating that you have coached a high number of clients is fine, but you can also reinforce people's impression of your professionalism by getting your name and credentials in print as often as possible.

Also, writing articles makes good sense from a marketing standpoint. Seeing someone's photograph and contact information isn't nearly as powerful as seeing that information following an interesting and informative piece on some aspect of life coaching. You will encourage responses and feedback from those who read your articles. You will stand out more.

Come up with a brief, biographical blurb, about 50 words, to include at the end of your articles. Something like the following would be appropriate, followed by your contact information:

> "Marty Smith is a life coach in Sacramento, California. A former insurance salesman and IT consultant, he is a self-described refugee from the corporate world. He has served as president of the Sacramento Chamber of Commerce, and has written articles for Coaching in Style and Success. He lives with his wife, two children, and three dogs."

Editors naturally tend to be well-read individuals, and due to the significant exposure that life coaching has had in the media, a lot of them are already familiar with the topic. Approaching them to write an article about life coaching will be easier if you can show them how your particular piece is relevant to their publication, and why you are the person to write it. Emphasize any coaching and writing credentials that you have.

However, keep in mind that editors are very busy people, so keep any correspondence with them brief and to-the-point. Be prepared to follow up with a resume and, if you have them, writing samples. If you would like to read a few more pointers on writing pitch letters, you can read an online article entitled "How to Write a Great Pitch Letter" at **www. publicityinsider.com/pitch.asp**.

Writing for Newspapers

One of the best ways to establish yourself as an expert is to write an article or column for a newspaper. While most large daily newspapers already have columnists, there may be an opportunity to write for smaller newspapers that reach your target audience.

There are many possible topics you could write about: parenting tips for raising teenagers, ways to avoid burnout at work, etc. Make sure your article provides valuable information to the publication's readers. Articles that sound like an ad for your services are not likely to get published.

Newspapers may have dozens of editors, so make sure you target your submission to the appropriate one. Once you have written your first column or article, phone the editor to ask if they would be interested in seeing it. If so, they will probably ask you to email it. If they want to publish it, they may offer to pay you. However, even if they don't pay, you should consider letting them publish it in return for including your bio and contact information at the end of the article or column.

Writing for Magazines

Another good way to establish yourself as an expert is to write articles for magazines. There are literally thousands of magazines on a wide range of topics such as business, health, parenting, and more. Many magazines accept submissions from freelance writers. However, some magazines are a better bet than others.

Unless you are already an established freelance writer, you may not have much luck trying to sell articles to popular magazines such as *Reader's Digest, Time, Fortune,* or *Cosmopolitan.* Magazines like these are flooded with thousands of submissions every month, so the odds of having your article accepted for publication are slim.

You are more likely to have your article accepted if you submit it to smaller or lesser-known publications. Many smaller publications are hungry for well-written articles that provide value to their readers. In many cases, the writer's background doesn't matter. You can find a listing of magazines and their guidelines for writers in The Writer's Market. A one month trial subscription costs $5.99. Visit **www.writers market.com** to learn more.

Study a few issues of the magazine and see what types of articles that they publish. This should go without saying, but too many writers submit material blindly. You might have an idea for a story that complements one that appeared in a recent issue, or one that follows up on a series of articles with a certain theme. If a magazine recently did a profile on local entrepreneurs, you might write a piece about how life coaches work with new business owners or why entrepreneurs are drawn to life coaching. Maybe the magazine just published an article about the growing number of workers who are dissatisfied with their jobs, or are sick of the daily grind.

As a life coach, you may be able to offer them some alternatives. If you live near a major metropolitan area, you can probably find a corporation that has hired coaches to train or motivate employees. This might make a good feature for a local business magazine. Even magazines with a broader range of topics often have a business or lifestyle section, and either section might be appropriate for an article about life coaching.

Consider profiling local life coaches. Interview three or four with different specialties, e.g. career coaching, relationship coaching, spiritual coaching or health and wellness coaching. This is also a good way to network. Show how the same basic set of concepts applies to the various disciplines within life coaching. Or you could write an article about your particular coaching specialty, if you have one, but remember not to make the piece seem like just an advertisement.

Television and Radio Talk Shows

If you've always wanted to be an on-air personality, here's your chance. The best shows for coaches to appear on are morning and afternoon talk shows, and sometimes, depending on your specialty, business shows or business segments of news shows. Phone the appropriate producer at the local stations and let them know that you would be happy to appear and provide your expertise for their audience.

You will probably be asked to send some information; this is where your promotional materials come in handy. After you've sent them or dropped them off, give the producer a couple of days to look them over and ask for an appointment. When you contact them, be sure to emphasize how much the show's audience will benefit from an interview with you. Remember, shows want dynamic, interesting guests.

Also, keep in mind that many station employees are overworked and underpaid. If you can make their job easier you are much more likely to land an interview. The best way to make their job easier is to include a list of "frequently asked questions" with the letter or news release you send them. This is a list of questions that you think listeners might like the answers to (such as "What are some good ways to relieve stress?").

Whenever you are booked for a radio or TV show, arrange beforehand to have the interviewer say that you are a life coach and mention your telephone number and web address. If you are going to be appearing on TV, ask if they will display your contact information on the screen at some point during your interview.

What you say during the interview can also help to promote you. For example:

YOU: That's one of the things I cover at my website, www.ima-coach.com. What I say there is ...

Of course, bear in mind that mentioning your website works best if you have a short, memorable domain name (see section 6.2.3 for more on websites). It would be a bit difficult to say, "As I explain at my website, www.myinternetcompany.com/userpages/mypages/me.html..."

6.3.5   Publish Your Own Products

Publishing your own products is an excellent way to establish your expertise. You may also be able to increase your income by selling products at your presentations, on your website, and to your clients.

Book Publishing

Being a published author gives a tremendous boost to your credibility. "Yeah, right," you may be thinking, "All I have to do is write a book and find someone to publish it!" Well, that's one way to get published, but it's certainly not the only way. Publishing a book can be a time-consuming process if you do it the conventional way. Once the manuscript is written, it can take six months or more to find a publisher, then another 18 months from the time the publisher accepts the manuscript until it's finally in print. Sure it can help your credibility, but it's not exactly quick.

> TIP: If you want to publish the conventional way, you can find a list of publishers and the kinds of books they are looking for in Writer's Market. A one month trial subscription costs $5.99.

A much faster way to get a book published is to self-publish. Self-publishing is simply contracting with a printing company to produce your book. You can find printers that specialize in helping self-publishers by typing "self-publishing" into your favorite search engine.

There are many successful coaches and authors who have self-published. For example, John Gray, author of *Men Are From Mars, Women Are From Venus*, self-published his early books. Gray's *What You Feel, You Can Heal* was originally published in 1984 through his Heart Publishing Company.

Self-publishing a book can also add to your credibility—provided you do not volunteer the fact that your book is self-published. (Of course you would say it was self-published if you are asked.) The reality is that many people perceive self-published books to be less impressive than "real" published books. No matter how outstanding your book was, a potential client may believe it was "not good enough" to be accepted by a publishing house. A great idea is to create a company name for your publishing business using the tips in section 5.3 of this guide.

A recent development is publishing books "on demand." Unlike self-publishing, where the author keeps all the profits, publishing on demand typically pays the author a royalty (a percentage of the revenue from books sold). If you want to explore this option, look into Lulu.com (**www.lulu.com**) which has no upfront cost. You can find other companies that offer this service by typing a search term such as "publishing on demand" or "publish your book" into a search engine.

Before paying any company to publish your book, thoroughly review their contract. Also, realize that you will be responsible for selling the book yourself. Some authors are disappointed to find print on demand publishers generally do very little, if any, marketing for the books they publish.

Booklets

If you haven't written enough to publish a complete book, or if self-publishing a book is simply too expensive, a faster, cheaper alternative is to publish a booklet. There's no reason why "How to Set Goals For Yourself" couldn't be the title of a booklet.

Your booklet could be as simple as a few sheets of paper printed on both sides, folded in half and stapled in the middle. You can print booklets in any quantity quickly and inexpensively at a local printer such as FedEx Office or Staples. For example, you might be able to have 50 copies of a short booklet published for less than $25.

> **TIP:** Although this is a great technique for getting your foot in the door, it is not a way to "fool" people into thinking you are an expert if you really are not. Some potential employers will ask for a copy of your publication. So make sure you write a booklet packed with useful information and expert advice.

Depending on the content of your booklet, you can either offer it free as a way to market your services to prospective clients, or sell it through your website. Either way, consider publishing it as an e-book which you can email to people. You can create up to five e-books free of charge through the Adobe website at **http://createpdf.adobe.com**.

Recording Yourself

The quickest way to develop material for audio cassettes or CDs is by taping one of your live presentations. Electronics and office supply stores sell a variety of recorders which you can slip into a pocket to record your presentation. You should be able to find several different models for about $60-80, or even less if they're on sale.

Another option which can provide superior sound is a mini-disc recorder manufactured by companies such as Sony or Sharp. You can find them at electronics stores for a few hundred dollars. Sony also manufactures digital voice recorders at prices starting at around $40.

To ensure the recorder picks up your voice, you will also need a lapel or lavaliere microphone (a microphone you pin on your jacket). These are available for about $30. You will also need tapes to record on. To avoid disruption to your talk, find tapes that can record until you take a break, perhaps 90 or 120 minutes in length.

If you intend to produce a number of audio products, and have the budget, you might consider buying your own portable recording studio. For example, Expert Magazine offers a product for $895 which you can read about at **www.expertmagazine.com/st/audio/studio.htm**.

You could make copies yourself for only the cost of the tapes if you copy them yourself on a dual cassette recorder, or for only the cost of the CDs using the CD burner on your computer. However, if you want to make the best impression, a professional duplication company can provide you with attractive packaging. You can find companies that duplicate audio materials in the Yellow Pages, or by doing an online search for "duplication services." If you shop around, you can find companies that can duplicate 100 audio tapes or CDs for about one dollar each.

Newsletters

Publishing a newsletter will help you stay in touch with current and former clients, as well as people who may be interested in learning more about life coaching. Use a newsletter to inform readers of trends in the coaching field, as well as to let them know about new products and services that you are offering.

Coaches use newsletters to promote their books, DVDs, CDs or speaking engagements, but be sure that the content goes beyond just that. Make your newsletter enlightening and entertaining, not just an advertisement. For example:

- List ten tips for reducing stress at work.

- Write a book review.

- Talk about a motivational speaker you saw recently and how his or her advice applies to life coaching.

- Include a few inspirational quotes.

- Interview a successful entrepreneur or CEO.

- Reproduce an article or story about coaching that you read (but be sure to obtain permission first).

- Or just write on any topic that you feel applies.

Some newsletters contain just one article a month, or focus on one particular theme. This is just one option. Read other coaching newsletters to get a feel for them. There are plenty of free coaching newsletters to which you can subscribe. You can glean valuable information on current trends, as well as make contacts and possibly find clients.

A monthly or quarterly newsletter via email works best. You can put more time and thought into what you want to say. Keep the length to five or six pages for a monthly newsletter, a little longer for a quarterly newsletter. A newsletter should complement your coaching practice, not replace it. Include a link on your website for people to subscribe to your newsletter, and a link on your newsletter to your website. When you speak with clients or potential clients, ask permission to put them on your mailing list.

Come up with a clever name for your newsletter. Some examples of names are: The Coaching Connection; Your Life, Part I (II, III, etc.); Making the Most of Everything. You do not want a name that is too obscure or confusing, or subscribers might assume that it is junk email and simply delete it unread. (Before using a name, make sure it's available. Refer to section 5.3.2 for tips on choosing a name.)

By opening a free publisher's account with Ideamarketers, you can read monthly articles on dozens of topics and subtopics, including coaching. If you read an article that you think would be appropriate for your newsletter, simply click on a link to request the writer's permission to reproduce the article. Since the writers are posting their work specifically to get publicity, almost all of them will say yes.

For about $15 per month to start, you can also upgrade to a premium publisher's account which will allow you to customize a newsletter or e-zine and give you access to the entire library of articles, instead of only those published within the past month.

Ideamarketers also offers free writers' accounts, where you can publish articles of up to 14,000 characters, including spaces, which translates to approximately four single-spaced pages of text. Although you will not receive any financial compensation, you will have the opportunity to post your name, bio and contact information. A counter lets you know how many people have viewed your article. You may open both a publisher's and a writer's account at no charge.

Visit Ideamarketers at **www.ideamarketers.com** and read some of their sample articles. You can also subscribe to several free newsletters.

6.4   Marketing to Corporate Clients

Many of the techniques described in this chapter can be used to market to corporate clients. For example, executive coach Timi Gleason, a former human resource director and consultant, says networking often comes into play when corporate coaches get hired. Since most have already put in significant time in the corporate world, they have already established a number of contacts and references who can assist them. If someone at Company A doesn't have any openings, he or she knows someone at Company B who might, etc.

Executive coach Kevin Nourse agrees that networking is very important when marketing your services to corporate clients and offers this advice:

> "Align yourself with specific industries. In the past five years, I have develop strong ties in the port authority industry that initially started out in my work with the association. Eventually, I began getting visibility among port leaders who belonged to the association. By developing industry knowledge and reputation, port leaders have been more likely to hire me as a coach and a consultant.
>
> Speak and write. Consistent with the previous point, I have been doing a lot of speaking and writing which has resulted in some very lucrative client engagements. For example, I was asked to speak on

leadership at the annual convention for the port authorities as well as write an article on leadership for their monthly trade publication. As a result, my name is being aligned with the industry in a very visible way – web searches using Google, for example, show a number of hits associated with speaking and writing I have done for that industry.

Give away business. Periodically I come across client opportunities that are not a good fit for me. I then pass along these leads to other coaches/consultants, which inevitably causes them to pass along leads to me also. I do this without expectation that another coach will return the favor, but this is often what happens."

If you don't have personal contacts like these, you can approach companies directly. While the human resources department often contracts with trainers, it is a good idea to also approach "decision-makers" in the appropriate departments because they may have the authority to hire you. If you offer sales training, you could also contact the vice president of sales, sales directors, and sales managers throughout the organization.

Realize that it may take months to break into a particular organization. Contacting as many decision-makers as possible within that organization can help improve your odds of getting hired more quickly.

Some coaches mail their brochures or information packages to prospective clients. If you decide to try this, make sure you target companies and decision-makers in each organization who are most likely to be interested in your services. You can go through a business directory, such as the Chamber of Commerce membership list, or the Yellow Pages and selecting those companies who might benefit from your specific knowledge. Mention in your letter that you will follow up with a phone call in a few days, and do so. Few coaches generate business from a mailing alone.

6.4.1 Proposals

Submitting proposals to prospective companies is another method Gleason recommends. After researching a company and assessing its current needs, the coach outlines the steps that he or she will take to meet those needs.

In some cases a client will actively solicit proposals by advertising in a business publication or by contacting coaches or trainers who have come to their attention through networking, the Yellow Pages, online, etc. This process is called a Request for Proposal, or RFP. When you submit your proposal, you are making a "bid" to do the work.

An RFP is a written statement of the client's specific needs and information about the client's organization. The RFP outlines in detail what the client's project entails and why they want to hire a coach; what they expect in the project proposals received from such outside consultants; and the kinds of expertise required.

RFPs typically will offer an overview of the company and its business structure, some background on the planned project, how and where to submit your proposal, how the proposal should be formatted, and what specific papers, documents and other submissions need to be included. It will also include the project's proposed budget, time frame, and any other conditions the project is subject to, as well as eligibility requirements for those wishing to submit a proposal, including the client's selection process and hiring criteria.

Here is an example of the type of information expected in a proposal:

- A description of your company

- Demonstration of your capability to develop and deliver the program

- Detailed description of the approach you will take in the training

- A proposed timetable

- A fixed price quotation for development and delivery of the program

- Specific resources (such as trainers) that you will assign to the project

- References from organizations you've done similar programs for

- An explanation of how you will measure results of the training

RFPs usually will include the following sections:

Introduction

The introduction often includes an overview of the organization and its organizational structure, a brief summary of the project and how it fits into the client's overall business objectives, a summary of the specific objectives for the project being considered, details of the project budget, and an explanation of why the client believes the services of an outside consultant are required.

Scope of Work/Services

This section details the work the client needs the coach to perform. The scope of work or services obviously will vary from project to project and will be within your own area(s) of expertise for the most part or you wouldn't be considering responding to it. The client will outline exactly what services or work you are expected to provide for the project and may specify in this section any reports on performance and progress (i.e. how you are meeting the objectives) required during and at the end of the project. The client may also request from you in this section any specific background documentation regarding your qualifications for performing the work or services required by the project.

Contract Deliverables

During the course of the work being performed you may be required to submit certain plans, reports and other documents analyzing and detailing project planning, implementation, identification of any issues affecting the services provided and a detailed outline of cost allocations for the project as each stage is implemented. This section will detail what those requirements are.

Proposal Instructions

This section details the format for your proposal submission and what you must include in your proposal package. The client will specify where and to whom you will submit your proposal, and the format of any documents you provide. This may include seemingly trivial things like the maximum length of documents and line spacing (e.g. 15 single-spaced pages).

Proposal instructions may include other specifics about various forms, reports and other documents to be provided. Some examples are:

- Technical Proposals: detailing methodologies, evaluation of objectives and identification of issues, draft work plans, etc.

- Management Proposals: including who will do the work, how the work will be organized and managed, and the relevant experience of participants

- Budget/Cost Proposals: how the project budget will be allocated including labor and other expenses, identification of staff and the work they will do including their rates of pay, a breakdown of costs per project objective, etc.

- Human Resources Proposals: labor and related issues such as time and costs, expertise specifics, details about any partner(s) and ancillary staff you will be bringing with you, etc.

- Any documents requiring signatures

To see some examples of RFPs you can check out the American Planning Association's website (**www.planning.org/consultants/requestsearch. htm**), which maintains a list of RFPs for government and other contracts.

Responding to Proposals

If the client has a formal request for proposal process you will use that as the guideline in preparing your proposal. When you submit your proposal, you are making a "bid" to do the work.

The bid process may also require you to make an oral presentation. The organization requesting the RFP will usually hold a session (sometimes called a bidding meeting) for interested parties to attend in order to learn more about the project before submitting their response to the RFP. This is the time to ask questions and elicit clear answers. The more clearly you understand the goals and purpose of the project, the better your chances of being the successful bidder.

When responding to an RFP, make sure your response is submitted before the stated deadline and answers all of the questions accurately. Keep a current personal or company resume on file for these occasions, and don't overstate your qualifications to win a bid.

Include written references from past consulting projects—even where you provided a service for free—and include a list of qualifications. Advise them of your availability and make certain you point out exactly how you will meet their objectives and what services are not within the scope of your contract. The client may not be obligated to award the contract to the lowest cost bidder. Instead, they may make their decision based on a number of factors, including the company's previous experience with similar projects.

Why Organizations Ask for Proposals

Sometimes the request for a proposal may come "out of the blue" from an employer you haven't approached. The beginning corporate coach typically thinks this is great news. After all, why would they ask for a proposal if they were not interested? Actually, there are a number of reasons employers ask for proposals:

It May Be Necessary for the Job

In some cases, a proposal is necessary for the job. For example, many government departments require the decision-maker to review written proposals from several different prospects before a contract is awarded. They will often have formal RFP guidelines such as those discussed above for you to follow. Likewise, some large companies require written proposals following strict submission guidelines.

If you pay attention to how they communicate with you, you should get a sense of how your proposal will be treated when it is received. Are they encouraging? Do they return your calls promptly? Do they sound positive about your chances? If the answer is "yes" and you want the job, then submitting a proposal is probably worth your time and energy.

It May Be a "Brush Off"

Some clients find it difficult to say "no" and want to avoid a confrontation. They can delay saying no by having you submit a proposal. The client can then say it is "under review" until you either give up or they finally work up the courage to tell you they are not interested.

It May Be Used to Confirm a Hiring Decision

The most common reason some types of clients ask for proposals is because they want to have written comparisons of several coaches. Often, they have a "preferred" coach they want to hire, and the purpose of the written proposal is to help them confirm their decision, or show their supervisor or a hiring committee that they have "shopped around."

> TIP: If you are the preferred candidate you will know it. The client will have discussed the project with you in detail, and you will have reached a tentative agreement to do the work. They will explain that their regulations require them to review written proposals and may even assure you that it will be "just a formality."

If you are the preferred coach and you want the job, then it is worth your time to put together a proposal confirming the details you have discussed with the clients. Otherwise, your time might be better spent focusing on clients who are seriously interested in you.

Creating a Winning Proposal

What to Include in Your Proposal

If the client has not given you any formal guidelines you can still put together a winning proposal following the outline of RFP components listed earlier in this section. Be sure to include:

- A description of your company

- A detailed description of the qualifications you will bring to the project and how those fit into the client's objectives

- A description of the methodologies you will use to meet the needs of the project and how those will benefit the client

- A detailed budget of cost and expense allocations and specific resources you will use in completing the objectives on time and within the budget

- References from other organizations for whom you have done similar projects

A number of companies specialize in writing proposals. You can find them by doing a web search for "writing proposals" and "contract." An excellent resource is the ProposalWriter.com website with links to proposal writing and government contracting at **www.proposalwriter. com/links.html**. You may also find the book *Proven Proposal Strategies to Win More Business*, by Herman Holtz, to be helpful.

For more information on how clients choose business coaches, see **http:// sbinfocanada.about.com/cs/management/a/choosetrainer.htm**.

6.4.2 Meeting with Corporate Clients

In most cases, while you may submit a written proposal, you will get work without going through a formal RFP process. In such cases, you may not be in competition with other coaches, but simply need to show the company why they should invest in your services.

When preparing for a meeting, says Timi Gleason, the corporate coach should find out who is going to be there, and what the expectations for the meeting will be. A notepad and pen are very important, as well as enough business cards to give to everyone present, and extra information packages to hand out. Prior to the interview, the coach should prepare a list of references to send at a future date, depending on the outcome.

Prepare a list of questions to ask the decision-makers. During this "needs analysis" you may have to adjust your line of questioning as you find out more about whatever the organization's needs or current difficulties that they may be experiencing. Do they want you to address lagging sales? Is there a lot of tension between managers and employees? Do they want someone who can help workers develop more effective team-building strategies? Then you can further explain how you can meet those needs. You can find some Sample Questions for a Training Needs Analysis on the next few pages.

Sample Questions for a Training Needs Analysis

1. Who is this training for?

   _____

   _____

   _____

2. What kind of training programs have they had in the past?

   _____

   _____

   _____

3. Were those programs effective or not? Why?

   _____

   _____

   _____

4. Why do you want to hold the current training?

   _____

   _____

   _____

5. What are the specific problems you want solved?

   _____

   _____

   _____

6. What specific topics do you want to be covered?

_____

_____

_____

7. What are the results you expect from this training?

_____

_____

_____

8. What do you need to be satisfied with the training?

_____

_____

_____

9. What do the participants want from attending this program?

_____

_____

_____

10. Is there anything else you think I need to know?

_____

_____

_____

11. Do company practices support this training?

_____

_____

_____

The final question can help give realistic expectations for the training. For example, if you are being asked to train customer service representatives to give more personal attention to customers, but the company awards bonuses based on how quickly customer calls are handled, the training is unlikely to achieve its objective.

Based on the information you receive from the needs analysis, you can explain how hiring you will meet those needs. Your proposal can include a cover letter, a summary of topics that will be covered, the proposed length of the program (e.g. two days or three hours per week for 10 weeks, etc.) and your fee. If you have already reached agreement on what needs to be done, you might simply submit a contract covering these points. (See the sample training contract in section 5.7.3.)

7. Succeeding as a Life Coach

Using the information, techniques and resources provided in this book, you should be well on your way to establishing your own successful coaching practice. In this chapter we offer some bonus ideas to help you ensure client satisfaction, followed by expert career advice from successful life coaches. We wish you the best of luck as you set out in your new career, and hope you enjoy many years of happiness and fulfillment as a life coach!

7.1 Ensuring Client Satisfaction

To help ensure success, remember to keep in mind the following points about good client service:

- Don't overwhelm clients with forms and checklists. While taking notes will make it easier for you to manage information, some people will be turned off by rigid insistence on writing everything down and being assigned written homework. It is essential for clients to assess their goals and aspirations, but some clients will be more inclined to make mental notes. Don't spend so much time preparing paperwork that you forget the essentials of coaching: good rapport, effective communication and the drive to inspire.

- Respect that different clients will respond better to different methods. Some of the exercises in this book will work fabulously with some people, while other exercises may need to be tweaked, or not used at all. Be creative and develop your own techniques, incorporating what you see, experience and learn.

- Resist the temptation to butt in. When you spend considerable time talking with someone and getting to know him or her, you may be tempted to offer too much input. The coach should listen more and talk less. A good coach cares about his or her clients, but also respects them enough to realize that they are capable of making the right decisions.

- Be of service. You don't have to do everything strictly on the clock. An occasional unscheduled phone call or spontaneous email lets clients know that you are supportive. If one of your clients is looking to meet the right woman for a relationship, you might call and let him know that you heard about a big singles' event in his area. Maybe you came across a website that would be of particular interest to another client, and decided to send her the link.

- Do little extras for clients to give them good customer service. Send them birthday or Christmas cards. Make impromptu phone calls to congratulate them on accomplishments and milestones. These little gestures go a long way.

- Periodically follow up with old clients. If you coach someone for three or six months, don't simply forget him or her after the coaching relationship formally ends. Make an occasional phone call, or send a card or an email to ask how things are going. Maybe the client needs coaching with something else, or knows a friend or colleague who might be interested.

- Enjoy yourself. People who become life coaches are not doing a job, they are living the life that they want to live. Few other careers offer you the opportunity to work at home, set your own hours, and choose the people you work with.

- Finally, be an inspiration to others. Let them know that if you can do it, they can, too.

In the next section you can read comments and insights from some of the many experts we interviewed for this guide. You'll see that they echo in their commentary and advice the basic principles we've provided elsewhere in the book.

7.2 Advice from the Experts

The many experts we interviewed to create this guide offered an amazing amount of excellent advice for our readers. Throughout this book, you have already read and have been guided by their contributions and their knowledge. We would like to offer you some additional thoughts from our experts who, at one time, were all in the position that you are now in, setting out on a new path to become a life coach. Following are some of their best tips for those new to this richly rewarding profession and wondering how to maximize their chances of success.

Starting Out

"There are two things that I would like all prospective coaches to know. The first is that coaching is the most enjoyable job in the world, but you have to be prepared for the reality of self-employment (i.e. you will spend as much time marketing and administering your business as you will coaching clients). The second is that an investment in coach training is never wasted. Even if you decide not to pursue a coaching business, you will be a happier person for the rest of your life as a result of what you learned by studying coaching."

— *Barbra Sundquist, Mentor and Business Coach*
www.BarbraSundquist.com

"It may take awhile for your coaching practice to take off, so protect yourself and have enough savings that you can buy what you need for your business, support your family, plus still have an emergency reserve in case of lean times, especially when you are just starting out. You want to focus on coaching your clients, building a practice and come from a place of abundance, not an anxious, scarcity mode."

— *KC Christensen-Lang, Happiness Is…*
www.toolsforpositiveliving.com

"Some coaches build their practices overnight, others do not. Many coaches focus on mimicking the methods that successful coaches have used to build their practices. This is useful, but only to the degree that the method is in alignment with who you are as a coach. In other words, if your strength is writing rather than speaking, focus on publishing articles rather than getting speaking engagements. Focus on what you love to do, and find a way to market yourself through that medium. Don't fall victim to thinking there is only one way to coach or to market yourself. And don't worry about alienating people because you are being "too" spiritual, new age, or unusual, if that is your style. As long as you are being true to yourself, you will find clients who have been looking for you even longer than you've been dreaming about how you want to do your work."

— *Jenna Avery, Life Coach for Sensitive Souls*
www.highlysensitivesouls.com

"It was a difficult concept at first that people would pay me to do this kind of work and that I deserved to get paid for it. Take it seriously. If you want to do this work, do it; however, plan for success. You may want to keep your day job until you have secured the education and built the clientele to stand on your own."

— *Laura Meyer, Divorce Recovery Coaching*
Unlimited, LLC
www.divorcerecoverycoach.com

"Be really clear with yourself about the difference between a coaching hobby and a coaching business. Coaches tend to be lifelong learners, which is great but doesn't always contribute to the bottom line. Decide how many hours a week you will spend in non-revenue generating activities such as taking classes, volunteering, reading newsletters, participating on discussion lists and talking with coaching colleagues. I've known coaches who have literally spent years participating in those activities to the exclusion of actually building a business. In a viable business those activities should be no more than 20% of the work week or about 8 hours tops."

— *Barbra Sundquist, Mentor and Business Coach*
www.BarbraSundquist.com

"In my work mentoring new coaches, [my own] work/life balance is also a huge challenge. If you can tap into the larger vision for your business and your life, you'll find that you get results more easily and have more time for life, outside of work. As a new coach, you may also feel stressed and find it difficult to slow down. If you're stressed, it will serve both you and your client to work on your own stress management and, eventually, visioning on what you want for your practice and your life. Unless you can take a deep breathe and slow down, you won't have any space to reflect on what you really want. Figuring out what you really want is the first step in making choices and, eventually, creating balance."

— *Amber Rosenberg, Pacific Life Coach*
www.workingmotherscoach.com

Understand Your Relationship with Your Clients

"I invested a significant amount of time and energy working with my coach to develop a clear way to explain what I do to prospective clients. I found that people had a hard time grasping the concept of coaching because it is somewhat abstract, as well as being a relatively new profession. Now I talk about the challenges they face, the vision I have for them, and the solutions I offer to help them get there."

— *Jenna Avery, Life Coach for Sensitive Souls*
www.highlysensitivesouls.com

"The key to becoming a life coach is knowing one's self first before going into coaching. Mature personal awareness is key. Not all teachers have the gift of teaching and the same is true for coaches. Many helpers are ill-suited for the role, in my opinion, for they neither truly know themselves nor have helped themselves first. Conversely, not all clients want to change."

— *John Fox, Life and Marketing Coach*

"I find it highly effective when the counselor is willing and able to form a real partnership with their client by relinquishing the notion that as a life coach, their primary responsibility is one of making their client "feel better." Most of my clients want to know who or what is to blame for their problems, issues or unhappiness. I think the challenge is helping clients understand that accountability on every level, emotional, physical and spiritual is the only real path to empowerment because it's the only way to change what isn't working in their lives. And for that reason, the only path to the personal fulfillment that comes with finding the things that do. But, like any profession with clients, there would always be some clients that are just too needy, wounded or self-absorbed to ever benefit from your services."

— *Marguerite Manning, Cosmic Karma*

"Coaching assumes the client has everything she needs to find her way forward, and that it is not therapy or even directive. It is all based on the magic of questions: the right question at the right time and offered in the right way. It gives back the power to individuals, so solutions and dreams-come-true come from the inside out instead of being manipulated through circumstances."

— *Marlee Ledai, Go Girl Coach*
www.gogirlcoach.com

"What I like most about being a life coach is helping clients find their own answers and seeing light bulbs go off when they begin pursuing their passions. I would consider myself a holistic coach – I coach the whole person rather than just what someone does for a living."

— *Laura Meyer, Divorce Recovery Coaching Unlimited, LLC*
www.divorcerecoverycoach.com

"A new life coach needs to be patient and know that a client can't change or release their "stuff" unless they want to. Even if you can clearly see what the issues are, you need to allow the client to decide when he/she is ready to release it. You have to be willing to call them on their "stuff", explain why they need to release it, show them how they can release it, be there for them and assist them in releasing it, but if they are not willing to, that is their choice."

— *Christy Whitman, Personal Empowerment*
www.christywhitman.com

Find a Niche

"Niches are good to have. I bring many years of experience and a varied background so I can move in and coach clients in different settings and services. Beginning coaches may want to start with areas/clients they feel most comfortable working with, what they know best, what they have experience in. Coaches do best if they are passionate about what they are offering and truly care about the needs of that particular client. They can always expand to other types of clients later."

— *KC Christensen-Lang, Happiness Is…*
www.toolsforpositiveliving.com

"It is really important to get certified and pick a niche in which you want to market yourself. If you think you are going to coach 'everyone' you are going to spread yourself too thin in your marketing strategies. You have to think of this as a business. You are not in the business of life coaching; you are in the business of marketing your life coaching business."

— *Christy Whitman, Personal Empowerment*
www.christywhitman.com

"I primarily offer coaching through my program called Embrace Your Essential Self. I take my clients through a specific set of processes and skills training within a specific timeframe. Many people find that they prefer this approach to coaching as opposed to an ongoing, open-ended relationship; though I do have a few clients that I work with that way as well."

— *Jenna Avery, Life Coach for Sensitive Souls*
www.highlysensitivesouls.com

"It's not surprising to anyone who knows me that I am now a freelance writer and spiritual life coach. The concept for my life-coaching, and ultimately the outline for my program, Your Contract With The Universe was born as all the spiritual beliefs and scientific principles I embraced came together for me to form one amazing belief system."

— *Marguerite Manning, Cosmic Karma*

"I chose to start doing group coaching for my programs because it allows more people to receive the information, the individuals find it helpful to hear other people that are going through the exact same thing they are, and it is more cost effective than just one-on-one sessions. I get so excited when I receive phone calls and emails from my clients that I coach one-on-one or in my group coaching classes (for example: The 5 Week Abundance Principle Coaching Program, The 4 Week Creating Your Ideal Body Course, The 4 Week Magnetizing & Manifesting Course, and The 4 Week Attracting Your Perfect Partner Course) and they have amazing breakthroughs or they meet their partner, get a job promotion, get a higher paying job, attract more clients to their business, or release weight."

— *Christy Whitman, Personal Empowerment*
www.christywhitman.com

More Guides to Build Your Business

Increase your income by offering additional services. Here are some recommended FabJob guides to help you build your business:

Get Paid to Speak

Imagine having an exciting high paying job that lets you use your speaking skills to make a difference in people's lives. The **FabJob Guide to Become a Motivational Speaker** will teach you how to...

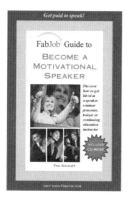

- Sound like a polished professional speaker

- Get speeches written for you

- Get hired to speak for conferences, seminar companies, conventions, corporations, schools, colleges, cruise ships, non-profit organizations, and continuing education programs

- Get jobs through speakers agencies

- Profitably present your own seminars

Get Paid to Give Business Advice

Imagine having a respected, high paying career where executives turn to you for advice on running their businesses. In the **FabJob Guide to Become a Business Consultant** you will discover how to ...

- Carry out a business consulting project step-by-step from conducting a needs analysis to presenting recommendations to the client

- Gather information through surveys, case studies, interviews, or focus groups

- Get hired by a consulting firm or as an internal consultant for a corporation

- Start your own consulting business, price your services, and get clients

- Be certified as a professional consultant

Visit www.FabJob.com to order guides today!